The Complete Idiot's Reference Card

10 Strange-But-True Moments in Canadian History

1. A Montreal bookseller is convicted of peddling obscene material after he is caught selling copies of D.H. Lawrence's critically acclaimed novel *Lady Chatterley's Lover*. (1960)

2. A *Maclean's* magazine article reports that by the year 2000, Canadians will probably have two-and-a-half times as many leisure hours as working hours. (1962)

3. Pierre Berton gets himself in hot water with the readers of *Maclean's* magazine by speaking out in favour of premarital sex. (1963)

4. Quebec City police chief Gerard Girard sends 50 patrolmen out to enforce a law that forbids women from displaying their thighs in public. (1965)

5. Journalist Peter Gzowski describes colour television as "a nice gimmick...that isn't that much of an improvement over black and white." (1966)

6. CBC TV refuses to air a Penman's men's underwear commercial on the grounds that "no treatment could make a men's underwear commercial acceptable at the present time." (1968)

7. *Chatelaine* magazine asks a matchmaker to describe the ideal mate for the country's most eligible bachelor, Pierre Elliott Trudeau. (1969)

8. *Chatelaine* magazine tells its readers about the Voice of Man In Toronto (VOMIT)—an anti-feminist group whose members welcomed "release from a lifetime's service as a free meal ticket for an intellectually inferior woman and the brood she forces on us." (1970)

9. Paul Anka's hit single "You're Having My Baby" enrages U.S. feminists so much that the National Organization for Women (NOW) awards Anka their annual "Keep Her In Her Place Award." (1974)

10. Bob and Doug McKenzie (a.k.a. Rick Moranis and Dave Thomas) sell 300,000 copies of a record album based on their highly popular SCTV segment, "Great White North." (1981)

alpha books

tear here

10 Really Bad Fads That Should Have Been Stopped At The Border

1. Elephant pants
2. Day-Glo clothing
3. Go-go boots
4. Hot pants
5. Polyester leisure suits
6. Mood rings
7. Pet rocks
8. Toe socks
9. Platform shoes
10. Deely boppers

The 10 Most Memorable Inventions to Come to Canada During the '60s, '70s, and '80s

➤ The birth control pill (1961)
➤ Disposable diapers (1961)
➤ The stretch suit (a.k.a. "the sleeper") for babies (1962)
➤ The miniskirt (1965)
➤ Colour television (1966)
➤ The microwave oven (1972)
➤ Generic grocery products (1978)
➤ Home computer (1978)
➤ Post-It® Notes (1980)
➤ Cellular phone (1985)

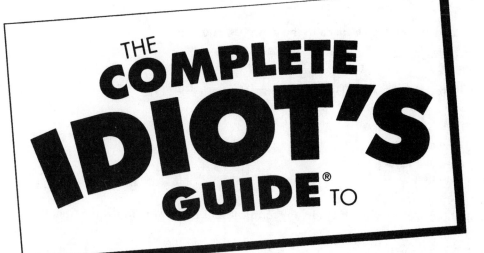

THE
COMPLETE
IDIOT'S
GUIDE® TO

Canada in the '60s, '70s, and '80s

By Ann Douglas

alpha books

Prentice Hall Canada Inc., Scarborough, Ontario

Canadian Cataloguing in Publication Data

Douglas, Ann, 1963–

The complete idiot's guide to Canada in the '60s, '70s, and '80s

Includes index.

ISBN 0-13-084952-9

1. Popular culture – Canada. 2. Canada – History – 1963– . I. Title

FC95.4.D68 1999   306'.0971'09045   C99-931801-2

F1021.2.D68 1999

Prentice-Hall Canada Inc.
Scarborough, Ontario

Prentice-Hall, Inc., Upper Saddle River, New Jersey
Prentice-Hall International (UK) Limited, London
Prentice-Hall of Australia, Pty. Limited, Sydney
Prentice-Hall Hispanoamericana, S.A., Mexico City
Prentice-Hall of India Private Limited, New Delhi
Prentice-Hall of Japan, Inc., Tokyo
Simon & Schuster Southeast Asia Private Limited, Singapore
Editora Prentice-Hall do Brasil, Ltda., Rio de Janeiro

ISBN 0-13-084952-9

Editorial Director, Trade Group: Andrea Crozier
Acquisitions Editor: Nicole de Montbrun
Copy Editor: Doris Cowan
Production Editor: Jodi Lewchuk
Art Direction: Mary Opper
Illustrations: Craig Francis
Cover Image: Photodisk
Production Coordinators: Barbara Ollerenshaw and Kathrine Pummell
Page Layout: Gail Ferreira Ng-A-Kien

1 2 3 4 5 RRD 03 02 01 00 99

Printed and bound in the United States of America.

Visit the Prentice Hall Canada Web site! Send us your comments, browse our catalogues, and more.
www.phcanada.com.

Contents at a Glance

Contents

Foreword

"If you can remember the sixties, you weren't really there." It's an old saw that conjures up all the clichés about the decade of peace, love, grooviness—and lots of drugs. But the funny thing is, whether we actually lived through the '60s, '70s, and '80s in Canada or not, our memories of what happened and of who we were get reduced to cliché, and occasionally nostalgia. We remember a few iconic images, a couple of noteworthy songs, and a handful of faintly embarrassing trends.

Who were we as Canadians in the recent past, though? How did we live? What were our great debates about? How have we changed and what's remained the same? Ann Douglas sets out to answer these questions in *The Complete Idiot's Guide to Canada in the '60s, '70s, and '80s*. It's a breezy trip down memory lane, and a refresher course in pop culture and social history. It also fills in some blanks about how we got to where we are at the end of the 1990s, through chapters on politics, family life, pop culture, economics, and trends.

It's also an update on what you might have missed. As a thirtysomething Canadian, for instance, my memories of the 1960s don't include much beyond Mr. Dressup and my favourite pair of clam digger pants. I was intrigued to read about things like how cooperative the Canadian government was with the U.S. during the Vietnam War; or, on a lighter note, just why the CBC refused to air ads about men's underwear!

In some cases, we may already know "how it all turned out," but not how the debate actually unfolded. We tend to take for granted, for instance, that the '60s saw the rise of the "second wave" of feminism, but it was not without substantial debate in society, and in the popular press. What we now take for granted was often the subject of intense, and sometimes bone-headed, debate. If some of the issues, like childcare, are still a source of heated debate, others seem positively silly in retrospect. Why was the coming of the metric system such a big deal?

It's also a chance to look at how politics has changed, and what's fallen off the "political radar screen." Why is the late '90s the era when we talk about taxes, and debate about the environment has all but vanished? Why have so many of the debates that had us worked up in the 1980s virtually disappeared? At the same time, it's a little spooky to read the debates about equality, regionalism, Quebec separation, and realize how little has changed on some fronts.

Of course, it's not all the serious stuff of politics and economics. Pop culture had a big role to play in who we were in the last few decades. In *The Complete Idiot's Guide to Canada in the '60s, '70s and '80s* you'll relive some of the hilarious, and sometimes spine-tingling trends that had Canadians in a tizzy. From Twister to pet rocks (the company, at one point, was shipping three to five thousand rocks a day), to Day-Glo clothing and Madonna wannabes, we've had some pretty weird trends. It puts '90s fads like piercing and tattooing into perspective. The '90s may live on as the decade in which Martha Stewart turned running a home into an Olympic event, but it's helpful to remember that in the '70s harvest gold colour schemes were a necessity for the well-turned-out suburban home. You'll relive it all in Ann's book, so break out the platform shoes and be prepared for some red-faced laughter.

One of the biggest changes we've seen since the '60s has been the rise of consumer technology, a development well documented by Ann. We've seen the proliferation of home computers, gadgets and electronic mass media. If your head is spinning over the high cost of the latest gadget, just be patient. Prices do seem to come down a bit. In 1976, for instance, the humble answering machine sold for more than $400.

Definitely Not the Opera, the CBC radio show I host, is all about pop culture. We often find ourselves looking for anecdotes and archival material about our pop past. The funny thing is, while there are innumerable sources of information about the U.S., there's surprisingly little about Canada. Think of the images burned into our brains: kids dancing in the mud at Woodstock, Nixon resigning, Ronald Reagan. In *The Complete Idiot's Guide to Canada in the '60s, '70s, and '80s*, you'll revisit distinctly Canadian moments like Expo '67, the "fuddle duddle" flap, and the demise of the stubby beer bottle.

American influence on popular culture here is undeniable, as a tour through the top television shows and pop songs shows. You'll see how our concern for our own culture next to the American giant, and our love-hate relationship with the States is nothing new. We wrung our hands over our "branch plant economy" in the 1960s, and fiercely debated free trade in the '80s.

From the silly to the serious, there are all kinds of interesting nuggets of information about how we lived in the '60s, '70s, and '80s. From mini skirts to Rubik's cubes, take an entertaining and distinctly Canadian tour of pop culture, politics, and daily life.

Nora Young,

Host of CBC radio's *Definitely Not the Opera*

Introduction

Wondering what's behind all the hype about the 1960s? Eager to find out for yourself if the 1970s and 1980s were really as bad as everyone says? You've come to the right place. *The Complete Idiot's Guide to Canada in the '60s, '70s, and '80s* will tell you everything you need to know about three of the most fascinating decades in this century. What's more, the book will do so in a straightforward and clear fashion rather than leaving you in a purple haze....

Only in Canada?

You'll note that the title of this book contains the word "Canada." Despite what you might think the word wasn't pasted into the title in a rather obvious attempt to keep the Canadian content police happy–although, frankly, that's not such a bad idea! The word is there for a perfectly valid reason. Unlike books which look at the '60s, '70s, and '80s through American eyes, this book looks at these three decades through Canadian eyes instead.

That's not to say that this book is devoid of American content, however. You'll find plenty of information on North American-wide fads and television shows, important events in U.S. politics, and so on–basically anything that would have mattered to Canadians at the time. What's important is that you'll be looking at those events from the viewpoint of a Canadian–and someone who's not afraid to poke a little fun at the Americans, no less!

How to Use This Book

The book has been organized to make it easy for you to make sense of all the weird and wonderful happenings that occurred during these three eventful decades. (Trust me: a lot happened. You'll thank me for the no-nonsense, nuts-and-bolts approach later on!)

Here's how the book is divided up and what you can expect to find in each section:

Part 1: The Sixties describes the highlights of one of the most colourful decades of the century–and I'm not just referring to the day-glo clothing. You'll find out about life in suburbia, the sexual revolution, the counterculture, the peace and environmental movements, the women's movement, the Quiet Revolution in Quebec, the October Crisis, and a whole lot more. You'll even find out what well-known Canadian writer caused a furor at *Maclean's* magazine by speaking out in favor of premarital sex; and how the matchmaker hired by *Chatelaine* magazine described the ideal bride for Canada's most eligible bachelor, Prime Minister Pierre Elliott Trudeau. (Kind of leaves you wondering if Margaret missed that issue.)

Part 2: The Seventies examines the wacky fads and outlandish fashions that managed to infiltrate the border during what can only be described as a ten-year-long lapse in good taste. You'll get the chance to relive great moments in the life of the Canadian rec room–like Canada's 11th hour victory over the Soviets in the 1972 Canada-U.S. hockey series and those stomach-wrenching "Another Great Recipe From Kraft" commercials. (Who would have thought you could use peanut butter and Miracle Whip in the same recipe?) You'll also find out about a Toronto deejay's valiant attempts to recruit members to his Disco Destruction Army and what mood rings had to say about the emotional state of Canadians during those long winter months.

Part 3: The Eighties tells you everything you need to know about the decade when "yuppie" became a household world. You'll find out about the Canadian board game that took the world by storm, the rise of the political right, the controversy surrounding the free trade agreement, and a series of gloriously bad fads that would have done the '70s proud. Along the way, we'll pause for a moment to remember that kinder, gentler time in our nation's history when beer could be enjoyed in a stubby.

If you stop reading the book at this point, you'll miss out on some of the best stuff. In the appendices, you'll find a detailed glossary (your guide to '60s, '70s, and '80s-speak!), a comprehensive timeline filled with juicy facts that you won't find anywhere else in the book, leads on the hottest retro pop culture web sites (including one where you can try your hand at an online Rubik's Cube), and a list of recommended readings for the keeners in the audience. (You know: the guys who wore pocket protectors back in the 1970s.)

Extras

Throughout the book, you'll find a few other bells and whistles that are designed to call your attention to important or especially nifty details:

Boomer Bytes

These are cool facts or statistics that would do the folks at Trivial Pursuit proud.

Newsflash!

These are concise summaries of the hottest news stories from the past–things that every Idiot needs to know.

Blast From The Past

These are catchy quotes that help to bring the past to life. You'll hear from historians, journalists, and everyday people who witnessed some of those important events this century.

Say What?

These are quick definitions of important terms that would otherwise leave you scratching your head.

Movers and Shakers

This is your chance to meet people who left their mark on the '60s, '70s, and '80s.

As you can see, there's a lot of great material in this book—material that you won't find anywhere else. So slip into those elephant pants and get ready to enjoy a one-of-a-kind trip back in time to Canada in the sixties, seventies, and eighties.

Acknowledgments

One of the lessons that my parents managed to drill into my head when I was growing up in suburbia was the importance of saying thank you. (I know: it may seem quaint in the post-punk rock era, but you're going to have to bear with me as I run through a laundry list of acknowledgements.)

First of all, I'd like to thank all of the editors I worked with at Prentice Hall Canada during the writing of this book: Robert Harris, Dean Hannaford, and Joan Whitman, who came up with the idea for the book and then thought of me when it was time to shop around for an author; and Andrea Crozier, Nicole de Montbrun, Jodi Lewchuk, Doris Cowan, and the rest of the Prentice Hall team, for making me feel like I was writing the most important book in the universe, even though I knew they were dealing with dozens of other titles.

I'd also like to thank the folks who assisted me when I was researching this book: Dave Preston, beer expert extraordinaire, for filling me in on that dark chapter in Canadian history when the stubby disappeared from the beer store shelves ; Brian Davidson, research officer, Canadian Bankers Association, for sending lots of fun bank-related trivia my way; my research assistants Janice Kent and Barb Payne, for service above and beyond the call of duty; and the staff of the Trent University library for helping me to work with those tortuous devices known as microfilm readers and not calling the cops the night I accidentally got locked in the library.

Finally, I'd like to thank that really cool guy that I met in geography class back in 1978. We've been together for two decades, four children, and ten books. If that isn't love, what is?

Part 1

The Sixties

Bob Dylan certainly got it right when he sang his now-classic ballad "The Times They Are a-Changin'." More than any other decade this century, the sixties were a decade of change—a period in which traditional ideas about sex, love, and marriage were turned on their head overnight; and the nightly news was filled with stories of protests, sit-ins, and rallies organized by anti-war, civil rights, women's rights, gay liberation, and environmental activists. Is it any wonder we continue to be fascinated by this turbulent time, almost forty years after the fact?

Chapter 1

Sex and Drugs and Rock 'n' Roll

In This Chapter

➤ The sexual revolution

➤ "Turn on, tune in, drop out"

➤ Sixties rock 'n' roll

In August of 1966, *The Globe and Mail* observed that Canada was experiencing "a curious mood of rebellion, of irresponsibility, of resentment" and that "Canadians are doubting all former stable things."

Whether Canadians were prepared to admit it or not, the newspaper's observations were bang on. Canada was in the midst of a social revolution the likes of which had never been seen before. But unlike most revolutions, which are fought by beret-sporting militias, this war was being waged by the teenage offspring of Joe and Jane Canuck. They wore their uniform of long hair, granny glasses, beads, peace medallions, and bell-bottoms by day and then went home to "crash" in their parents' suburban bungalows at night. In between, they managed to drive their parents crazy with their unconventional views on peace, love, war, and everything in between.

The Generation Gap

Boomer Bytes

There were two million babies born in Canada between 1945 and 1948—the earliest years of the so-called "baby boom." This first wave of boomer babies entered their teen years during the early 1960s, a period of unprecedented social unrest.

Much as the older generation might have wished that members of the younger generation would hop into a Volkswagen bug and disappear into the sunset, Canadian society had no choice but to take notice of these placard-waving young people. There were simply too many of them to ignore. In his book *The Years of Protest 1960–1970,* Alan Edmonds describes the effect that these teenaged baby boomers had on Canadian society: "By the end of the decade, people under twenty-five were so numerous they represented an irresistible force—a massive bulge in the social structure that the Establishment seemed unable to harness and use to its own ends. The young did not, as they had as recently as the fifties, represent a subculture. Instead, they created what came to be known as a counter-culture."

The counterculture challenged every symbol and value the older generation held dear. They rejected the "Canadian dream" of getting married, starting a family, and buying a bungalow in suburbia. They pooh-poohed the idea of waiting until after marriage to have sex. They sported buttons with deliberately provocative sayings like "God Is Dead," "Make Love, Not War," and "Turn On, Tune In, Drop Out." And they grew their hair long and dressed themselves in outlandish fashions. (Some young people even wore replicas of the Iron Cross—the German Army's highest award for valour—something that older generations of Canadians who had lived through the horrors of the Second World War treated as a slap in the face.)

Given the differences between the older, more conservative generations and their

Blast from the Past!

"The parent generation was obsessed with its own affairs: newer and brighter houses and basement-to-bedroom broadloom, second cars, dishwashers, and deciding whether ten- and twenty-year-old marriages were worth saving. Thus it didn't at first notice the changes that would, within a few years, totally disrupt its way of life."

—Alan Edmonds, *The Years of Protest: 1960–1970*

younger, experience-hungry counterparts, is it any wonder that Canadians, like their neighbours to the south, suddenly started bemoaning the "generation gap"?

Behind Closed Doors

During the 1960s, Canadians' attitudes towards sexuality changed dramatically. The definition of what constituted "obscene material" was thrown out the window. Birth control stopped being taboo and became a ticket to worry-free sex. Growing numbers of young people admitted to having sex outside of marriage. And Canadian society became more tolerant of "the love that dare not speak its name"—homosexuality.

From "No, No" to "Go-Go"

In 1960, a Montreal bookseller was convicted of peddling obscene material. His crime? Selling copies of D.H. Lawrence's critically acclaimed novel *Lady Chatterley's Lover.* When well-known Canadian authors Morley Callaghan and Hugh MacLennan jumped to the bookseller's defence, arguing that the book was a work of art, they were denounced by the Health League of Canada for having "contributed to the spread of adultery, prostitution, and venereal disease in Canada."

Fast-forward by ten years and you discover a very different Canada. By the early 1970s, a smorgasbord of sexually explicit material was widely available in most Canadian cities. Even Toronto the Good had its share of adult cinemas that showed soft porn movies, restaurants that had semi-nude waitresses, bars that featured bare-breasted go-go dancers, and bookstores that specialized in pornography.

This is not to say that old-fashioned Canadian moral standards had completely gone the way of the dodo bird, however. In 1965, Quebec City police chief Gerard Girard sent 50 patrolmen out to enforce a law that said that women weren't permitted to display their thighs in public. (Girard lost the battle for the public good the following year when the miniskirt made its memorable Canadian debut.)

Girard wasn't the only one trying to safeguard the morals of Canadians. The Canadian Broadcasting Corporation (CBC) was also doing its part to keep the airwaves free of anything that might even remotely smack of smut. In fact, in 1968, it refused to air a Penman's men's underwear commercial on the grounds that "no treatment could make a men's underwear commercial acceptable at the present time." That decision led Tom Moore, the commercial's producer, to voice his frustrations to *Maclean's* magazine: "They'll show pit commercials for Ban. They'll cut bras in *half,* for godsake. So we bend over backward to do a pleasant underwear thing and it's a no go. Arbitrarily, without even seeing it, some dictatorial pinhead turns us down."

The tug-of-war between the old morality and the new was described in memorable terms by Marshall Delaney in an article in *Saturday Night* magazine in August of 1969. He described a trial in which an expert witness had been called to shed some light on

Blast from the Past!

"We've opened up to the extent that we'll accept brassieres and foundation garments, but still no panties or men's underwear I'm afraid."

—Barry Donnelly, assistant supervisor of the CBC's commercial acceptance department, explaining to *Maclean's* magazine in 1968 why the CBC was unwilling to air a Penman's men's underwear advertisement

whether a particular play was or was not obscene. The judge who was presiding at the trial asked the witness if he thought that there would be a backlash against sexually explicit material in entertainment, with "the great silent majority" rising up in fury against the new immorality and demanding a return to stricter censorship. The witness politely said no. When one of the lawyers present at the trial later asked him why he hadn't taken a harder stand on the issue, the witness had this to say: "The only honest answer would have been: 'No, Your Honour, that backlash isn't going to happen because the only people who want it are people your age, and you're going to be dead pretty soon.'"

The Pill

On August 18, 1960, the Searle Drug Company in the U.S. began marketing the birth control pill. One year later, the Canadian government approved it for sale in Canada.

Because it was still illegal under the Criminal Code to "offer to sell, advertise, publish an advertisement of or [have] for sale or disposal any means of preventing conception," the introduction of the birth control pill didn't create the same kind of waves in Canada as it had in Britain and the U.S. Canadian doctors were too worried about the legal ramifications of spreading the word about this new contraceptive method to chat it up to their patients—even those who were respectable married women!

It wasn't until the university campuses got on the birth control bandwagon that the word really began to get out. In 1965, the University of British Columbia started providing its students with information about birth control. Other universities soon

Blast from the Past!

"Gaining access to the Pill in the face of parents and conservative medical practitioners was, in some communities, more difficult than buying LSD or grass."

—Doug Owram, *Born at the Right Time: A History of the Baby Boom Generation* followed suit, and suddenly the floodgates opened. While it was very difficult for unmarried women to get doctors to prescribe the birth control pill before 1966, virtually any woman who wanted to go on the Pill could get a prescription by 1970.

It's not hard to figure out why the Pill gained such widespread acceptance in such a short period of time. It eliminated the fear of unplanned pregnancy, and it addressed society's growing concerns about the population explosion. (In 1962, *Saturday Night* magazine had warned that by 2026, there wouldn't even be standing room on the surface of the earth for all the planet's inhabitants.) The Pill made it possible for young women to live out the slogan that appeared on so many buttons during the 1960s: "Make Love, Not Babies."

The Sexual Revolution

The Pill played a huge role in the sexual revolution during the 1960s, but it wasn't the only factor responsible for the younger generation's growing willingness to hop in the sack without a marriage licence, the moral equivalent of the *Good Housekeeping* Seal of Approval! Young people had far greater opportunities for sexual experimentation than previous generations had enjoyed.

In their book, *Canadian Women: A History,* authors Alison Prentice, Paula Bourne, Gail Cuthbert Brandt, Beth Light, Wendy Mitchinson, and Naomi Black explain this phenomenon: "In the past, if young people left their families before marriage, they usually went to live with a surrogate family so that their lives were still carefully monitored. During the late 1950s and 1960s, it became more common and more acceptable for the young to leave home to live on their own or with people their own age while working or completing their education." Many of these young people who were living on their own weren't just hitting the books: they were also hitting the sack—although, to be fair, young women still tended to limit their premarital rendezvous to the man they eventually hoped to marry.

Newsflash!

In June of 1963, *The Financial Post* reported that a birth control pill was in the works for men. It wasn't the first such pill to be tested, but it certainly seemed to be more promising than previous efforts on this front: "This one does not have the undesirable side effect of an earlier pill which made a man's face go bright red when he took a drink of alcohol after he had taken the pill," the paper reported.

Boomer Bytes

In early 1960s, UWO sociologist William Mann reported that there was no sexual revolution on campus: only 13 percent of female students and 35 percent of male students had ever had sex.

There was also a lot more talk about sex, notes historian Doug Owram in his book *Born at the Right Time: A History of the Baby Boom Generation*: "By the time the first baby boomers reached university...sexuality was freely depicted in both literature and movies in ways that would have been completely unacceptable only a decade earlier. With each

Newsflash!

Young people weren't the only ones who were having sex. Pierre Sévigny, John Diefenbaker's associate minister of national defence, was found to be having an affair with Gerda Munsinger, a German immigrant. When the RCMP warned Justice Minister Davie Fulton that Munsinger was a prostitute and consequently a security risk, Diefenbaker reprimanded Sévigny but refused to ask for his resignation. The Munsinger affair earned itself a place in the history books for being Canada's first major parliamentary sex scandal.

Newsflash!

In May of 1963, Pierre Berton got himself in hot water with the readers of *Maclean's* magazine when he wrote an article that spoke out in favour of premarital sex. In his article, Berton wrote about "the Great Twentieth Century Hoax, whereby every adolescent is taught that sex is the key to everything—but he can't enjoy it for another ten, fifteen, or twenty years." Berton went on, "Having goaded the infants into a state of emotional and romantic frenzy to which intercourse, rather than cold baths, must be the obvious release, we are going to have to accept teenage sex as matter-of-factly as we now accept the other facets of togetherness....I would rather have them indulge in some good, honest, satisfying sex than be condemned to a decade of whimpering frustration brought on by the appalling North American practice called 'petting.'"

The letters from readers came fast and furious: "Who is Pierre Berton that you honor him by squandering a whole page on the trash he writes?" asked a reader in Stockholm, Saskatchewan. Another reader said simply, "I would like to offer my sincere sympathy to Mr. Berton's wife."

Berton's column stopped appearing in the magazine shortly thereafter.

passing year, adolescents grew into a world that shielded them less and less from the powerful and enticing world of sexuality."

The availability of such sexually explicit materials was the source of much concern. In her 1967 book *Sex and the Teen-Age Revolution, Vancouver Sun* columnist and future Liberal MP Simma Holt gave her take on the situation: "Today's young people have too much materially and too little spiritually. They are besieged with movies, television, magazines, books extolling sex and the fast life."

Regardless of which factor or factors were responsible for the rapid liberalization of views on sexuality, there was no way to put the genie back in the bottle once it broke free. Over the course of ten years, premarital virginity went from being the cornerstone of mainstream morality to an almost quaint tradition that was upheld only by conservative religious and ethnic groups.

Coming Out of the Closet

At the beginning of the 1960s, homosexuality was a crime in the eyes of the law, a mortal sin in the eyes of the church, and a psychological disorder in the eyes of the medical profession. According to Alvin Finkel, Margaret Conrad, and Veronica Strong-Boag, authors of *History of the Canadian Peoples: 1867 to the Present,* "Gay civil servants, RCMP officers, and members of the armed forces were fired as a matter of policy, and gay men—but not lesbians—were barred from immigration to Canada."

Attitudes toward homosexuality became more liberal as the decade progressed. The sexual revolution and the civil rights movement encouraged greater tolerance of gays

Newsflash!

One of the most significant events in the gay liberation movement took place at the Stonewall Inn in Greenwich Village, New York. On Friday, June 27, 1969, police raided the Stonewall Inn—a bar that catered to gay men—because the facility didn't have a liquor licence. The bartenders, a bouncer, and a number of cross-dressers on the premises were arrested. Patrons of the bar began throwing rocks and bottles at the police when they were forced out of the bar. "Gay power" became their rallying cry. According to Irwin and Debi Unger, authors of *The Times Were a-Changin'*, "The Stonewall riot was the Boston Tea Party of the gay community. The courageous defiance of the police by the New York homosexual community electrified gays everywhere in America and ignited a full-fledged liberation movement."

Newsflash!

In January of 1962, *Maclean's* published an article called "The Unmarried Wives" which served as an exposé on the horrors of "living in sin." While the majority of the article was devoted to talking about the social fallout of common-law arrangements, the writer of the piece, McKenzie Porter, also reported the findings of a study that challenged the conventional wisdom about this type of relationship.

Porter summarized the findings of a study by Ann F. Foster, a social worker on the staff of Toronto's Neighbourhood Workers Association. In her study, Foster compared the relationships of 40 legally married couples and 40 common-law couples and reached some shocking conclusions: "She found that the common-law husbands were more regular workers, better providers, and less given to philandering than the legal husbands. While the common-law wives were heavier drinkers, and more promiscuous than the legal wives, they were superior housekeepers, and more attractive physically. The children from the common-law homes made fewer appearances in juvenile courts than those from lawful homes, and were markedly less prone to sexual delinquency."

and lesbians. In 1969, after making his now famous statement that the state had no business in the bedrooms of the nation, Prime Minister Pierre Elliott Trudeau ushered in legislative changes that removed some of the restrictions against homosexual relationships between consenting adults.

Turn On, Tune In, Drop Out

In 1962, a Harvard University psychology instructor named Timothy Leary experimented with LSD for the first time. He was so blown away by the experience that he became an LSD zealot, singing the praises of this particular drug so loudly and enthusiastically that he got himself fired from Harvard.

In the years that followed, Leary created an organization called the International Foundation for Internal Freedom (IFIF) and went about preaching the benefits of his drug use. He told young people to "turn on" (get in touch with "the universe within"), "tune in" (connect with the world around them), and "drop out" (take a break from work, school, or whatever was preventing them from getting in touch with themselves). In his book *The Politics of Ecstasy*, he made LSD use sound positively respectable: "The discipline of LSD is without a doubt the most complex and demanding task that man on this planet has yet confronted. I often tell college students, "If you want to get a Ph.D., count on four years after you graduate....But for your LSD, count on thirty years at least."

It wasn't Leary who ultimately sold young people on the merits of drug use, however. It was their rock-and-roll icons who deserve the credit—or blame—for that. Big-name entertainers like Mick Jagger admitted to using drugs, and rock-and-roll artists like Bob Dylan and Jefferson Airplane sang songs that alluded to the joys of taking drugs.

Illicit drug use became increasingly popular with young Canadians, many of whom made the trek to Haight-Ashbury, San Francisco, in 1967 so that they could be part of the so-called Summer of Love. Unlike previous generations of drug users—a small number of Canadians had been using heroin for decades—these drug users were extremely vocal about the merits of their drugs of choice: marijuana, hashish, and LSD.

Boomer Bytes

LSD guru Timothy Leary didn't have to work very hard to convince Canadian students of the merits of dropping out. According to an article in *Maclean's* magazine in February 1963, one in three Canadian students had dropped out of school by the time they finished grade eight, and seven out of ten didn't stick around long enough to finish high school.

There were also a lot more drug users than ever before. The number of charges laid under the Narcotics Act more than tripled between 1966 and 1968. (See Table 1.1.)

Table 1.1 Number of Charges Laid Under the Narcotics Act

1960	516
1961	520
1962	376
1963	394
1964	376
1965	465
1966	567
1967	1234
1968	1713
1969	4032
1970	8596

Source: Doug Owram, Born at the Right Time: A History of the Baby Boom Generation

All the talk about illicit drugs was making Joe and Jane Canuck more than a little nervous. Growing public concern about the drug issue led the federal government to propose a classically Canadian solution: the government appointed a royal commission to look into the role that governments and the courts should play in prohibiting and regulating the use and distribution of drugs. In a series of four reports published between 1970 and 1973, the Royal Commission on the Non-Medical Use of Drugs (a.k.a. the LeDain Commission) recommended that people no longer be charged for merely possessing marijuana, that the penalties for other marijuana offences be reduced, that there be no increase in the penalties for other types of drug offences, and that drug addicts receive medical treatment rather than court-imposed criminal sanctions. The commission also pointed out that adult attempts to scare teenagers away from drug use had backfired: rather than encouraging them to steer clear of LSD and other substances, the fear-mongering tactics had only served to make drug use more exciting.

Rock 'n' Roll

Some of the most memorable music produced during this century was created during the 1960s. The powerful beat and compelling lyrics that had been made famous by black musicians in decades gone by were borrowed by a new generation of white musicians, and black musicians like Jimi Hendrix and Aretha Franklin finally found their spot at centre stage.

Much of the music of this era celebrated the use of psychedelic drugs. Singer Janis Joplin, who died at the age of 27 from a heroin overdose, summarized the feelings of many

Blast from the Past!

"In the late Sixties, young idealists and rebels, eight hundred at a time, were given full control of an eighteen-story highrise in the heart of English Canada's largest city. Rochdale College it was, an untested, bold idea on Bloor Street at the edge of the University of Toronto campus, a ten-minute walk from the Ontario Legislature. Rochdale College, a twin tower of raw concrete and straight lines [that opened in 1968], the largest co-operative student residence in North America, the largest of the more than 300 free universities in North America, and soon to be known across the country as the largest drug supermarket in North America."

—David Sharpe, *Rochdale: The Runaway College*

drug-using performers when she told *Life* magazine: "I'd rather have ten years of superhypermost than live to be seventy sitting in some goddam chair watching TV."

In addition to listening to songs that were inspired by psychedelic drugs, young people also listened to artists such as Bob Dylan, Joan Baez, Pete Seeger, and the folk trio Peter, Paul, and Mary—artists who frequently appeared at protest rallies against the war in Vietnam and for civil rights, the women's liberation movement, the gay rights movement, and the environmental movement.

Blast from the Past!

"We used to have about eight national anthems in Canada and no love songs. Well, now we have the love songs and we're also getting songs that tell you how the country feels."

—Singer Ian Tyson, "Musicians Play a Canada Rock," *Maclean's* magazine, February 4, 1970

The Canadian Scene

While the radio station playlists were dominated by musical acts from the U.S. and Britain, some homegrown artists did manage to attract their share of air time during the 1960s. Here's what you need to know about the hottest Canadian musical acts of the decade.

Ian and Sylvia

Ian and Sylvia Tyson (known simply as "Ian and Sylvia") were two of the most influential folk artists of the 1960s. They were known for their unique sound—a blend of country, rock, and folk—and were among the first folk musicians to use electric guitars. Their most famous song, "Four Strong Winds," written by Ian Tyson, was an international hit in 1962. The duo also had their own TV show on CTV during the 1970s. (The show was initially called *Nashville North* but was subsequently renamed *The Ian Tyson Show* after Ian and Sylvia split up. At that point, Sylvia began to host a CBC Radio show called *Touch the Earth*.) The two went on to enjoy solo careers during the 1970s and 1980s, but never achieved the same degree of fame as they had experienced when they were performing together.

Gordon Lightfoot

Gordon Lightfoot began his recording career in 1960, playing a key role in the burgeoning Canadian music scene that was centred around Yorkville in the early 1960s. He enjoyed a series of hit singles during the 1960s and 1970s, including the "Canadian Railroad Trilogy," "Early Morning Rain," "Alberta Bound," "Cotton Jenny," "If You Could Read My Mind," "Carefree Highway," "Sundown," and "The Wreck of the Edmund Fitzgerald." He's widely considered to be one of the most influential Canadian performers of all time. Consider what the Canadian Music Hall of Fame has to say about

the "Canadian Railroad Trilogy," the song that he was commissioned to write in honour of Canada's Centennial: "Few contemporary performers have so well captured the adventure, the hardship, the tragedy and the elation that goes into building a country, through lyric and melody, in a single epic song."

Leonard Cohen

Leonard Cohen has already established himself as one of Canada's most successful poets and novelists by the time he recorded his first record, *The Songs of Leonard Cohen*, in 1968. His most famous song, "Suzanne," became a hit record for American singer Judy Collins. He continued to record albums throughout the 1970s and 1980s and enjoyed a period of tremendous popularity in the late 1980s and early 1990s as other artists began to record large numbers of his songs. He was even the subject of a hilarious song by singer Nancy White: "Leonard Cohen's Never Gonna Bring My Groceries In" appeared on her 1990 album *Momnipotent*.

The Band

The Band got its start as the Hawks, Ronnie Hawkins' (a.k.a. the "Hawk") backup band during the early 1960s. They played the Toronto nightclub scene until they hooked up with Bob Dylan in 1968, changed their name to the Band, and toured the U.S., Australia, Britain, and Europe. The group released its debut album, *Music from Big Pink*, shortly thereafter, an album that featured such hit songs as "The Weight," "Caledonia Mission," and "Chest Fever." Their next album, *The Band*, was released in 1969. It soared to ninth spot on the U.S. charts and sold over one million copies, largely due to the popularity of the album's three hit songs: "Up on Cripple Creek," "The Night They Drove Old Dixie Down," and "Rag Mama Rag." Along the way, they became the first North American band to appear on the cover of *Time* magazine.

The Guess Who

The Guess Who got their name from a marketing gimmick. According to their bio in the Canadian Music Hall of Fame Web site, the group purposely left its name off a 1965 single called "Shakin' All Over." (They had good reason to leave their name off the record: at that point, the Winnipeg-based group was performing under the name Chad Allen and the Expressions!) Deejays dubbed them the Guess Who and the name stuck. Five years later, they had their biggest hit, "American Woman," which went right to the top of the American Hot 100. (The year before, they'd also had a lot of success with "These Eyes.")

Newsflash!

Before 1960, most of the records sold in Canada featured foreign musical acts. That began to change during the 1960s as music—both homegrown and foreign—began to play an increasingly important role in Canadian popular culture. A 1970 ruling by the Canadian Radio-Television and Telecommunications Commission requiring that AM broadcasters play a minimum of 30 percent Canadian material each week gave the Canadian music industry a badly-needed jumpstart and helped to lay the groundwork for the phenomenally successful 1990s.

Neil Young

Neil Young got his start in the coffee houses of Toronto's Yorkville district during the 1960s. He enjoyed a series of hit records with both Crazy Horse and Crosby, Stills, Nash, and Young and, in the 1990s, Pearl Jam. His best-known songs include "Only Love Can Break Your Heart," "Heart of Gold," "My My, Hey Hey (Out of the Blue)," and "Harvest Moon." He has often been described as the music world's greatest chameleon—an artist who is able to reinvent his style with each album.

Woodstock

The most noteworthy musical event of the 1960s was an outdoor concert on a farmer's field near the tiny New York State hamlet of Woodstock, which ran from August 15 to 17, 1969. The brainchild of hippies Michael Lang and Artie Kornfield, Woodstock was promoted by two wealthy young people, John Roberts and Joel Rosenman. (The four connected when Lang and Kornfield read Roberts and Rosenman's ad in *The New York Times*. The ad read: "Young men with Unlimited Capital looking for interesting, legitimate investment opportunities and business propositions.")

The four men managed to attract such big-name performers as Creedence Clearwater Revival, the Jefferson Airplane, Janis Joplin, Jimi Hendrix, the Grateful Dead, the Who, Santana, Richie Havens, Joan Baez, Joe Cocker, and Arlo Guthrie. The result was, in the words of Irwin Unger and Debi Unger, authors of *The Times Were a-Changin': The Sixties Reader*, "three frenzied days of music, pop, acid, grooving, skinny-dipping, and lovemaking, along with rain, mud, garbage, broken limbs, dysentery, freak-outs, two deaths, and one birth."

The concert promoters had hoped for attendance of 75,000, but 400,000 young people turned out for the concert. The latrines, food stands, and ticket booths were overwhelmed, and the majority of those attending the concert got in free. Consequently, even though the concert was a tremendous success, it didn't turn a profit for the organizers. It did, however, take on a mythic quality as a high-water mark for the counterculture world of the 1960s.

Blast from the Past!

According to Irwin Unger and Debi Unger, editors of *The Times Were a-Changin': The Sixties Reader*, Woodstock's organizers faced one unexpected expense: "Abbie Hoffman, the bad boy of the counterculture,...threatened to bad-mouth the festival on the street and create chaos at Woodstock if he and his friends were not given payola. The promoters sent $10,000 to Hoffman and associates on the Lower East Side."

The Least You Need to Know

➤ During the 1960s, Canadians' attitudes towards sexuality changed dramatically. Ideas about what constituted obscene material loosened up considerably. Birth control became socially acceptable. Sex before marriage became the norm for university students. And society as a whole became more tolerant of homosexuality.

➤ Young people experimented with illegal drugs such as marijuana, hashish, and LSD. They were spurred on by the former Harvard psychology instructor, Timothy Leary, who encouraged them to "turn on, tune in, drop out."

➤ The hottest Canadian musical acts of the 1960s included Ian and Sylvia, Gordon Lightfoot, Leonard Cohen, the Band, the Guess Who, and Neil Young.

➤ The musical highlight of the 1960s was Woodstock, a concert in New York State that ran from August 15 to 17, 1969, and attracted such big-name entertainers as Creedence Clearwater Revival, the Jefferson Airplane, Janis Joplin, Jimi Hendrix, the Grateful Dead, the Who, Santana, Richie Havens, Joan Baez, Joe Cocker, and Arlo Guthrie.

Chapter 2

I Am Woman

> ## In This Chapter
>
> ➤ The role of the pill in jump-starting the women's liberation movement
>
> ➤ The myth of the happy housewife
>
> ➤ The anti-feminist backlash
>
> ➤ Will that be one paycheque or two?
>
> ➤ The liberalization of the country's divorce and abortion laws

"Today nearly a million women in Canada and more than eight million other women throughout the world are happily swallowing the pill and wondering how on earth their mothers, let alone their grandmothers, ever managed to lead reasonably normal lives without it. They are part of the first generation in history in which women have been given a real choice about when to marry and when to have children. The pill has freed them from the tyranny of pregnancy—the oldest, the most natural, and thus the harshest tyranny of all." Thus wrote Douglas Marshall, in *Maclean's* magazine in March of 1967.

The birth control pill played an enormous part in making the women's liberation movement of the 1960s possible. For the first time in history, women had an almost foolproof method of controlling their fertility. This allowed them to decide when—or

whether—they wanted to have children and to plan their lives accordingly. Many decided to postpone marriage and children indefinitely. (After all, if you could have worry-free sex outside marriage, there wasn't the same incentive to make a trip to the altar.) Others decided to get married, but chose to work for a while before starting their families.

In an article entitled "The surprising social revolution we've started with the Pill" that appeared in *Maclean's* magazine in March of 1967, journalist Douglas Marshall highlighted some of the changes that had occurred since the introduction of the birth control pill. In addition to pointing out that the birth rate was declining and the number of women in the workforce increasing, Marshall noted that even the quality of married life was being improved by the birth control pill: "It is in the years immediately after marriage that the pill truly opens up a brave new world for modern couples," he wrote. These couples no longer had to worry about being "burdened by children" right away—something that gave them the opportunity to get to know one another and get their finances on solid ground before the babies started to arrive. There were also a lot fewer shotgun weddings, he noted. (Prior to the introduction of the birth control pill, as many as 50 percent of all first-time brides were pregnant when they walked down the aisle!)

The birth control pill wasn't solely responsible for the women's liberation movement, of course. It simply arrived on the scene at the right time. Growing numbers of Canadian women were already expressing dissatisfaction with their role in life. Now that they had this magic little pill to help them to control their fertility, they were able to take a good hard look at the rest of their lives—a situation that set the stage for revolution.

Happy Days?

The 1950s were a great time to be alive—unless, of course, you happened to be a housewife. As historian Stephanie Coontz notes in her book *The Way We Never Were: American Families and the Nostalgia Trap*, "a successful 1950s family...was often achieved at enormous cost to the wife, who was expected to subordinate her own needs and aspirations to those of both her husband and her children." In fact, as early as 1949, *Life* magazine was reporting that "suddenly and for no plain reason" women were "seized with an eerie restlessness."

Large number of women turned to alcohol or tranquillizers in order to hide from their feelings of dissatisfaction. According to Coontz, tranquillizers were developed in the

1950s to meet the needs of unhappy housewives. They were an overnight success: American women consumed 462,000 pounds of tranquillizers in 1958 and 1.15 million pounds in 1959. If everything was picture perfect *a là Leave It to Beaver,* then why were so many women popping pills? And why was every major American women's magazine using the word "trapped" to describe the plight of the suburban housewife?

The Feminine Mystique

Clearly the stage was set for Betty Friedan to write her 1963 bestseller, *The Feminine Mystique,* a book that described for the first time "the problem that has no name"—the boredom and despair of suburban housewives. The book was provocative and not afraid to break the silence on a topic that many considered taboo—how housewives really felt about their lives.

Blast from the Past!

"I think we will see within the next two years a massive rebellion of women that is at least comparable in magnitude to the black revolution or the student protest."

—Dr. Richard E. Farson, a psychologist and academic from the California Institute of the Arts in Los Angeles, quoted in the October 1969 issue of *Chatelaine*

"If a woman had a problem in the 1950s or 1960s, she knew that something must be wrong with her marriage or with herself," Friedan wrote. "Other women were satisfied with their lives, she thought. What kind of woman was she if she did not feel this mysterious fulfillment waxing the kitchen floor?"

The book hit a nerve with women across North America, many of whom went on to organize "consciousness-raising groups" so that they could share their feelings with other women.

B Is for Backlash

It didn't take long for men to start getting a little hot under the collar when it came to the women's movement. In the October 17, 1964, issue of *Maclean's* magazine, Sidney Katz expressed the feelings of many Canadian men when he stated that he'd already had enough of the women's movement: "For several years now, the Western world has been inundated with a tidal wave of articles, books, studies, radio and TV programs, speeches, conferences, panels, and symposia dealing with the dilemma of the modern housewife, and I, for one, have grown tired of it."

Journalist Eric LeBourdais echoed Katz's sentiments six years later when he wrote a controversial article stating that it was men, rather than women, who were being oppressed. The article—which was entitled "What men have to gain. Sex object? It's a lot worse being a 'work' object"—appeared in the November 1970 issue of *Chatelaine.* LeBourdais wrote: "The Lib ladies obviously don't realize it, but they're doing men their greatest favor since the discovery of fire. That's when mankind stopped wandering and

19

Blast from the Past!

In November of 1970, *Chatelaine* told its readers about the Voice of Man in Toronto (VOMIT)—an anti-feminist group whose members welcomed "release from a lifetime's service as a free meal ticket for an intellectually inferior woman and the brood she forces on us."

life's chores got split up, with the women keeping an eye on the cave and the kiddies, while the men went out to forage for food."

That same issue of *Chatelaine* contained a tongue-in-cheek rebuttal from journalist Barbara Frum who talked about the things that women stood to lose because of the feminist movement: "Soon they'll have to lose their ignorance about the complicated things. The option will be closed to slough off the brain-wearying decisions about insurance policies, mutual funds, mortgage contracts. Away will go the privilege of being wide-eyed and WOW about oil changes, horsepower, kilowatts, amperes, market longs and market shorts, term vs. annuity, NATO, SEATO, GATT, DC-AC, EEC, IRA, PQ, NLF, Yalta, Potsdam."

It wasn't just men who were objecting to the women's movement, of course. There were some outspoken female critics, too, like journalist Sheila H. Kieran who wrote an article titled "Who's downgrading women? Women" for *Maclean's* magazine in August of 1968. "As long as women remain apathetic, as long as they confuse temperament, tears, and shrillness with femininity, as long as they insist on special pleading, they will be treated with the easy-going contempt they deserve," she wrote.

Kieran wasn't the only woman who had reservations about the direction that the women's movement seemed to be taking. The majority of Canadian women found it hard to relate to the more radical elements in the women's movement—a point that *Chatelaine* editor Doris Anderson, herself a committed feminist, hammered home in an

Boomer Bytes

During the 1960s, *Chatelaine* magazine took a gutsy stand on a variety of issues, including divorce, abortion, and feminism. At the same time, the magazine remained true to its women's magazine roots, publishing articles on cooking, decorating, and dieting! The April 1969 issue featured an article with weight loss tips from such celebrities as politician John Turner, athlete Nancy Greene, broadcaster Adrienne Clarkson (who was to be named Governor General of Canada in 1999), actor Bruno Gerussi, and journalist June Callwood; and the November 1969 issue featured "The Thinking Woman's Diet"—a 914-calorie exercise in deprivation!

editorial in the magazine's November 1970 issue: "Some radical groups have cut themselves off from men. Most women probably believe there is nothing to be gained by sexual apartheid or guerrilla warfare."

A number of Canadian women—particularly those who belonged to the more affluent classes—felt that they had little to gain from women's liberation. "To try to convince the woman who has just ankled her way though the deep-pile broadloom on her way to the two-car garage to drive away from her dream bungalow filled with every huckstered Brandname in the world by a generous, hardworking husband—to try to tell that woman she's been had at the bargaining table of marriage is to grasp the frustration of every evangelist for women's liberation," wrote Barbara Frum in the November 1970 issue of *Chatelaine*. "Who in her suntanned, taut-bodied, carefully cultivated mind is going to surrender the benefits of a subsidized life for the privilege of being her own man?"

Another Royal Commission

In 1966, Laura Sabia, president of the Canadian Federation of University Women, called together representatives of 30 national women's organizations to discuss their common concerns. The group, which began calling itself the Committee on Equality for Women, called for the establishment of a Royal Commission on the Status of Women. When Prime Minister Lester B. Pearson seemed to be dragging his feet on this issue, Sabia threatened to march two million women to Ottawa to ensure that the group's demands were taken seriously.

The Royal Commission on the Status of Women was formally established in February of 1967. Its mandate was "to inquire and report upon the status of women in Canada, and to recommend what steps might be taken by the Federal Government to ensure for women equal opportunities with men in all aspects of Canadian society...."

The commission received submissions from across the country. It heard that women held less than 1 percent of the top decision-making jobs in business, industry, and government even though they made up more than half of the Canadian population; that only 9 percent of professionals were female; and that there were very few daycare facilities to care for the children of women who worked outside the home.

The commission issued its report in 1970. The report stated that women should be free to choose employment outside the home; that caring for children was a responsibility to be shared equally between mothers, fathers, and society as a whole; that special treatment related to maternity would always be necessary; and that women would need special treatment for an interim period to overcome the adverse effects of discriminatory practices. The report, which *Toronto Star* reporter Anthony Westell described as "a bomb already primed and ticking...packed with more explosive potential than any device manufactured by terrorists...a call to revolution," represented the agenda for feminists during the 1970s and beyond.

According to Alison Prentice, Paula Bourne, Gail Cuthbert Brandt, Beth Light, Wendy

Mitchinson, and Naomi Black, authors of *Canadian Women: A History,* by the time the commission tabled its report, the majority of Canadian women were determined to get their share of "the just society" promised by the newly elected prime minister, Pierre Elliott Trudeau. For the first time, they began rejecting the conventional definition of the good life: "a home of one's own, a car in the driveway, a fridge in the kitchen, and 2.5 kids in the 'rec room' watching *Les Plouffe* or *Father Knows Best.*"

Will That Be One Pay Cheque or Two?

At the start of the 1960s, Canadian women had yet to make significant inroads into the workforce. While it was acceptable for childless married women—or women with school-aged children—to work outside the home, society had grave reservations about having mothers of preschoolers holding down jobs in the paid labour force. Consequently, it wasn't until well into the 1970s that it became commonplace for women with preschoolers to work outside the home.

Most historians agree that what led large numbers of women to re-enter the workforce en masse during the 1960s and 1970s was a desire to keep up with the Joneses. "The advent of television provided yet another and more powerful medium through which advertisers could convince Canadians that [a variety of household] products were essential to an improved standard of living," write Alison Prentice, Paula Bourne, Gail Cuthbert Brandt, Beth Light, Wendy Mitchinson, and Naomi Black in their book *Canadian Women: A History.* "For most families, the purchase of expensive consumer items was possible only if there were more than one wage earner in the family."

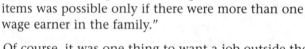

Blast from the Past!

"Organized society is still opposed to the idea of married women making any substantial contribution to the world outside the four walls of a house."

—Marguerite Ritchie and Mollie Gillen, writing in the April 1960 issue of *Saturday Night* magazine

Of course, it was one thing to want a job outside the home, but quite another thing to get one. In August of 1960, journalist Dean Walker wrote about the factors that kept women out of the workforce in an article in *Canadian Business:* "Although psychologists are convinced that mentally, physically and emotionally women are as capable as men of handling management problems, industry is armed with a blind eye and a telescope and does not get the message. As a result, a huge and attractive pool of talent, possibly our most neglected national asset, is untapped."

Throughout the decade, there continued to be considerable discussion in the media about the problems experienced by women who were re-entering the workforce. Journalist Jack Schreiner described the need for childcare and childcare income tax exemptions in an article in the December 12, 1964, issue of *The Financial Post.* And *Chatelaine* ran a special "back to work" editorial package in its August 1969 issue. (The

Boomer Bytes

In 1964, 31 percent of Canadian workers were women—up from 23.2 percent in 1950. "This growth is due chiefly to the number of women older than 35 who are returning to work. Federal Department of Labor officials have estimated that more than 80 percent of the 554,000 jobs for women created in the 1950s were filled by married women," noted journalist Jack Schreiner in the December 12, 1964, issue of *The Financial Post*.

editorial package contained a curious mix of feminist rhetoric and practical "how to" advice. One of the articles—"How women who work cope with meals"—provided valuable tips to women who were wondering how they could possibly put in a day at the office and still manage to have dinner on the table at the end of the day. One of the women interviewed in the article used the timer on her automatic oven so that she could have a pot roast on the table by 6:30 p.m. Another whipped up casseroles the night before so that dinner would be ready to pop in the oven the moment she arrived home from work. A third admitted to purchasing ready-made meals: "A deli is a girl's best friend," she confided.)

In an article that appeared in the November 1970 issue of *Chatelaine,* editor Doris Anderson stated the magazine's position on the role of women as the decade rolled to a close: "Femininity can't be defined by job roles. Women aren't women because they have special aptitude with vacuum cleaners, cooking pots, diapers, and typewriters. Those are the jobs society has always assigned to women, that's all."

The Abortion Debate

In 1968, the federal government changed section 208 of the Criminal Code, which outlawed abortions except when the procedure was necessary in order to save a woman's life. A woman could now obtain an abortion if she could prove to a hospital abortion committee that an unwanted pregnancy was damaging her mental health.

The move was controversial, stirring up heated debate between the pro-life and pro-choice

Boomer Bytes

Between 1954 and 1965, there were 226 therapeutic abortions and 50,000 to 100,000 illegal abortions performed in Canada.

camps. While the pro-life forces found any liberalization of the country's abortion laws unacceptable, the pro-choice forces felt that the changes hadn't gone far enough. Doris Anderson called for further abortion law reforms in an editorial in the October 1969 issue of *Chatelaine:* "A year ago, we got a new abortion law making it possible for a woman to have a legal abortion in Canada if she could (a) convince a board of three or more doctors that her health, mental or physical, would be in danger if she had a baby; and (b) find a doctor willing to perform the operation. (In a town with only one doctor or only a Catholic hospital—lots of luck.)...The government must have lots of other worries on its collective and almost totally male mind. It probably wishes the agitation about abortion would go away. But the problem for women is too real for it to go away....We can't wait the customary Canadian twenty, ten, or even five years for this reform. We need it now."

Till Divorce Do Us Part

There was considerably less controversy when the newly elected Trudeau government decided to liberalize the country's divorce laws. The majority of Canadians felt that divorce-law changes were long overdue.

Prior to 1969, divorce was illegal in Quebec and Newfoundland. Couples in these provinces who wished to end their marriages had to ask the House of Commons to pass a private act of Parliament. The situation in the other eight provinces was only marginally better: adultery was the only legal grounds for divorce.

Boomer Bytes

There were 50,000 to 100,000 Canadian couples living common-law by the late 1960s.

Because the divorce laws in Canada were so rigid, Canadians who hoped to end their marriages frequently ended up leaving the country in order to obtain a divorce. These divorces—which were granted by countries such as Mexico—weren't legally recognized in Canada, but as journalist Alan Edmonds noted in an article in *Maclean's* magazine in September of 1967, they allowed people to live common-law with a clear conscience: "Mostly, they are people who cannot get divorced and must pay this as conscience money; they've met someone else who won't live with them 'in sin'—except on the strength of a spurious document in Spanish which most lawyers admit is 'about as legally valid as toilet paper.'" Edmonds noted that these so-called "Mexican divorces" could be obtained for as little as $1,000—including the cost of plane tickets!

Many unhappily married Canadian couples were relieved when the federal government decided to liberalize the divorce laws, expanding the grounds for divorce to include cruelty, desertion, and marital breakdown, and eliminating the need to have a "guilty party" in order to end a marriage. For many Canadian couples, these divorce law changes meant that they were finally free to live happily ever after.

The Least You Need to Know

➤ The birth control pill made the women's movement possible because it provided women with a virtually foolproof method of controlling their fertility.

➤ During the 1960s, women began talking about "the problem that has no name" —the boredom and despair experienced by many suburban housewives.

➤ Many men and some women were opposed to the so-called women's liberation movement.

➤ While the number of women in the workforce continued to increase during the 1960s, it wasn't until the 1970s that large numbers of women with preschoolers began working outside the home.

➤ The country's abortion laws were liberalized in 1968—something that sparked heated debate amongst members of both the pro-life and pro-choice camps.

➤ The country's divorce laws were modernized in 1969. For the first time, Canadian couples didn't have to hang the blame for marriage breakdown on a single "guilty party."

Chapter 3

Oh, Baby!

In This Chapter

➤ Escape to the suburbs

➤ What the best-dressed babies were wearing

➤ Toys, games, *Romper Room*, and more

"Our suburbs were wondrous places. Built through the 1950s, they offered the split-level ranch-type life that, for a while at least, fulfilled most Canadians' dreams of property and possessions," writes Alan Edmonds, in his book *The Years of Protest 1960–1970.*

At the start of the 1960s, the post-war baby boom was still going strong, and Canadian families were packing up and moving to the suburbs. Most Canadian parents believed that paradise was to be found in the bedroom communities that were springing up just outside the country's major cities. Families with young children were looking for neighbourhoods where there were plenty of trees and parks to enjoy—something that the suburbs promised to deliver.

Pleasantville Revisited

A typical suburban neighbourhood was sprinkled with cookie-cutter homes that were designed to appeal to families within roughly the same income bracket. Sure, there was usually more than one model of house to choose from, but they all looked strikingly similar. For one thing, 80 percent of the homes were bungalows. For another, they were all roughly the same size—1,000 to 1,200 square feet—a size that did not exactly allow for Scarlett O'Hara staircases or other architectural extravagances.

Part of the appeal of the suburbs, of course, was their very uniformity. You didn't have to worry about someone constructing a monster home beside your tiny little bungalow. (At least, not yet!) In fact, the founding mothers and fathers of Etobicoke—a suburb of Toronto—went to great lengths to ensure that all of the streets in the community maintained that prized uniformity. Residents were required to cut their grass at least once each week, to keep hedges and fences in the front yard at a height of less than two and a half feet, and to refrain from building backyard bird houses. (I haven't figured that one out yet.) According to Alan Edmonds, author of *The Years of Protest 1960–1970*, Etobicoke was the first community in Canada to demand that garbage be placed in plastic bags for collection—"gift-wrapped garbage," it was called!

Most suburban homes tended to be free of knick-knacks and to boast easy-to-clean surfaces for floors, walls, and furnishings—and for good reason. Between one-third and one-half of the residents of a typical suburb were children under age 14—hardly the velvet chesterfield crowd! These suburban homes were also equipped with the latest appliances, although not every family boasted a clothes dryer yet, and only a select few had one of those newfangled devices that could wash dishes automatically. (See Table 3.1.)

Table 3.1

The percentage of Canadian households that had various household appliances in 1966:

Refrigerator	96 percent
Electric stove	69 percent
Freezer	23 percent
Dishwasher	3 percent
Clothes washer	86 percent
Clothes dryer	25 percent

Source: **The Toronto Star**

In February of 1963, *The Financial Post* published an article which described the hottest trends in the Canadian housing market. People were looking for "storms and screens on every window, decorated rooms, paved driveways, sodded lawns back and front, finished roads with curbs and streetlights, and underground wiring." Four-bedroom homes were also becoming quite popular, the article noted: while only 3 percent of homes built a decade earlier had boasted this many bedrooms, 20 percent of homes being built in 1963 had four bedrooms.

Here's Looking at You, Kid!

There's a reason why Jane and Joe Canuck were on the lookout for a four-bedroom home. The baby boom was still going strong at the start of the 1960s with a "typical" family having three or four children.

Of course, some families were still having six, seven, or eight children—a throwback to generations past. These families got a good blasting from journalist Sidney Katz in the October 19, 1963, issue of *Maclean's* magazine. He wrote: "Big families are an anachronism. Houses aren't built for them. Most incomes are pitifully inadequate to support them and most couples aren't emotionally equipped to rear half a dozen children in the environment of modern North American life." (Bet a lot of couples reached for the birth control pills after reading Katz's article!)

Boomer Bytes

By 1960, two-thirds of Canadian households had one car and 10 percent had two or more cars.

—Source: Douglas Owram, *Born at the Right Time: A History of the Baby Boom Generation*

A New Way to Have Babies

In October of 1967, *Maclean's* magazine reported on a shocking development: a Canadian hospital—St. Joseph's in Hamilton, Ontario—was allowing fathers to be present in the delivery room when their wives were giving birth!

Certain members of the medical establishment were less than thrilled about this development. One Montreal obstetrician who was interviewed in the article didn't make any effort to hide his feelings: "It's true the husband is present at the laying of the keel, but I'm damned if I think he has any right to a place at the launching."

Boomer Bytes

By 1966, Canada had a larger proportion of children in its population than any other Western nation: 34 percent. The corresponding figure for the United States was 21 percent.

Dr. William Allemang, a professor of obstetrics at the University of Toronto, tried to reassure the magazine's readers that the new trend towards natural childbirth was "a fringe thing in the field of obstetrics"—more of a fad than anything.

The Birth of Disposable Diapers

In 1961, Procter and Gamble invented Pampers, the world's first disposable diaper. Disposable diapers cost about 10 cents apiece, which may explain why they only managed to capture 1 percent of the diaper market during their first year in production.

Newsflash!

One of the most horrific stories to hit the headlines during the 1960s was the tragedy of the thalidomide babies.

Between 1957 and 1961, large numbers of pregnant women around the world took thalidomide to relieve morning sickness. At least 20 percent of babies whose mothers took the drug during their fourth to eighth weeks of pregnancy suffered severe deformities. Some had crude hands joined to their shoulders or foot-like appendages that were attached to their hips rather than normal hands and legs. Approximately 8,000 babies were affected worldwide.

Thalidomide was available in Canada for less than one year, but during that time four million tablets of the drug were purchased. Despite the fact that the Canadian government first heard warnings about the drug's effects in December of 1961, the drug wasn't ordered removed from drugstore shelves until four months later.

"The history of thalidomide will be cited by doctors, researchers, and governments for years to come," wrote journalist June Callwood in the May 19, 1962, issue of *Maclean's*. "It most certainly will alter attitudes, methods of testing, and regulating all over the world."

Newsflash!

In March of 1962, *The Financial Post* reported that it had "good news for busy mothers." There was now a one-piece stretch suit on the market that covered a baby from the neck down. More than 600,000 of these "sleepers" had been sold during their first year on the Canadian market—not bad for a country in which just 500,000 babies were born each year.

Over time, however, disposable diapers became the trendy, modern way to handle diapering—something that allowed the disposable diaper companies to capture 85 percent of the $3.5 billion Canadian diaper market by 1990.

Parenting by the Book

If there was one parenting authority that Canadian parents turned to time and time again during the 1960s, it was Dr. Benjamin Spock, the Connecticut-born author of *Dr. Spock's Baby and Child Care*.

First published in 1945, *Dr. Spock's Baby and Child Care* went on to sell 50 million copies in 42 languages—an achievement that made it the second bestselling title of all time. (The Bible is number one.)

Dr. Spock tried to reassure parents that they could rely on their gut instincts when it came to parenting:

"Trust yourself. You know more than you think you do," he wrote in the opening lines of the book. He also emphasized the psychological aspects of parenting, encouraging parents to feed their infants on demand rather than according to a strict and arbitrary schedule.

Not everyone agreed with what Dr. Spock had to say. Some called him "the father of permissiveness" and blamed him for the wanderlust of the hippie generation. He also got a lot of heat because of the stand he took against the Vietnam War. In 1968, he was convicted of aiding draft resisters and sentenced to two years in jail—time that, in the end, he didn't serve. Still, his influence was enormous: when he gave GI Joe the thumbs down in 1967, orders for the previously popular toy halved overnight.

Babes in Toyland

Wondering what could be found in a typical child's toy box during the 1960s? Let's lift up the lid and take a peek.

Barbie Meets Ken

After being a swinging single for the first two years of her existence, Barbie finally met the man of her dreams in 1961. That's when Mattel began manufacturing Ken. Ken and Barbie stayed together for six years, but then separated for two years from 1967 to 1969, when Ken temporarily went out of production. (Barbie's younger sister Midge also went out of production in 1967, something that must have led more than a few little girls to wonder if Ken and Midge had decided to set up in a Barbie Dream House of their own.)

Twister

One of the hottest games of the 1960s was Twister, a party game that asked players to twist their bodies into pretzel-like contortions without falling over on top of the other

Blast from the Past!

"When they are dealing with purely factual material, advice books are a great boon to new parents....But advice books always exceed the factual matters and go on to give what-to-do advice on matters such as discipline, tantrums, pacifiers—all subjects on which the experts don't agree among themselves at any given time, and on which their views have changed over the years."

—Journalist Sheila H. Kieran, writing in the July 3, 1965, issue of *Maclean's* magazine

Boomer Bytes

Between 1959 and 1989, 500 million Barbie dolls and one billion sets of Barbie clothes were sold around the world. That works out to an average of 45,662 Barbies and 91,324 outfits sold each day!

players. It was played on a polka-dotted plastic sheet that was spread out on the floor. The game was invented by Chuck Foley, an American father of nine. He recently explained the game's appeal to a reporter from *The Dallas Morning News*: "The biggest problem people had in entertaining was worrying about people enjoying themselves and not getting into corners. [Twister] pulled people together."

Yo-yos

While the yo-yo was nothing new—it had actually been around for years—there was a bit of a yo-yo renaissance during the 1960s and 1970s. According to the History Channel Web site, three U.S. presidents—Kennedy, Johnson, and Nixon—were seen playing yo-yo in public, and political activist Abbie Hoffman was caught "walking the dog" during a Congressional hearing.

Boomer Bytes

Here are some of the proudest moments in toy history, circa 1960:

➤ Barbie's boyfriend Ken is introduced (1961)

➤ Lego comes to Canada (1961)

➤ Frisbees hit the Canadian market (1962)

➤ Canada's owl-like Ookpik toy achieves international stardom (1964)

➤ GI Joe comes on the market (1965)

➤ The Superball is introduced. At one point Wham-O is manufacturing 170,000 balls per day (1965)

—Sources: *Toronto Star*; Jane Stern and Michael Stern; *Sixties People*, Doug Owram, *Born at the Right Time: A History of the Baby Boom Generation*

The Least You Need to Know

➤ Throughout the 1960s, the place to be for families with young children was the suburbs. Family after family moved into the 1,000-to-1,200-square-foot "cookie cutter" bungalows that dotted the suburban landscape.

➤ Natural childbirth came into vogue and one Canadian hospital started allowing fathers into the delivery room.

➤ Thalidomide was pulled off the market after it was linked with severe deformities in developing babies. It was available in Canada for less than one year.

➤ Disposable diapers and stretch sleepers were two of the most lasting inventions of the 1960s.

➤ Parents continued to turn to Dr. Spock for parenting advice, despite the fact that he was attracting criticism for being "the father of permissiveness."

➤ Toy crazes of the 1960s included Barbies, Twister, Frisbees, Ookpiks, GI Joe, and the Superball.

Chapter 4

Fun and Games

In This Chapter

➤ Canadians' love-hate relationship with the CBC

➤ Colour TV comes to Canada

➤ What shows Canadians were tuned in to

➤ Fashion and fads, 1960s style!

➤ A year-long birthday celebration

Pop culture fads spread like wildfire during the 1960s. Thanks to the power of TV, what was hot in California or New York one day could be all the rage in Halifax or Vancouver the next. Canadians tuning in to American television shows like *The Ed Sullivan Show* could check out the latest trends in fashion or hear about the latest dance fad at the very same time that Americans were finding out about them. Suddenly, it didn't matter if you lived in Toronto or Buffalo: you were part of an increasingly homogeneous North American culture.

That's not to say, of course, that Canadians were prepared to abandon the Maple Leaf in favor of the Stars and Stripes. If anything, the flood of American culture made some Canadians more determined than ever to celebrate their Canadian identity. (Perhaps that explains why many of the decade's most heated debates related to the role of the

Boomer Bytes

In 1952, a TV set cost $400—approximately 20 percent of the average annual income of a Canadian household or roughly $10,000 in 1999 dollars.

CBC: whether the corporation was living up to its mandate of promoting Canadian culture or was too quick to cash in on advertising dollars by airing the more commercially successful American television shows!)

In this chapter, we're going to look at the TV shows, fashion trends, and fads that made the sixties such an unforgettable decade; and take a quick trip back to 1967, when Canada invited the entire world to its birthday party.

TV Nation

When the first Canadian television stations went on the air in Toronto and Montreal in 1952, only 26 percent of Canadians were able to pick up television signals. By 1960, the situation had changed dramatically: more than 90 percent of Canadians were able to tune in to one or more of the 59 TV stations that were broadcasting in Canada by that time.

After Canada's first private broadcaster, CTV, was licensed in 1961, the Canadian television market became more competitive. The CBC found that it was increasingly necessary to carry popular American TV shows rather than Canadian-made TV shows if it was going to be able to compete for advertising dollars.

Movers and Shakers

Herbert Marshall McLuhan (1911–1980) attracted a lot of attention during the 1960s because of his studies of the effects of mass media on thought and behaviour.

A professor of English at the University of Toronto, McLuhan distinguished between "hot media" (e.g. print or radio), which are full of information and require less sensory involvement from the reader or listener, and "cool media" (e.g. the television or the telephone), which are relatively lacking in information and require the sensory involvement of the viewer or listener. McLuhan concluded that the message was affected by the medium chosen: "The medium is the message."

An academic with tremendous insight into the changing nature of communication, McLuhan predicted and described the effects of the Internet and virtual reality as early as 1964, noting that it would eventually be possible to form relationships based solely on electronic communication.

Boomer Bytes

While there might not have been a lot happening on the small screen during the 1960s, there was plenty happening at the National Film Board (NFB). The NFB had focused primarily on documentaries during the immediate post–war years, but in the early 1960s, it became involved in the production of dramatic feature films for theatrical release. The 1960s were truly the NFB's golden age. After that time, government cutbacks and the growth of the commercial film industry would reduce its importance in the feature film arena.

That's not to say that the CBC abandoned its commitment to Canadian television, however. During the 1960s, it produced a number of highly popular shows, including *Wojeck, Quentin Durgens MP, This Hour Has Seven Days, Man Alive, The Nature of Things, Mr. Dressup,* and *The Friendly Giant,* among others.

Despite this string of successes, more often than not, the CBC found itself in the hot seat because of its programming decisions. This attack by Douglas Marshall, writing in *Maclean's* magazine in October of 1968, was typical: "The CBC...gives the illusion of dictatorship. It is run by people who seem to believe they are members of a jittery banana-republic regime constantly on the verge of another coup. Nobody knows whose head will roll tomorrow and everybody is so busy protecting his own back that the feelings of the [viewers]...are the last thing to worry about." The title of Marshall's article? "Viewers of Canada, unite! After all, it's OUR $12 million."

In Living Colour

While it's hard for us to imagine life without it, the initial response of Canadians to colour TV was decidedly underwhelming.

"There just isn't any demand," one dealer told *The Financial Post* in August of 1966—just weeks before the CBC's first colour broadcast on October 1, 1966. "When people start asking for them I'll place an order. Until then, I have no intention of building up an expensive inventory." (While an averaged-sized black-and-white television set could be had for $200, colour television sets of the same size cost between $700 and $2,000.)

Perhaps Canadians were a little reluctant to fork over that amount of money until they were sure about what they would get for their investment. Despite the fact that the CBC had invested $15 million to make the switch to colour broadcasting, Canadians still couldn't be sure that they'd be able to enjoy watching their favourite programs in

colour. ("If problems with lighting can be overcome, hockey will...be televised in color," a CBC spokesman told *The Financial Post*.)

Even Peter Gzowski gave colour TV the thumbs down. In an article titled "What's so great about color TV?" that ran in the March 5, 1966, issue of *Maclean's*, Gzowski warned Canadians that they were going to be less than dazzled by their new colour TVs: "Adjusting the controls on a color set is no more difficult than warming up a Boeing 707. In front, besides the regular knobs for vertical and bright and so on are two labelled 'color' and 'tint.' 'Tint,' apparently, is for the fine tuning, after you get everything else in balance. Me, I can't ever seem to get to that stage: I'm still fiddling with a set of knobs at the back of the set that control the individual colors, red, green, and blue. On a few occasions, I've been able to get everything roughly in balance, but, so far at least, it doesn't stay that way for long."

One Big Happy Family...

Most of the shows that Canadian families tuned in to during the 1950s and 1960s were decidedly white bread. The name of the game seemed to be produce programming that was guaranteed not to offend the sensibilities of the folks who controlled the purse strings at the big advertising agencies. The result was a middle-class, white Protestant universe that was ruled by kindly fathers, saintly mothers, and mildly mischievous but never downright rotten children. The best examples of this type of television show were such American imports as *Father Knows Best* (1954 to 1962), *Leave It to Beaver* (1957 to 1963), *My Three Sons* (1960 to 1972), *The Donna Reed Show* (1958 to 1966), and *Ozzie and Harriet* (1952 to 1964)—shows that continued to live on long after the shows' producers pulled the plug, thanks to the miracle of reruns.

Even shows that stepped outside the mould by tampering with the recipe for "the perfect family" were careful not to overstep the bounds of good taste. One of the best-kept secrets in the weird and wonderful world of TV sitcoms was the fact that Carol Brady of *The Brady Bunch* was actually a divorcée rather than a widow. (The powers that be in TV land had decided that the North American viewing public wasn't quite ready for a show that focused on a divorced woman!) Other shows airing at the time took a similarly conservative approach: shipwreck or no shipwreck, there was no hanky-panky to be had on *Gilligan's Island!* (See Table 4.1.)

Table 4.1 Don't Touch That Dial: The Hottest New Shows to Debut During the 1960s

Year	The hottest new shows to debut that season
1960	*The Andy Griffith Show*
	Checkmate
	The Flintstones
	My Three Sons
1961	*Ben Casey*
	Rocky and Bullwinkle
	The Defenders
	The Dick Van Dyke Show
	Dr. Kildare
1962	*The Beverly Hillbillies*
	The Lucy Show
	McHale's Navy

1963	*The Fugitive*
	My Favorite Martian
	The Outer Limits
	The Patty Duke Show
1964	*The Addams Family*
	Bewitched
	Gilligan's Island
	The Man from U.N.C.L.E.
	The Munsters
1965	*Big Valley*
	Get Smart
	Gidget
	Green Acres
1966	*Batman*
	The Monkees
	Star Trek
1967	*The Carol Burnett Show*
	Ironside
	The Smothers Brothers Comedy Hour
1968	*Hollywood Squares*
	Mod Squad
	Rowan and Martin's Laugh-In
1969	*The Brady Bunch*
	Hee Haw
	Marcus Welby M.D.

Sources: The Toronto Star's Starweek Magazine, *February 6 to 13, 1999; Charles Panati*, Panati's Parade of Fads, Follies and Manias: The Origins of Our Most Cherished Obsessions.

All the News That's Fit to Print—and Then Some!

Not all of the popular shows were imports, of course. One of the most watched television shows of the 1960s was *This Hour Has Seven Days* (October 4, 1964, to May 8, 1966)—a home-grown news and public affairs program known for its outrageous and irreverent style. According to Alan Edmonds, author of *The Years of Protest 1960–1970,* the show once staged a sketch showing the Pope being asked to referee a baseball game, and on another occasion it invited leaders of the Ku Klux Klan on the show—then confronted them with a black interviewer!

Over time, the popular show became an embarrassment to CBC management, which decided to cancel it in the spring of 1966—a move that drew even more calls of protest than the infamous Pope sketch!

What the Kids Were Watching

Grownups weren't the only ones who were glued to their TV sets, dreaming of the time when someone would invent a wireless remote control. Kids were also getting hooked on the tube.

One of the most popular Canadian children's television shows of all time was *Mr. Dressup,* which aired from 1967 until 1996. Host Ernie Coombs and puppet sidekicks Casey and Finnegan delighted children with a low-glitz mixture of art activities and make-believe. (Casey and Finnegan actually packed it in a few years sooner than *Mr. Dressup!*)

The Friendly Giant was another Canadian show that was aimed at the preschool set. The show—which ran from 1958 to 1985—was hosted by Bob Homme (the friendly giant!) and sidekicks Jerome the giraffe and Rusty the rooster. The show was set in a castle. (The raising and lowering of the drawbridge was one of the highlights of each episode.)

Blast from the Past!

"Hardly anyone really likes commercials. In fact, program flush-rating charts kept at municipal waterworks indicates most of us don't even watch them—we go to the bathroom instead."

—Elizabeth Graham, writing in the March 16, 1966 issue of *Maclean's* magazine

Romper Room was similarly popular with children under five. In the fall of 1966, CTV started broadcasting *Romper Room* from coast to coast. (Up until that time, the Canadian version of the American show had only been broadcast from CTV's studio in Hamilton, Ontario.) By that time, *Romper Room* was being broadcast in 15 different countries. There were 143 local versions of the show, all virtually identical in format and style because each of the *Romper Room* teachers was personally trained by the show's creators, Bert and Nancy Claster of Baltimore, before making her on-air debut.

Boomer Bytes

Maclean's magazine reported in its April 22, 1961, issue that one out of three children were watching television by the age of three, four out of five by the age of five, and nine out of ten by the time they reached Grade 1.

Jocelyn Dingman of *Maclean's* explained the show's appeal to the children (known as "Do Bees" for "do be good") who tuned in: "Many children [of three, four, and five] lead rather solitary lives, and part of the show's fascination for them is that they can watch children their own age play, sing, and eat cookies....Hardly anything else on television is suitable for children under five. They love commercials, but wander away during the shows."

While *Romper Room, The Friendly Giant,* and *Mr. Dressup* kept preschoolers entertained, there wasn't the same amount of home-grown programming for their older brothers and sisters. By default, school-age kids tuned in to such American imports as *Roy Rogers, Lassie, The Mickey Mouse Club, Walt Disney,* and the Canadian version of the *Howdy Doody Show.*

Ready to Wear

Fashion made the man—and the woman—during the 1960s. You didn't have to wear a button that expressed your political beliefs (although many young people opted to do that anyway!) Your clothes got the message across for you.

Boomer Bytes

Some of the best commercials of the 1960s, according to *Advertising Age* magazine:

➤ Maxwell House's "Good to the Last Drop" commercial for ground coffee

➤ Lyndon Johnson's 1964 presidential campaign advertisement, which showed a young girl picking petals from a daisy, followed by a nuclear explosion

➤ the Marlboro Man cigarette commercial, which changed the target market for the cigarette from women to men

➤ an uncharacteristically sexy Noxzema advertisement that had a former Miss Sweden cooing "Take it off. Take it all off."

You can read about the magazine's other favourite commercials from this decade by visiting: the *Advertising Age* magazine web site at www.adage.com

Young matrons tried to achieve the Jackie Kennedy look, sporting pillbox hats, two-piece suits with semi-fitted tops and huge buttons, A-line skirts that fell to mid-knee, low-slung sensible pumps, and wraparound sunglasses that curved around the sides of their heads. They completed the look with flamboyant bouffant hairdos that left their hair feeling as sticky and matted as candy floss.

Members of the younger generation went for far flashier outfits.

Some wore the "elephant pants" made famous by entertainers Sonny and Cher: pants that flared out at the knee so dramatically that they were large enough to fit an elephant's ankle.

Others went for the tie-dyed look popularized by hippies in San Francisco's Haight-Ashbury district, a look that became the uniform of the Woodstock generation well into the 1970s. (The fact that it was an alternative look didn't stop manufacturers from trying to cash in. It wasn't long before department stores were offering tie-dyed sheets, rugs, and curtains as well as commercially manufactured—as opposed to home-made—T-shirts and tank tops.)

Still others wore granny dresses—dowdy, ankle-length dresses that would have done any granny proud and that caught on with young women who wanted to cast a vote of disapproval against the hottest fashion trend of the decade—the miniskirt.

And anyone who was hip was sure to be sporting a pair of granny glasses (half-frame glasses).

For those who dared to wear them another hot fashion item was go-go boots—white leather, rising to mid-calf—a style inspired by the miniskirt-clad go-go girls who wore them as they danced in suspended cages at chic American nightclubs. (Nancy Sinatra's song "These Boots Are Made for Walkin'" became the anthem of the go-go boot crowd.)

Newsflash!

On May 10, 1969, *The Financial Post* reported that a French researcher had discovered that girls who wore miniskirts developed more fat on their thighs than those who wore longer skirts. "The evidence of fleshy increase is apparently so convincing that an American farmer has decided to shave the hind legs of all his cattle and pigs in the hope of obtaining an extra bonus of meat," the newspaper noted.

Newsflash!

In the summer of 1966, Canadians went mad for Wm. Neilson Ltd.'s new Super Swirl ice cream. Flavours included Mad Mad Mocha—coffee ice cream with chocolate sauce—as well as Strawberry Spin, Merri-Mint, Raspberry Dazzle, and Leaping Lemon. "I have been in this business 26 years, but I have never seen sales go like this before," one Neilson official told *The Financial Post*.

Fads

The 1960s also saw their share of fads. Here are a few of the more memorable:

➤ *Troll dolls.* By 1963, young women in college and high school had taken to carrying around troll dolls—hideously ugly dolls that were supposed to bring good luck to their owners.

➤ *Lava lamps* were a source of instant entertainment, whether you were straight or stoned. Over two million lava lamps were sold in the U.S. between 1965 and 1970.

➤ *Black lights* made clothes that had been washed in phosphates glow in an eerie fashion—which made them a perennial favourite at parties.

➤ *Day-Glo clothing* went one step better. Because of the fluorescent dyes and resins they contained, they glowed in ordinary daylight.

Dance Crazes

The hottest dance craze of the 1960s was the twist—a dance that was all the rage in 1961. Here's how Chubby Checker described his now-classic dance to a journalist: "It's like putting out a cigarette with both your feet and coming out of a shower and wiping your bottom with a towel to the beat of the music. It's that simple."

Other popular dances during the decade included the "mashed potato" (a variation on the twist), the "swim" (which involved moving your arms in a swim-like motion), and the "Watusi" (which involved moving your arms like a surfer).

Wasn't That a Party?

In 1967, Canadians had good reasons to dance. They were celebrating the country's 100th birthday. Canadians were in the mood for a party: literary works were commissioned, cultural centres sprouted up across the country, canoeists followed the paths first used by the fur traders, and mountain climbers made their way to the top of previously unconquered peaks in the Rockies.

Not everyone was hit with a case of centennial fever, however. Michael Bliss—a Toronto high school teacher who was about to start his postgraduate work in history at the University of Toronto (and who would eventually become one of the country's best-known historians!)—made a rather convincing case for cancelling the whole damned thing.

Newsflash

During the late 1960s, small publishing houses began to pop up in cities across the country. Two of the most noteworthy publishing houses to emerge during this period were Coach House Press (established in 1965) and House of Anansi (established in 1967). Coach House Press authors included Leonard Cohen, bp Nichol, George Bowering, and Michael Ondaatje; while House of Anansi 's included Northrop Frye, Margaret Atwood, and Dennis Lee (one of the co-founders of the press).

"What really happened in 1867?" he wrote. "Nothing much, really....Why [then] are we so intent on deluding ourselves that anything important happened in 1867? I suggest that it's a symptom of sincere but misguided nationalism. We can't bear the idea of our history being so dull; secretly we envy the Americans, whose national history at least started with a resounding bang. Confederation, by contrast with 1776, was scarcely a whimper."

Expo '67

At the heart of Canada's year-long birthday celebration was Expo '67, the first world exhibition to take place on North American soil. While Expo '67 was the centrepiece of Canada's centennial celebrations, it only ended up happening at all because the USSR cancelled its own plans to host the world exhibition that year—a move that enabled Montréal mayor Jean Drapeau to convince the Bureau International des Expositions in Paris that Canada was prepared to step in.

The Canadian Corporation for the 1967 World Exhibition was established to organize and run the event. It was set up as a three-way partnership between the federal government (50 percent), the Québec government (37.5 percent), and the city of Montréal.

The Corporation decided that the ideal site for

Blast from the Past!

"In the year 2000, Canadians will probably have two-and-a-half times as many leisure hours as working hours and, if the trend continues, assembly lines and business conferences will probably become those slight annoyances Canadians will have to put up with for the few brief hours they spend away from their hobbies."

—Shirley Mair, writing in the January 27, 1962, issue of *Maclean's*

the exhibition would be Ile Ste-Hélène, a park in the centre of the St. Lawrence that was linked to Montréal by the Jacques Cartier Bridge. The island was expanded using land reclamation techniques that involved using silt and rock dredged from the bottom of the river. What's more, a new island—Ile Notre-Dame—would be created to provide further space for the exhibition. When river bottom sources of landfill proved insufficient, it became necessary to bring in landfill by dump truck, which quadrupled the cost of building on the site.

The theme chosen for Expo '67 was Man and His World—derived from the title of a book by the French author, poet, and aviator Antoine de Saint-Exupéry, *Terre des Hommes*. The exhibit was divided into five sections: Man the Creator, Man the Explorer, Man the Producer, Man the Provider, and Man and the Community.

Running from April 27 to October 29, Expo '67 attracted more than 50 million visitors—not including the five million admissions by performers, members of the press, official visitors, and employees. While Expo '67 cost the Corporation approximately $283 million, the return to taxpayers was roughly double that amount.

The Least You Need to Know

➤ By 1960, more than 90 percent of Canadians were able to tune in to one or more of the 59 television stations that were broadcasting in Canada at that time.

➤ The CBC first broadcast in colour on October 1, 1966.

➤ One of the most popular—and most controversial—TV shows of the 1960s was *This Hour Has Seven Days,* a gutsy news and public affairs show.

➤ Popular children's shows included *Mr. Dressup, The Friendly Giant,* and *Romper Room.*

➤ The 1960s were the golden years of the National Film Board.

➤ Fashion trends included the Jackie Kennedy look, elephant pants, tie-dyed everything, granny dresses, granny glasses, go-go boots, and of course the miniskirt.

➤ Fads included troll dolls, lava lamps, black lights, and Day-Glo clothing.

➤ On the dance floor, couples grooved to the twist, the mashed potato, the swim, and the Watusi.

➤ In 1967, Canada celebrated its first Centennial. The highlight of the year's celebrations was Expo '67, the first world exhibition to be held on North American soil—an event that attracted 50 million visitors.

➤ Two of the most noteworthy publishing houses to emerge during the 1960s were Coach House Press and House of Anansi.

Chapter 5

Political Animals

In This Chapter

➤ The Kennedy magic

➤ The Cuban missile crisis

➤ Trudeaumania

Television forever changed the rules of the political game. It was no longer enough to be smart, hard-working, and capable: you also had to know how to work your magic in front of the unblinking eye of the television camera. As a result, certain politicians who might have been able to coast to victory in the radio and newspaper era saw their chances of winning an election melt away under the hot television lights, while others—like U.S. President John F. Kennedy and Canadian Prime Minister Pierre Elliott Trudeau—added another credential to their already stellar CVs: that of media star.

The Kennedy Magic

It's easy to forget that the 1960 U.S. presidential campaign was a tough battle for John F. Kennedy to win, and that, in the end, it came down to a photo finish. Although it's almost impossible to imagine it now, given the mythology that now surrounds JFK, the contest could have gone either way: Kennedy ended up defeating Richard Nixon by a mere 113,000 votes out of the 68,800,000 that were cast.

What clinched the election for Kennedy were two important factors: his choice of a running mate and his stellar performance during the televised presidential debates.

If Kennedy hadn't hooked up with a Texas Protestant running mate, Lyndon Johnson, he might have lost enough of the Southern Democratic vote to lose the election. (Kennedy was a Catholic from the north—something that wasn't likely to score points with the large Protestant constituency in the deep south.)

And if he hadn't come across as a confident and capable leader during the televised presidential debates, he might have fallen victim to Republican charges that he was too youthful and inexperienced for the job. Godfrey Hodgson, author of *America in Our Time: From World War II to Nixon—What Happened and Why,* had this to say about Kennedy's on-air charisma: "It was no accident that John Kennedy, the first President to understand the power of television and to make himself a master of it, was also the first President elected after television had achieved primacy among the news media."

A Winning Style

Kennedy continued to work his magic after his inauguration. In the April 7, 1962, issue of *Maclean's* magazine, Washington correspondent Ian Sclanders described the incredible popularity of Kennedy and his family: "The active and attractive Kennedys have, since they moved into the White House, become America's favorite family, America's favorite television performers, the glamorous characters in America's favorite true-life story. Because this is so, political observers are wondering whether Kennedy is the prototype for future presidential candidates and whether, to get elected henceforth, it will be necessary to be handsome and articulate, to have a background of great wealth and an Ivy League education, and to have a pretty wife and appealing children."

There was no denying it: Kennedy *had* led a charmed life for someone so young. Just 43 when he became president, Kennedy had already enjoyed a distinguished military career; he was a successful politician; and had written a Pulitzer Prize–winning book, *Profiles in Courage,* which described a series of American political leaders who had defied public opinion and voted according to their consciences. He had also married well, hooking up with socialite Jacqueline Lee Bouvier along the way.

That Dark Day in Dallas

When Kennedy was assassinated in Dallas on November 22, 1963, Canadians as well as Americans went into mourning. *Maclean's* columnist Ian Sclanders described the effect that Kennedy had on those around him in an article that appeared after Kennedy's

Newsflash!

One of the scariest moments during the 1960s occurred in October of 1962, when U.S. President John F. Kennedy demanded that the Soviet Union remove its missiles from Cuba. The situation came so close to exploding that Kennedy called on Canada to put its North Atlantic Air Defence (NORAD) forces on alert in the event that the Soviet Union refused to back down. (While Canadian Prime Minister John Diefenbaker secretly put the troops on alert right away, he didn't announce that he had done so for three days because he was concerned that Kennedy was being overly belligerent with the Soviets. This delay annoyed Kennedy no end, and led the U.S. government, which was already infuriated by Diefenbaker's economic policies, to work to ensure his defeat in the following year's federal election!) In the end, the Soviets agreed to withdraw the offending missiles and the crisis was averted.

Canadians were more than a little put off by the American president's hard-nosed stand on the issue. In the aftermath of the crisis, journalist J.B. McGeachy wondered whether the U.S. would show similar aggression towards Canada if it were to elect a socialist Prime Minister—like the Canadian Commonwealth Federation's Tommy Douglas: "What happens if Canadians elect Tommy Douglas as Prime Minister?" he asked. "Would the U.S. army, commanded perhaps by Goldwater, invade?

"This isn't a fantastic idea," he continued. "Socialism, which is Douglas' political creed, is equated with communism in millions of American minds. Besides, Douglas' party, the CCF, wants to quit NATO. If Canada went socialist and pacifist at the same time, wouldn't the Kennedy reasoning call for an American military occupation?"

death: "I watched Kennedy campaign for the presidency when I first came to Washington. I saw him sworn in as president. I appreciated his easy banter at press conferences, marveled at his grasp of facts and figures. I was often moved by his words; they were the most moving words of any American since Lincoln. Now I stood in the street and watched his coffin go by."

Sclanders concluded his tribute to Kennedy by voicing a hope that Congress would pass the various pieces of legislation Kennedy had managed to bring forward during his 1,000 days in office so that his death would seem "a little less wasteful and a little less sad."

The Trudeau Style

While Pierre Elliott Trudeau was no John F. Kennedy, he was like a breath of fresh air to a Canadian electorate that was used to politicians who were almost uniformly lacking in both charisma and style.

Trudeau got his political feet wet in Quebec, where he actively campaigned for political and social reform and worked hard to oppose the Union Nationale government of Maurice Duplessis.

It didn't take Trudeau long to come to national attention once he decided to try his hand at federal politics. With a series of stellar careers behind him (he was a constitutional lawyer, a professor of law, an author, and one of the founders of the highly respected Quebec review *Cité Libre*), Trudeau joined the federal Liberal party in 1965 and was elected to Parliament. After assuming the role of parliamentary secretary to Prime Minister Lester B. Pearson, he became the federal Minister of Justice in 1967—a position that put him in the national spotlight when he liberalized the country's laws on abortion, homosexuality, divorce, and national lotteries.

A little arm-twisting from his Liberal Party colleagues persuaded him to throw his hat into the ring for the 1968 leadership contest, which he ended up winning on the fourth ballot.

In an article that appeared in *Maclean's* in May of 1968, Douglas Marshall described how television helped to propel Trudeau to victory: "Back in the days of steam radio, Trudeau would probably have taken a year to achieve what TV did for him in three months. But television didn't create Pierre Elliott Trudeau any more than it staged the Liberal convention. TV simply made it easier for the Trudeau bandwagon to reach its inevitable destination."

The Right Man for the Times

Trudeau assumed his spot at centre stage at exactly the right time in the country's history—a period in which Canadians were feeling particularly good about themselves and their country, the result, no doubt, of the year-long navel-gazing exercise known as Centennial Year!

He was hip, youthful-looking, and an intellectual who seemed to have both fresh ideas and a willingness to make things happen. He grew his hair long and wore sandals in the House of Commons, and after he was elected he set aside money for such youth-oriented projects as youth hostels, conferences on poverty, folk festivals, and co-op housing developments. Somehow he managed to appeal to members of both the younger and older generations—no small feat at a time when the generation gap seemed positively unbridgeable. He also had a flair for the dramatic: at one point, the cameras caught him twirling a carnation between his teeth!

"His nonchalance, his indifference to accepted political strategy of campaign promises, his air of mocking superiority, his jackknives off motel diving boards, were in dazzling contrast to the earnest awkwardness of Robert Stanfield [the Conservative candidate]," recalls veteran journalist June Callwood in her book *Portrait of Canada*.

And then there was his sex appeal—a characteristic not often associated with Canadian prime ministers! As Douglas Stuebing noted in his book *Trudeau: A Man for Tomorrow*, "An inescapable aspect of the Trudeau revelation has been his devastating effect on

Blast from the Past!

"Pierre Elliott Trudeau was pop culture. Swept to power on the crest of a wave of rock-star hysteria called 'Trudeaumania,' triumphant in the rainbow-coloured nationalist afterglow of 1967, Trudeau turned the country into spectacle itself, the glamorous movie it had only ever dreamed of becoming, with Pierre Elliott Trudeau both its director and its star."

—Geoff Pevere and Greig Dymond, *Mondo Canuck: A Canadian Pop Culture Odyssey*

women. There seems to be no middle ground in the feelings that women have for Canada's Prime Minister." At various times before and after his marriage, Trudeau was linked with singer Barbra Streisand, actress Margot Kidder, classical guitarist Liona Boyd, among others; when he finally married he was over 50, and his bride was 30 years younger. He went on to father a child when well into his golden years—something that no doubt earned him the respect of others his age during the pre-Viagra era!

Even celebrities like Beatle John Lennon were known to become starstruck in Trudeau's presence: "If there were more leaders like Mr. Trudeau, the world would have peace," Lennon told the group of reporters who had congregated outside of Trudeau's office after Lennon had gone to Ottawa to meet with Trudeau in 1969.

Newsflash!

Not all of the new government's ideas were popular. An article in the June 7, 1969, *Financial Post* informed Canadians that the Post Office was thinking about introducing a national postal code system. "It might look like a license plate or a shorter version of your credit card number, but whatever the combination of numbers or alphabet chosen, it seems likely that the Post Office will opt for a national coding system."

The Rise and Fall of Trudeaumania

In July of 1969, *Chatelaine* published an article entitled "Whom Should Trudeau Marry?" The writer of the article, Daniel Cappon, sought out the services of a matchmaker to help him to paint a portrait of the ideal mate for Trudeau.

The matchmaker told Cappon that the woman that the PM eventually married should be "not too racy, a global jet-set type, for this might be too much to handle. Similarly, though very intelligent, she must not present a threat by being a scientific sophisticate

Say What?

Trudeaumania: Canadians' fascination with Pierre Elliott Trudeau, which peaked in 1968, the year when Trudeau was first elected Prime Minister.

(a physicist)....She really shouldn't have a PhD cum laude." At the same time, she should be "reliable, steady, quiet, rather than extravagantly flamboyant, hotheaded or scatterbrained." She might be a dancer, a skater, or an artist, or "Perhaps better still, she should excel auditorily rather than visually, and be a musician of sorts—a harp player?" Most important of all, she should be "independent enough...to be a challenge, but not so wild or unusual as to be impossible to tame...."

Whether Trudeau read the article before he met his future bride is anyone's guess, but if he did read it, he certainly didn't take the matchmaker's advice to heart. In 1971, Trudeau married 22-year-old Margaret Sinclair, the daughter of veteran Liberal James Sinclair. Margaret was "a stunning upper-class hippie princess who liked to dance, go barefoot, wear flowers in her hair and once claimed that her definition of culture was 'rock music,'" according to Geoff Pevere and Greig Dymond, authors of *Mondo Canuck: A Canadian Pop Culture Odyssey.*

Ironically, Trudeau's marriage to Margaret marked the end of his youthful appeal. Compared to her, he suddenly seemed middle-aged and decidedly less cool. Even worse, the two of them seemed to have so little in common. (During the 1970s, the Canadian people would find themselves in the rather uncomfortable position of looking on as the PM's marriage began to self-destruct in a particularly public and humiliating way.)

Trudeau's statesmanlike image also began to suffer. If he couldn't control the wild child he'd married—a woman who thought nothing of partying with the Rolling Stones at Studio 54 and who was rumoured to have hopped in the sack with one of the members of the bad boy rock band—how could he be trusted to run the country?

Newsflash!

Trudeau wasn't particularly popular with members of the federal civil service—especially the English-speaking ones. He was frequently accused of introducing policies that forced bilingualism down their throats. During the early 1970s, Trudeau sent group after group of reluctant civil servants through French immersion programs that turned out upwards of 1,000 graduates each year. The message was clear: if you wanted to get anywhere in government circles, you had to be fluent in both of the country's two official languages.

In the end, the Trudeaus divorced, and Pierre ended up with custody of their three boys—something that helped to rehabilitate his image somewhat. Even though the days of having women tossing flowers at his feet were long since behind him, he'd gained a new respectability as he made the transition from the country's most eligible bachelor to its most famous single father.

The Least You Need to Know

➤ After 1960, television began to play an increasingly important role in determining which politicians would be elected. John F. Kennedy and Pierre Elliott Trudeau were both extremely television savvy, knowing intuitively how to use the camera to their advantage.

➤ Americans engaged in an almost cult-like worship of the Kennedys from the time of John F. Kennedy's election in 1960 until long after his assassination in Dallas, Texas, on November 22, 1963.

➤ One of the scariest moments during the 1960s occurred in October of 1962, when U.S. President John F. Kennedy demanded that the Soviet Union remove its missiles from Cuba. A crisis that could have seen the two superpowers at war with each other was only narrowly averted.

➤ The Canadian public has always been fascinated with Pierre Elliott Trudeau, but the high-water mark of his popularity was in 1968, when "Trudeaumania" swept the country. He was hip, youthful-looking, and an intellectual who seemed to have both fresh ideas and a willingness to make things happen—the right man for the times.

Chapter 6

War and Peace

In This Chapter

➤ The Vietnam War

➤ The U.S. civil rights movement

➤ The October Crisis

The sixties were a tumultuous decade. Young people who disagreed with American involvement in the Vietnam War organized "teach-ins" and peace rallies that were designed to encourage others to oppose the war. Black Americans were becoming increasingly impatient with the slow process of change on the civil rights front, and there were outbreaks of rioting in many large U.S. cities. And on this side of the border, a growing number of Quebeckers started uttering a word that sent chills down the spine of most Canadians: *separation.*

The Vietnam War

The U.S. had been playing an active role in the Vietnam War since 1950, but most Canadians and Americans didn't pay a lot of attention to the war until the mid-1960s, when U.S. President Lyndon B. Johnson dramatically increased the number of American

Say What?

The domino theory: The American government's belief that if Communism became rooted in one country it would spread to neighbouring countries; U.S. political theorists felt that America should intervene to stop the process before it got under way. The expression was coined after U.S. President Dwight D. Eisenhower used a particularly colourful metaphor in a speech to reporters in 1954: "You have a row of dominos set up, you knock over the first one, and what will happen to the last one is the certainty it will go over very quickly."

troops engaged in the conflict. (The numbers jumped from 75,000 in 1965 to 375,000 in 1966, and to 500,000 in 1968.) Johnson, like his predecessor Dwight D. Eisenhower, felt that the U.S. had to do whatever it could to ensure that South Vietnam didn't fall to the Communist forces in North Vietnam—an event that they felt would lead to the spread of Communism throughout the region. (The belief that Communism would inevitably spread to other countries if left unchecked was known as "the domino theory.")

There weren't enough volunteers to produce the required number of troops, so Johnson had no choice but to turn to the Selective Service system, a.k.a. "the draft." Because students were exempt from the draft, relatively well-off young people were able to avoid the draft by enrolling in college. (Not surprisingly, college enrollment skyrocketed during the war.) Unfortunately, this meant that less privileged and minority youth were more likely to be drafted than their white, middle-class counterparts—a sore point with members of the African-American community in particular.

Boomer Bytes

A poll published in the October 1967 issue of *Maclean's* magazine revealed Canadians were as divided about the Vietnam War as their neighbours to the south. The poll showed that 66 percent of Montrealers and 39 percent of Torontonians thought that Canada should call for the U.S. to end its bombing of North Vietnam.

Canada's Involvement in the Vietnam War

Another popular strategy for avoiding the draft was to flee to Canada, and many Americans chose to do just that when the dreaded draft card showed up in the mail. Canadian immigration records show that 30,000 "draft dodgers" settled in Canada legally, but some Vietnam War experts estimate that another 50,000 lived on the run in Canada during the years of the war.

While the Canadian government liked to pretend that Canada was a neutral bystander during the Vietnam War, that simply wasn't the case. Whether it was prepared to admit it or not, Canada was squarely on the side of the United States and the South Vietnamese. Canada allowed the U.S. military to test its herbicide "Agent Orange" at CFB Gagetown in New Brunswick and to practise carpet-bombing runs over Suffield, Alberta, and North Battleford, Saskatchewan. It also sold billions of dollars worth of supplies to

Blast from the Past!

"When I read about an American soldier firing a clip of tracer bullets into a group of women and children in some Mekong hamlet, I feel a quiet thrill of pride. The vivid description of a fighter-bomber snarling across the hills near Khe Sang, spraying napalm, sends a surge of patriotism coursing through my veins. An eyewitness account of bombs wrenching at rice paddies along the Ho Chi Minh Trail stirs me like the cry of bugles. After all, I tell myself, it's our war, too."

—Walter Stewart, in a hard-hitting piece about Canada's behind-the scenes involvement in the Vietnam War that appeared in the March 1970 issue of *Maclean's* magazine

the Americans: $2.5 billion worth of war materials such as ammunition, napalm, aircraft shells, and explosives; and $10 billion worth of food, beverages, clothing, and other supplies.

Despite Canada's ongoing support of the American war effort, Canadian Prime Minister Lester Pearson managed to earn the wrath of U.S. President Lyndon Johnson when, in a speech at Temple University in Philadelphia in 1965, he urged the American government to temporarily cease bombing North Vietnam in an effort to bring about peace. The president didn't exactly welcome the prime minister's advice. In fact, he was outraged that Pearson had dared to criticize American foreign policy. (Johnson momentarily forgot that Canada had compromised its role on the International Control Commission to defend America's views of the conflict, and that it had agreed to spy on North Vietnam on behalf of the U.S.!) Rumour has it that the next time the two men were together, the giant Texan grabbed the smaller Canadian by the collar and shouted an obscenity at him. Apparently, Pearson was too stunned to reply.

Newsflash!

The use of Agent Orange—a pesticide that was employed to defoliate the jungle during the Vietnam War—didn't sit well with the growing number of Canadians and Americans who were becoming concerned about the environment.

By the late 1960s, there was widespread concern about air pollution, water pollution, solid-waste disposal, the world's dwindling energy resources, radiation, the use of pesticides, noise pollution, and other environmental problems.

This interest in environmental issues was sparked by the publication in 1962 of Rachel Carson's book *Silent Spring*. A highly respected American marine biologist, Carson warned of the dangers of DDT and other pesticides: "For the first time in the history of the world, every human being is now subjected to contact with dangerous chemicals, from the moment of conception until death." Within two years of the publication of *Silent Spring*, 40 states introduced laws restricting the use of pesticides. The book is widely credited with having encouraged millions of people around the world to hook up with the environmental movement.

Doris C. ONeil, editor of *Life: The 60s,* recalls how strong the environmental movement was by the time the first Earth Day was held on April 22, 1970: "By 1970 Earth was *the* cause, a link between people who shared little else other than the scary realization of their planet's fragility. Environmental and wilderness groups signed up hundreds of new members. Recycling became hip, and littering a mortal sin."

Canadians Who Served in Vietnam

Canadians also contributed to the Vietnam war effort by joining the U.S. Army. According to Tracy Arial, author of *I Volunteered: Canadian Vietnam Vets Remember*, approximately 30,000 Canadians volunteered for service.

Just like their American counterparts, Canadian Vietnam vets found it hard to attract much public support when they returned home from the fighting fields. In fact, the Canadian public seemed reluctant to even acknowledge their existence. One of the biggest slaps in the face they received was the refusal of the Canadian Legion to accept them as members until 1994—20 years after the end of the war. Until that point, they had been refused membership on the grounds that they had fought with foreign forces in a war in which Canada had no direct interest.

The names of the 101 Canadians who died while serving in Vietnam are recorded on the Vietnam War Memorial in Washington, D.C. According to *Maclean's* magazine, the number of dead is probably closer to 300, but identification is difficult, because in many cases, U.S. military records of the Canadians who served in the war give only the name of the U.S. city where they enlisted, not the name of the city where they were born.

Rallying for Change

Opposition to the war began to build after 1965, when Johnson began to dramatically increase the number of American troops who were committed to the conflict. When the first anti-Vietnam rally took place in New York in late 1964, it attracted only 1,500 protestors, but a rally in Washington a year later pulled in a crowd of 25,000. Many Americans who had initially thought it was treasonous to speak out against the war felt that they could no longer keep quiet about their government's misguided foreign policy decisions.

In mid-1965, anti-Vietnam protestors began burning their draft cards as a symbol of their opposition to the war. Congress stepped in and passed a law that made this act illegal.

In Canada, peace activists began carrying signs that read "End Canadian Complicity." They pointed out that Canada wasn't just profiting financially from the war. It was also allowing its representatives on the UN observer team in Vietnam to spy for the American army. (Not surprisingly, the anti-Vietnam movement in Canada was buoyed by the anti-American sentiment that was growing in the country at the time.)

Anti-Vietnam protests became bigger and more frequent on college campuses on both sides of the border. On May 4, 1970, members of the National Guard fired on student demonstrators at Kent State University, killing four people. The demonstrators had been protesting U.S. President Richard Nixon's decision to send 32,000 troops into Cambodia to stabilize the area and to eradicate enemy camps. One week later, two students were shot and killed by state troopers at Jackson State University in Mississippi. In the aftermath of the shootings, 500 campuses across the U.S. shut down in protest. Fifty shut down for the remainder of the semester.

Newsflash

John Lennon and Yoko Ono staged a "bed-in" for peace at the Queen Elizabeth Hotel in Montreal in the spring of 1969.

Boomer Bytes

By 1971, two-thirds of Americans wanted their government to pull out of the war in Vietnam.

The Beginning of the End

The turning point of the war, at least in terms of the amount of support on the home front, was the Tet offensive.

While both sides in the conflict had traditionally observed a ceasefire around the time of lunar new year, called Tet, in 1968 the North Vietnamese decided to launch a surprise attack on 100 cities and military posts. The Tet offensive resulted in large numbers of casualties on both sides: the South Vietnamese and the Americans ended up with 4,200 dead and 1,600 wounded while the North Vietnamese saw 45,000 killed and 100,000 injured. The horrific losses on both sides shook the American public's faith in the chances of victory. CBS anchorman Walter Cronkite asked the question that was running through many Americans' minds: "What the hell's going on? I thought we were winning this war."

Americans were shocked that military might wasn't enough to win this war—that napalm, incendiary bombs and highly toxic chemical agents used to defoliate the jungle and expose the enemy weren't enough to counteract the guerrilla tactics used by the North Vietnamese. "American soldiers found themselves in a war where a bicycle could contain a bomb; where a rice paddy could be full of sharpened, poisoned bamboo stakes called punji sticks; where children and old women could be the enemy," writes Doris C. ONeil in *Life: The 60s.*

"The Americans...are fighting the wrong war in the wrong place at the wrong time, and they are very far from winning it," concluded *Maclean's* magazine in February of 1968. "Can an Asian peasantry, whose strongest weapons are pride, patriotism and guts, defy the mightiest technological power on earth? After too many years of fighting, the answer seems to be that yes, the Vietnamese can."

More Bad News from Vietnam. Story at 11

The role that TV played in helping to create a backlash against the war is hard to overestimate. For the first time ever, Canadians and Americans were able to watch

Newsflash!

Americans were particularly horrified to learn about the My Lai massacre, which occurred on May 16, 1968, but wasn't public knowledge until 1969. At that point, Vietnam veteran Ronald Ridenhour threatened to spill the beans about the incident unless the U.S. Army launched an investigation. Over time, the American public learned that an American infantry company led by Lieutenant William L. Calley had marched into the South Vietnamese hamlet of My Lai, and slaughtered 347 unarmed civilians—mainly old men, women, and children. The My Lai massacre became a symbol of the brutality of the Vietnam War and helped to convince many Americans that it was time to pull the plug on the war entirely.

Blast from the Past!

"We should fix for the attacking platoon to be as photogenic as possible. We should try for state-by-state viewer identification—a John Wayne Texan is a must. We also need a Harvard-type playboy from New England, preferably from upstate New York, where our latest Nielsens took a hit. Throw in a misunderstood high-school dropout from Brooklyn, preferably brave; a hillbilly for laughs; and teenagers from the midwest, the deep south and the coast."

—Michael Carreck, writing a fictitious memo from one TV executive to another touting the viewer potential of the Vietnam War. The spoof, which ran in *Maclean's* in January of 1967, was entitled "Live from Vietnam! War could be bigger than *Bonanza*!"

the horrors of war right in their own living rooms. They didn't like what they were seeing.

"There is a growing sense of guilt," wrote American journalist Walter Lippmann at the time. "The American people are becoming revolted and ashamed by the spectacle of themselves engaged in a war where a big, rich, super-armed giant is trying to beat the life out of a dwarf. Less and less are Americans enjoying the idea of themselves in such an uncivilized, unchivalrous, inhumane role. This is the most unpopular war in American history. It is also the war which most deeply affronts the American conscience."

The Vietnam War was quite different from the wars that the country had waged in the past. "Americans had been prepared to make sacrifices in blood and treasure, as they had in other wars," explains Stanley Karnow in his book *Vietnam: A History.* "But they had to be shown progress, told when the war would end. In World War II, they could trace the advance of their army across Europe; in Vietnam, where there were no fronts, they were only given meaningless enemy 'body counts'—and promises.... The public, distressed by mounting casualties, rising taxes, and no prospect of a solution in sight, turned against the war long before America's political leaders did."

The Final Toll

The Vietnam War was a costly war for the American people, both in lives lost and in money spent on the war effort.

By the time the two sides signed the Paris Accord on January 31, 1973, 1.7 million people had lost their lives, 3 million had been wounded, and 13 million had been displaced from their homes. (The U.S. toll was 57,606 killed, 303,700 wounded, 766 taken prisoner, and 5,011 declared missing.)

According to Vietnam War expert Victor Levant, the U.S. dropped 7 million tonnes of bombs and 75 million litres of herbicide during the war and lost 10,000 helicopters and warplanes. The direct cost of the war to all the countries involved was $146 billion, but the indirect costs were more like $900 billion.

The war also took its toll on the American psyche—a point that Alan Axelrod hammers home in *The Complete Idiot's Guide to American History:* "The fact is that all America was a victim of the war, which had created a rift—to use a term from the era, a *credibility gap*—between citizens and government. Vietnam killed human beings, and it also killed trust."

Not-So-Civil Rights

While they were doing their best to win an unwinnable war overseas, Americans were also struggling to keep peace on the home front—no easy task, given that battle lines were being drawn between black and white Americans.

Hard as it is to believe today, segregation was the norm in the American South until the early 1960s. It was widely accepted that blacks and whites would drink from different drinking fountains, use different washrooms, and eat in different restaurants. When the government did order that segregation be abolished, it had to be prepared to back up those orders with force. In 1962, over 16,000 federal troops had to be called in to ensure the safety of the first black student to enroll at the University of Mississippi.

A Man with a Dream

The leader of the civil rights movement was Martin Luther King Jr., a Baptist minister who had come to national attention after assuming leadership of the Montgomery,

Blast from the Past!

"No doubt, it's reprehensible for the Alabamans...to act as they do. But do we really suppose that we are intellectually or morally superior to them? Are we quite sure that in the same circumstances (that is, if we had 54 million compatriot Indians or Eskimos or Negroes in Canada which would roughly duplicate the South African situation), we would behave any better? I, for one, doubt it."

—J. B. McGeachy, writing in the June 3, 1961, edition of *The Financial Post* about Canadians' tendency to be smug about their track record on the race relations front

Alabama, bus boycott of the late 1950s. (The bus boycott was organized after a black woman, Rosa Parks, was arrested and jailed for refusing to move to the back of the bus.)

In 1963, King organized a massive march on Washington, where he gave his famous "I have a dream" speech. The speech described his hopes for a freer America: "When we let freedom ring, when we let it ring from every village and every hamlet, from every state and every city, we will be able to speed up that day when all of God's children, black men and white men, Jews and Gentiles, Protestants and Catholics, will all be able to join hands and sing in the words of the old Negro spiritual, 'Free at last! Free at last! Thank God almighty, we are free at last!'"

The following year, King received the Nobel Peace Prize for his civil rights work. He then went on to expand the civil rights movement into the North and began attacking economic injustices as well as legal and social discrimination. Unfortunately, black frustrations about the slow pace of change led to rioting in many cities: a riot in the Watts section of Los Angeles in 1965, for example, resulted in the loss of 34 lives and more than $40 million in property damage. What's more, some of the more radical elements of the civil rights movement deserted King to follow Malcolm X, who preached that the white man was the devil incarnate, and Stokely Carmichael, who called for "total revolution" and sang the praises of "black power."

On April 3, 1968, Dr. King spoke to a crowd of cheering civil rights activists in Memphis, Tennessee, where he was lending support to 1,300 sanitation workers who had been on strike since February 12. He said, "I have been to the mountain top...And I've looked over. And I've seen the promised land. I may not get there with you. But I want you to know tonight, that we as a people will get to the promised land." The following day, he was killed by escaped convict James Earl Ray as he stood on the balcony at the Lorraine Motel, chatting with the Reverend Jesse Jackson and musician Ben Branch.

Senator Robert Kennedy urged mourners to avoid violence in the aftermath of King's assassination: "Those of you who are black can be filled with hatred, with bitterness and a desire for revenge. We can move toward further polarization. Or we can make an effort, as Martin Luther King did, to understand, to reconcile ourselves and to love." Despite Kennedy's plea, riots broke out in a number of U.S. cities, including New York, Boston, Raleigh, N.C., Jackson, Miss., Atlanta, and Memphis.

Not surprisingly, the civil rights movement spilled across the border. African-Canadians became more willing to speak out against racial discrimination. In 1969, following a student protest at Sir George Williams University (now Concordia University) in Montreal—a protest that resulted in the destruction of the university's computer system—the federal government began to provide funding to the Black United Front (BUF) and other similar organizations in an effort to defuse the Canadian black power movement's growing militancy. What's more, the Trudeau government decided, in 1971, to create the position of Secretary of State for Multiculturalism to look into ways to resolve the grievances of Canadians belonging to various cultural groups.

The Quiet Revolution

In 1960, the Liberal party under Jean Lesage won the Quebec provincial election, ushering in a period of rapid but peaceful change that would thereafter be known as the Quiet Revolution. Over the course of the next eight years, the government passed legislation designed to modernize virtually every aspect of Quebec life. The primary focuses of this program were education and economic development, but the reforms also included changes to the political system (including the introduction of laws that were designed to attack political patronage and limit election spending), the establishment of a provincial hydroelectric utility, and the creation of a provincial pension plan. The provincial government also became more willing to assert itself on the national stage, putting the federal government on notice that it wanted to withdraw from several federal-provincial cost-sharing programs. It even went so far as to attempt to establish relations with foreign countries directly, sidestepping Ottawa in the process. (The feds were not amused.)

Vive le Québec libre!

Just as important as the political changes that took place, however, was the cultural renaissance that took place in Quebec during this period. Francophones in Quebec began to think of themselves as Québécois rather than Canadian, and they became anxious to establish contact with the French-speaking world beyond Canada's borders.

This sense of Quebec nationalism reached its climax during the visit of Charles de Gaulle, the president of France, during Expo '67 in Montreal. De Gaulle created a political stir when he waved to crowds from the balcony of Montreal City Hall and shouted "Vive le Québec! Vive le Québec libre! Vive le Canada français! Vive la France!" It was hardly an appropriate sentiment for a visiting dignitary to utter during the country's centennial year—not unlike standing up at a wedding reception and trashing the bride! Not surprisingly, Pearson was quick to object to de Gaulle's comments, leading the French president to cut his visit short.

Blast from the Past!

"Liberals who think the Negro revolution is all but complete will find to their dismay, in the months and years to come, that the very process of struggling for certain limited rights has finally given the Negro a sense of selfness, of his identity as a Negro. The Negro revolution will therefore continue to accelerate as a newly confident American Negro moves at last to seize his rights—with or without the support of the white population."

—David McReynolds, writing in the February 1965 issue of *Saturday Night*

One Country, Two Languages

Canada's centennial year was a momentous year for Quebec for other reasons, too. René Lévesque, a prominent member of the Liberal party, decided to form a separatist party, the Parti Québécois (PQ)—a party that went on to capture a quarter of the votes in the Quebec provincial election the following spring. Another milestone was the release of the first volume of the report of the Royal Commission on Bilingualism and Biculturalism. The commission recommended that French and English be formally declared official languages and that they be given equal status in government, administration, and the courts. This recommendation ultimately resulted in the passage of the Official Languages Act in 1969.

Many English Canadians resented the Official Languages Act and the government's plans to promote official bilingualism. One Conservative member of the government earned the wrath of French-speaking Quebeckers—to say nothing of the tactless-remark-of-the-decade award!—when he stated, "The cold hard fact is that Canadians of French origin should be learning English as fast as they can instead of the English learning French." (It didn't help that he expressed his opinion that English was "the easier and more reasonable language to learn"!) The backlash against bilingualism continued through the 1970s.

Despite the backlash in certain quarters, however, the policy of official bilingualism led to far-reaching changes. In his book *The Years of Protest 1960–1970*, Alan Edmonds comments on some of these changes: "When the decade began, the French wording on a package of corn flakes occupied a quarter of the back of the package. By the mid-sixties, it occupied the entire back of the package, a change ordered as part of the growing federal programme of bilingualism. Canadian National Railways announced that it would have its name in both English and French painted on all its 100,000 box-cars. That meant having 'Canadien National' as well as 'Canadian National' on the railcars, a paint job that involved only one letter in the name and was then estimated to take thirteen years."

Blast from the Past!

"For Quebec today, the choice is not between two systems more or less favorable to its overall progress. The choice is simply one between a good life and a slow death. And we cannot play hide-and-seek with history by saying, 'We aren't ready yet...'"

—René Lévesque, writing about the benefits of separatism in his book *An Option for Quebec*, published in 1968

The October Crisis

On October 5, 1970, a radical cell of the Front de Libération du Québec (FLQ) kidnapped British trade minister James Cross, whom they saw as a symbol of British imperialism. Five days later, a second cell abducted Pierre Laporte, Quebec's minister of labour and immigration. Wealthy Montrealers lived in fear that they or members of their families could be the next targets of the kidnappers.

Newsflash!

In 1968, Quebec francophones were reading Pierre Vallières's book *White Niggers of America*, a book that argued that Quebeckers were "cheap labour that the predators of industry, commerce and high finance are so fond of, the way wolves are fond of sheep." Vallières—one of the founders of the Front de Libération du Québec (FLQ)—wrote the book during the four years he spent in jail for his involvement in FLQ bombings in Montreal. (He was arrested in New York City during a protest at the United Nations. The demonstrators were trying to convince the UN that Canada was violating the United Nations Charter of Human Rights with its treatment of the French-speaking citizens of Quebec.)

The FLQ, a radical separatist group, was upset by the recent victory of Liberal Robert Bourassa in the Quebec provincial election, believing that his victory had been engineered by the federalists, particularly the anglophone business community.

The FLQ was not a household word for most Canadians until after these high-profile kidnappings, although the group had been around since the early 1960s. Between 1963 and 1970, they claimed responsibility for 200 bombings. Their targets included McGill University, the home of Montreal mayor Jean Drapeau, and the Montreal Stock Exchange.

In exchange for an agreement to release the hostages, the FLQ demanded publicity for its manifesto, free passage to Cuba or Algiers for a number of terrorists ("political prisoners") who were then in detention, and $500,000 in gold bullion.

The federal government sent in soldiers to protect potential targets of terrorist action—a move that made many Canadians nervous. Prime Minister Trudeau had cutting words for those who dared to criticize his actions: "I think the society must take every means at its disposal to defend itself against the emergence of a parallel power which defies the elected power in this country and I think that goes to any distance...It's only...weak-kneed bleeding hearts who are afraid to take these measures."

When asked by CBC television reporter Tim Ralfe how

Boomer Bytes

Despite the Opposition's attempts to score political points at Trudeau's expense, public opinion was solidly behind Trudeau and his decision to invoke the War Measures Act. A poll taken at the time indicated that 88 percent of all Canadians and 86 percent of Quebeckers approved of the decision.

far he was prepared to go in holding out against the hostage-takers, Trudeau said, "Just watch me."

On October 16, the Trudeau government proclaimed the War Measures Act, banned the FLQ, suspended civil rights, and imposed martial law on the nation. Four hundred and sixty-eight people were arrested because they were suspected of belonging to the now-outlawed FLQ. (By the end of the year, all but 41 of them had been released.) The night after the War Measures Act was proclaimed, Laporte's body was found in the trunk of an abandoned car. (Two months later, Cross was freed by his captors, who were given free passage to Cuba in exchange for his life.)

The October Crisis neither weakened separatism nor ended the violence in Quebec. Over time, many FLQ members found another way to channel their pro-separatist sentiments: by supporting the Parti Québécois.

The Least You Need to Know

➤ Canadian immigration records show that 30,000 "draft dodgers" settled in Canada legally, but some Vietnam War experts estimate that another 50,000 lived on the run in Canada during the years of the war.

➤ Canada allowed the U.S. to test its herbicide, Agent Orange, at CFB Gagetown in New Brunswick and to practise carpet-bombing runs over Suffield, Alberta, and North Battleford, Saskatchewan. It also sold billions of dollars' worth of supplies to the Americans and spied on North Vietnam on behalf of the U.S.

➤ Approximately 30,000 Canadians served in the Vietnam War.

➤ The Tet offensive marked the turning point in the war—the point at which the American people decided that they wanted out.

➤ The U.S. civil rights movement was led by Martin Luther King Jr., a Baptist minister. In 1963, he led a massive march on Washington, where he delivered his famous "I have a dream" speech. The following year, he received the Nobel Peace Prize for his civil rights work.

➤ The Quiet Revolution took place in Quebec, profoundly changing the province's social, political, cultural, and economic life.

➤ In October of 1970, members of the radical separatist group, the Front de Libération du Québec (FLQ), kidnapped a British diplomat and a Quebec cabinet minister. To deal with the situation, Prime Minister Pierre Elliott Trudeau invoked the War Measures Act, a decision that the majority of Canadians supported.

Chapter 7

One Small Step

In This Chapter

➤ Space exploration

➤ The dawn of the computer age

➤ The backlash against technology

The sixties were years of tremendous technological change. At the start of the decade, there were only a handful of computers from sea to shining sea; by the end of the decade, computers had taken over the world of business and were poised to enter Canadians' homes as well. The truly momentous breakthrough on the technological front, however, happened some 240,000 miles from the earth's surface, when American astronaut Neil Armstrong took his historic first steps on the moon.

Out of This World

It's not hard to see why 600 million viewers around the world tuned in to watch Armstrong take his "one small step for man, one giant leap for mankind." Given the troubles that they had to deal with on Planet Earth—the Vietnam War, race conflicts, environmental concerns, and the battle of the sexes, to name but a few—

Blast from the Past!

One of the most popular films of the 1960s was Stanley Kubrick's *2001: A Space Odyssey* (1968). The movie,which had a computer named HAL as one of its main characters, took place on board a space ship en route to Jupiter. The film managed to tap into both the public's fascination with space travel and its fear of computers—a combination that paid off handsomely at the box office.

Blast from the Past!

"I believe this nation should commit itself to achieving the goal, before this decade is out, of landing a man on the moon and returning him safely to the earth. No single space project in this period will be more impressive to mankind, or more important for the long-range exploration of space; and none will be so difficult or expensive to accomplish."

—U.S. President John F. Kennedy, May 25, 1961, in a message to Congress

is it any wonder that so many people were happy to focus their attention on the heavens for a change?

"At home, no matter where you stood, the sixties looked messy and unreadable, like a painting viewed too close to make out anything but the texture of the brushstrokes and the smudge of color," write Peter Jennings and Todd Brewster in their book *The Century.* "Yet from out there, in the dark eternity of the universe, the planet projected a picture of harmony, an essentially beautiful orb, ordered and still."

One Giant Step...

Armstrong took his historic walk on the moon on July 20, 1969. He described the texture of the moon's surface as he took those first few steps: "The surface is fine and powdery. It adheres in fine layers, like powdered charcoal, to the soles and sides of my boots. I only go in a fraction of an inch, maybe an eighth of an inch, but I can see the footprints of my boots and the treads in the fine, sandy particles."

It had taken the U.S. billions of dollars of taxpayers' money and the labours of more than 400,000 people in assembly plants and control rooms across the country to make the walk possible. The space programs had even seen some casualties: two years before Armstrong's triumphant walk, three astronauts had burned to death in their space capsule during a mission that ended in tragic failure. Hardly anyone was dwelling on these facts, however, as Armstrong walked across the surface of the moon and into the history books. They were too mesmerized by what human beings—and technology—had managed to achieve.

And in Third Place, It's Canada...

Canada also established a presence in space during the 1960s—although it was far less flashy than the Americans'. On September 29, 1962, Canada launched its first satellite, Alouette I, one of four Canadian

Blast from the Past!

North Americans' fascination with life beyond Planet Earth was reflected in two popular TV shows of the 1960s: *The Jetsons* and *Star Trek*. The Jetsons, which premiered in 1962, focused on the adventures of George and Jane Jetson, a space-age family that lived in the Skypod Apartments in Orbit City with their children Judy and Elroy and the family dog Astro. *Star Trek*, which became one of the most popular television shows of all time in the years following its 1966 television premiere, described the adventures of the crew of the starship *Enterprise*. While die-hard Trekkers may find this hard to believe, *Star Trek* didn't pull in very many viewers during its first season. In fact, according to Edith Pavese and Judith Henry, authors of *TV Mania: A Timeline of Television*, it didn't become a hit until long after it went into syndicated reruns—proof, once again, that there is life after prime time.

satellites to be launched under an agreement signed with the U.S. National Aeronautics and Space Administration (NASA). The satellites were designed and built at the Defence Research Telecommunications Establishment in Ottawa (later renamed the Communications Research Centre of the Department of Communications). The launching of Alouette I allowed Canada to follow in the footsteps of the Soviet Union and the United States, to take its place as the third country to venture into space.

This Does Not Compute

In March 10, 1962, *Maclean's* magazine published an article entitled "The incredible things the thinking machines are doing for us—and to us." The article described how the computer was changing the world of business and predicted that the computers would ultimately help to create a world in which there were "shorter hours and higher earnings, undreamed of leisure and abundance."

The author of the article, Ian Sclanders, told the magazine's readers that there was no such thing as a typical computer. There was a huge variation in the size—and the cost—of these amazing machines. "They range in size from giants that weigh tons to compact models that fit comfortably in a modest office," he wrote. "Many are leased rather than sold, and in Canada the rent is as much as $135,000 a month and as little as $350 with the monthly rental equalling a forty-eighth of the purchase price." (If you stop and do the math, you'll see that the bargain-basement model he was describing rang in at a hefty $16,800!)

Boomer Bytes

By 1968, a single silicon chip could hold 256 bits of RAM—more RAM than a room-sized computer had been able to hold just a few years earlier.

Boomer Bytes

There were home computers on the market in the U.S. by the late 1960s, but they were anything but affordable. Neiman-Marcus advertised a "kitchen computer" in its 1969 Christmas catalogue. The price? An eye-popping $10,600!

Developments on the computer front hit the headlines of Canadian newspapers time and time again. In 1963, *The Financial Post* reported that 24 of the top 30 universities in Canada had installed computers. (The first university to do so was the University of Toronto, which, between 1947 and 1951, had built Canada's first computer—a monolithic contraption large enough to fill a room!) In 1966, the paper reported that a rental business in "of all things" used computers was beginning to flourish in Canada. And in 1967, it reported on the glitches and growing pains that many businesses were experiencing as they dragged themselves kicking and screaming into the computer age. (In an uncharacteristically cynical moment, the paper noted that "Experience with computers is quickly showing that they have one thing in common with man: they can look very busy but may not actually be producing anything of value.")

Home Is Where the Computer Is...

By the end of the decade, computers had dropped so much in price and had become so affordable that many Canadians could actually envision the day when there would be a computer in every home.

Constance Mungall, a Canadian journalist, didn't just have to imagine what it would be like to have a computer in her home, however. In early 1970 she and her family got to experience it first-hand—something that apparently gave them the distinction of having Canada's first home computer.

It wasn't actually a home computer, however. It was a business computer that had been adapted for home purposes so that Mungall could give *Chatelaine's* readers a taste of what was to come. She wrote about her family's experiences in an article titled "We lived with a computer" that ran in the April 1970 issue of the magazine.

Mungall was very impressed with what the computer was able to do for her and her family. In addition to being capable of storing an astounding 131,000 words—about 250 typewritten pages—it kept track of what cooking ingredients she had around the house, logged her daily calorie count, and reminded her which family members were due for dental checkups! Still, all these accomplishments paled in comparison to what computers would be able to do for her in the future, she noted: "I can easily foresee that I could, when the already existing computers of all the utilities, the big department stores, the banks, the government are linked, do twice as much work in just a little more time. I could do all my banking, pay all bills, buy through the catalogue, make hair appointments and medical appointments, check the stock market, buy or sell, not to mention research some subject for my magazine or radio writing. All this could be done without leaving the house or dialing any telephone number except the computer's."

Mungall told *Chatelaine's* readers that the computer age was now upon them, ready or not: "Give it less than ten years, and they'll be as commonplace as color TV: in fifteen or twenty years, they'll cost about as much as a telephone, and every house on the street will have a terminal like ours."

Boomer Bytes

There were technological advances on other fronts as well. On March 19, 1966, *The Financial Post* predicted that "perhaps as many as one third of all the cars in Canada" would have air-conditioners in the future.

The Downside

Of course, not everyone was thrilled about the dawn of the computer age. Many people wondered what would happen to the human beings who found themselves out of a job as computers and robots replaced them in offices and on assembly lines. There was also a lot of fear that some workers—women in particular—would find themselves shut out of the higher-paying computer industry jobs that were springing up by the thousands. These were issues that Canadians would continue to grapple with during the remaining decades of the century.

The Least You Need to Know

➤ Six hundred million television viewers from around the world tuned in to watch U.S. astronaut Neil Armstrong walk on the moon on July 20, 1969, an event he himself described as "one small step for man, one giant leap for mankind."

➤ On September 29, 1962, Canada launched its first satellite, Alouette I—the first of four Canadian satellites to be launched under an agreement signed with the U.S. National Aeronautics and Space Administration (NASA).

➤ The fascination with the space race helped to inspire both TV shows such as *The Jetsons* and *Star Trek* and movies like *2001: A Space Odyssey.*

➤ Canada's first computer was built at the University of Toronto between 1947 and 1951. It was a monolithic contraption, large enough to fill a room.

➤ By 1968, a single silicon chip could hold 256 bits of RAM—more RAM than a room-sized computer had been able to hold just a few years earlier.

➤ Not everyone was thrilled about the dawn of the computer age. Many people were worried about the job losses that would inevitably occur as computers and robots replaced human beings in offices and on assembly lines.

Chapter 8

The Good Old Days

In This Chapter

➤ Boom times for the Canadian economy

➤ Living in the shadow of the giant next door

➤ Canadians love credit cards

➤ The Great Canadian meltdown!

A Gallup poll taken early in the 1960s revealed that 95 percent of Canadians were happy with their lives—a figure that earned them the right to declare themselves the happiest people in the world.

You didn't have to be a rocket scientist to figure out what was behind this national outbreak of happiness. Canadians had a lot to be happy about. These were, after all, boom years for the Canadian economy. Despite a brief recession at the start of the decade—when the unemployment rate had soared to a hair-raising 11.2 percent—the economy was extremely healthy. In 1965, the country's gross national product soared past the $50 billion mark for the first time ever. Add to that the fact that inflation was low throughout the decade and you can see why Canadians were grinning from sea to shining sea.

Blast from the Past!

An article entitled "Skirts and stocks: do they swing together?" appeared in the August 20, 1966, edition of *The Financial Post*. The article suggested that anyone who wanted to know where the market was heading need only look at the length of women's skirts: "Put aside your graphs and stock charts and concentrate on the fall trend in hemlines when trying to figure out which way the market will go," wrote reporter Amy Booth. "So far this century, hemlines often have been a faithful reflection of stock market trends....In 1965 the British introduced the spectacular mid-thigh miniskirt. Like the miniskirt, however, the long upswing in stock prices had gone about as high as it could go—and the market leveled out."

The Have-Nots

That's not to say that the situation was picture-perfect for every Canadian, however. Government statistics showed that one in four Canadians was living in poverty. Those most likely to be experiencing hard times were natives, African-Canadians, francophones, recent immigrants, families led by women, and those living in the Atlantic provinces or the North. There was also considerable economic disparity from province to province: average weekly wages in 1961 ranged from a low of $57.03 in Prince Edward Island to a high of $85.20 in Ontario.

More Trouble in Paradise

And then there was the problem of labour unrest. It seemed that every Canadian with access to a sign and a can of paint was walking the picket line protesting *something*. (Even housewives got in on the act, organizing boycotts against certain supermarkets to protest what they saw as unreasonably high prices.)

More often than not, the chief grievance was wages. Canadians wanted to be paid as well as their American counterparts. Over the course of the decade, there were strikes by postal workers, schoolteachers, railway employees, airline personnel, longshoremen, and production line workers. (In many cases, Canadian production line workers found themselves in the rather odd situation of having American union leaders negotiating on their behalf with the American head offices of Canadian branch plants.)

Blast from the Past!

If there was one group that Canadians agreed were overpaid and underworked, it was the politicians. Journalist J.B. McGeachy had this to say in an article entitled "Are MPs Overpaid at $10,000 a Year?" which appeared in *The Financial Post* on February 6, 1960: "If MPs want to demonstrate that they earn their pay, they should try being more original and independent, even outrageous and rebellious at times. While they are at it, they might shorten their orations. The time limit of 40 minutes is supposed to be a maximum and is no reason why every contribution should measure exactly 39 minutes, 60 seconds."

The Giant Next Door

A 1964 Gallup poll revealed that nearly half of Canadians were concerned about the amount of American investment in Canada. They certainly had good reason to worry. In 1960, nearly 75 percent of foreign investment had come from a single source—the United States. This made Canada extremely vulnerable to policy shifts in Washington as well as any downturns in the American economy. It was kind of like having most of your eggs in a single basket—except, in this case, you didn't actually own the basket.

Same Old Problem

Of course, it was nothing new for Canadians to be concerned about the effects of foreign investment. Back in 1957, the Royal Commission on Canada's Economic Prospects had highlighted the growing problems caused by the "Americanization" of the Canadian economy and had urged the government to exercise tighter control over foreign investment. (When the commission's chair, Walter Gordon, was appointed federal minister of finance following the election of 1963, he proved to be corporate America's worst nightmare. He introduced a 30 percent "takeover tax" on the sale of Canadian companies to foreigners; took steps to prevent foreign takeovers of Canadian banks, insurance companies, and other financial services; and introduced policies that were designed to prevent the Americans from gaining a stranglehold over Canadian media outlets.)

Despite Gordon's willingness to tackle the problem head-on, the amount of American investment remained high throughout the decade. By 1968, foreign companies controlled 57 percent of the Canadian manufacturing industry, 70 percent of the mining industry, and 80 percent of the petroleum and gas industries. (The Canadian government would respond to the threat to its petroleum and gas industries by forming Petro-Canada, a publicly owned petroleum company, in the 1970s.)

Branch Plant Syndrome

One of the biggest drawbacks to the large amount of foreign investment in Canada was a phenomenon known as "branch plant syndrome"—the tendency of large multinationals to open branch plants in Canada in order to bypass the tariff restrictions that they would otherwise face when they shipped goods across the border.

Branch plants brought jobs to Canada, but the jobs came at a price. For one thing, branch plants rarely got involved in research and development. They also tended to purchase any goods they required from the parent company's U.S.-based suppliers rather than looking for Canadian suppliers, and the profits that they generated were siphoned off for distribution to U.S.-based investors.

And Now the Good News...

Of course, it wasn't all doom and gloom with regard to Canadian-American economic relations. The Canada–U.S. Automotive Products Agreement of 1965 created a single North America–wide market for cars, trucks, buses, tires, and automobile parts. Because these goods could cross the border in both directions, tariff free, the Canadian automotive industry enjoyed a boom in export sales to the U.S.

Newsflash!

In 1965, consumer advocate Ralph Nader published a book that forced the automotive industry to pull up its socks. His book, *Unsafe at Any Speed*, exposed the industry's poor safety standards and led the U.S. Congress to pass a stringent auto safety act the following year.

Will That Be Cash or Chargex?

In 1968, four Canadian chartered banks launched Chargex—a nationally recognized credit card that gave consumers the freedom to charge their purchases regardless of where they decided to shop. (Until that time, Canadians who chose to use credit cards had ended up with a walletful of cards from different department stores and gas stations since it wasn't possible to use an Eaton's card at the local Shell station, nor was it possible to use a Gulf card at the Bay.)

Whether it was the introduction of the new Chargex card or the fact that more Canadians were getting into the habit of using plastic, Canadian consumers went a little charge-happy during the 1960s. By the end of the decade, the total credit debt in Canada had jumped from $223 per person in 1960 to $515 per person in 1969. As Alan Edmonds notes in *The Years of Protest 1960-1970,* "No one was sure whether [this increase] meant that Canadians suddenly had more faith in tomorrow than ever before, or whether we decided collectively that tomorrow might never come, so we might as well mortgage it to the hilt."

Boomer Bytes

In 1962, the Canadian dollar was worth 92.5 cents U.S. It remained fixed at this level until 1970, when its value was allowed to float again.

–Source: *The Globe and Mail*

Money to Burn

Of course, Canadians didn't just have money to *burn* by using their credit cards. They also had money to *melt.*

Until the mid-1960s, Canadian dimes, quarters, and half-dollars were made from 80 percent silver. In 1966, the price of silver increased dramatically, which meant that coins containing silver were actually worth more than their face value. This led the Royal Mint to decide to cut the percentage of silver in coins to just 50 percent.

Canadians weren't the only ones who were wrestling with this particular problem, of course. The folks in Washington also found themselves with vaults full of coins that were worth more than their face value.

While it was illegal in both countries to damage, deface, or melt coins, there was nothing that either government could do to prevent people from melting U.S. coins in Canada or from melting Canadian coins in the U.S. and then selling the melted coins to a silver dealer. As a result, millions of coins found their way across the border in both directions, a situation that led to a shortage of small change in stores!

Newsflash!

One of the hottest-selling books of the 1960s was Morton Shulman's get-rich-quick book, *Anyone Can Make a Million,* which described how he had made a fortune playing the stock market, offering "surprising techniques and closely-guarded secrets of the pros." The Toronto doctor would subsequently achieve great fame as Toronto's chief coroner and an outspoken crusader on behalf of anyone who had been wronged by fraud or corruption in high places.

Coin merchants set up shop in towns along the Canada–U.S. border as well as in some of the country's largest cities. They offered a 20 percent premium on the face value of old coins: if you handed over an old quarter, you'd pocket 30 cents worth of new coins for your efforts. While this sounds like a rather tedious way to make a fortune, some enterprising Canadians managed to do just that: according to Alan Edmonds, author of *The Years of Protest 1960-1970,* one Vancouver man managed to finance his Hawaiian honeymoon solely through his coin trading habit, and a parking meter clerk in Quebec City managed to squirrel away enough coin-related profits over a three-month period to buy a new car!

In 1968, the price of silver shot up even further and both Ottawa and Washington started minting coins that didn't contain any silver at all.

The Least You Need to Know

➤ The 1960s were boom years for the Canadian economy.

➤ They were also years of unrest on the labour front, with the Canadian public having to deal with strikes by postal workers, schoolteachers, railway employees, airline personnel, longshoremen, and production line workers, to name but a few.

➤ A 1964 Gallup poll revealed that nearly half of Canadians were concerned about the amount of American investment in Canada.

➤ By 1968, foreign companies controlled 57 percent of the Canadian manufacturing industry, 70 percent of the mining industry, and 80 percent of the petroleum and gas industries.

➤ The Canada–U.S. Automotive Products Agreement of 1965 created a single North America–wide market for cars, trucks, buses, tires, and automobile parts.

➤ In 1968, four Canadian chartered banks launched Chargex—a nationally recognized credit card that gave consumers the freedom to charge their purchases regardless of where they decided to shop.

➤ In 1966, the price of silver increased dramatically, which meant that coins containing silver were actually worth more than their face value. As a result, millions of coins were shipped across the U.S. border, where they were melted and sold to silver dealers.

Chapter 9

God Is Dead

In This Chapter

➤ Religion during the 1960s

➤ Jesus freaks

➤ Other forms of spiritualism

When John Lennon announced that the Beatles were "more popular than Jesus Christ," and *Time* magazine ran a cover story that asked "Is God Dead?" many people were scandalized. Others, however, simply shrugged their shoulders and accepted these anti-religious sentiments as a sign of the times. After all, if young people were determined to challenge every conceivable type of authority, why should the church be exempt?

By 1960, the religious revival of the 1950s had disappeared. Canada's religious leaders were left with nothing but fond memories of expanding congregations and a construction boom that had seen new churches springing up all over the country. And the growth trend hadn't just stopped, it had reversed—churches were actually losing members, and they would go on losing them for decades to come. (In 1945, 60 percent of Canadians attended church weekly, and 82 percent stated that they belonged to a church; by 1990 only 23 percent of Canadians were attending church regularly, and just 29 percent claimed to be members of a church.) The decline in

Boomer Bytes

In 1965, 83 percent of Roman Catholics attended church regularly. By 1986, this figure had dropped to 43 percent.

Sunday school enrolment was particularly apparent during the1960s: By 1970, there were only half as many children attending Sunday school as there had been in 1960.

The Uncomfortable Pew

Desperate times call for desperate measures. In 1963, the Anglican Church of Canada decided that it was time to engage in some heavy-duty navel gazing in order to pinpoint the reasons why the pews were becoming increasingly empty on Sunday mornings. The Anglican Church gave the job of determining what was behind this mass exodus from the country's churches to a rather unlikely candidate, Pierre Berton.

Berton was the former church editor for a Vancouver daily newspaper and perhaps Canada's best-known (and sometimes most hated!) journalist at the time. He was chosen to do the research because he was not a member of the faith community, and thus would be able to look at the situation objectively. (He admitted, in the introduction to his book *The Comfortable Pew,* that he'd stopped going to church during his college years because he found far more interesting ways to spend his time: "Mine was a rebellion born of apathy. More compelling interests entered my life: summers spent in mining camps, winters spent at college.")

Not everyone was thrilled that Berton had been given this assignment. In fact, even within the Anglican Church itself there was sharp disagreement about whether bringing Berton on board had been a smart thing to do. (The Anglican dioceses of Toronto and Calgary were particularly outspoken on the issue.) A debate raged in newspapers across Canada about Berton's suitability for the job. "I shall not buy or read [the book]," one writer declared. "Pierre Berton will finish us off," said another.

The controversy surrounding Berton's book led it to become an immediate bestseller when it finally hit the bookstore shelves in 1965. And if it was controversy that Canadians wanted, Berton was happy to deliver. With the Anglican Church's blessing, he had expanded the scope of his book to include all of the major non–Roman Catholic Christian denominations—which meant that he was able to outrage a far greater number of people by what he had to say!

Berton started his book by noting that he was writing his book "in an age when people change their churches as easily as they change their domiciles, choosing often enough the handiest church in their suburbs"—assuming, of course, that they even bothered to go to church at all.

He went on to pin the blame for the decline in attendance on the churches themselves, arguing that they were "weak, tardy, equivocal and irrelevant" and that they were desperately out of touch with the needs of Canadians: "Church leaders are woefully behind the times and it is safe to say that large numbers of them do not know what is happening or do not want to believe it when they are told."

He concluded his book by telling his readers in no uncertain terms that the church had to accept the fact that, in the future, "many who call themselves Christians will not necessarily 'go to church' at all—will not even identify themselves with a congregation or a specific denomination." Then he posed the big question—one that caused a stir at more than one church potluck supper: "Will the Church then reject these people or ignore them, simply because they refuse to take out exclusive membership cards in the religious club?"

Boom, Bust, No Echo

A point that Berton failed to make in his book, which in retrospect is certainly worth considering, is that the massive decline in church attendance had a great deal to do with the coming of age of that most infamous of generations, the baby boomers.

Once they entered their teen years, this huge group of young people began questioning the authority of the churches. In the end, they decided that the churches were sadly out of touch with the real world.

Consider what Peter C. Emberley had to say about the baby boom generation's rejection of the established churches in a recent article in *Maclean's* magazine: "For the generation weaned on positive thinking and the inherent goodness of all human prompting, the old theological language of sacrifice, discipline, guilt and sin is a problem. So are doctrinal and credal authority—expressions of a religion that is censorious, judgmental and restrictive, extinguishing openness and joy. Baby boomers' schooling, after all, dwelled on creativity and originality.... Baby boomers also struggle with the fitful relation of religion to scientific reason—how to reconcile the apparent contradictions of modern

Blast from the Past!

"The Boomers broke a long-established pattern. For centuries, the values of one generation were passed on to the next. But the sheer numerical weight of the Boomers changed this. The Baby Boom generation heavily outnumbered their parents. When they decided to go off in search of new, modern values there wasn't much anybody could do to stop them."

–Source: *Canada and the World Backgrounder*, May 1998

skepticism and ancient mystery, laboratory experiment and psychic experience, individual autonomy and cosmic piety."

The boomers wanted the church to modernize, to recognize the equality of people of different races and sexes, and most important of all, to accept that non-traditional ideas might have some validity. In many cases, the churches simply turned a deaf ear.

Blast from the Past!

"Wanted—for sedition, criminal anarchy, vagrancy, and conspiring to overthrow the established government."

—An excerpt from a "Wanted" ad for Jesus Christ—a popular poster during the 1960s

Jesus Freaks

That's not to say that young people were abandoning religion en masse. Some were turning to religion, attending pep rallies where they could hook up with other born-again Christians. They called themselves "Jesus People" but their detractors gave them a less positive label: "Jesus freaks." They professed to be getting high on Jesus Christ.

The Jesus People movement lasted only about five years—from 1969 to 1974, approximately—but it continues to have an impact to the present day. The movement encouraged the traditional churches to allow casual attire at worship services, to install hi-fi speakers in the sanctuary, and to adopt a more conversational style of preaching. It also encouraged the growth of the Christian book publishing and gospel music industries on both sides of the border.

Searching for Truth

Not all young people turned to the established religions or even their hipper offshoots in their search for meaning and truth. Some turned to Eastern religions, cults, and even the occult.

These young people believed that it was necessary to look elsewhere for inspiration. "Christianity was rejected, because it was seen as the tribal religion of the white Western bourgeoisie and as the ideological justification for capitalism, for imperialism, even for racism," explains Godfrey Hodgson in his book *America in Our Time: From World War II to Nixon—What Happened and Why.* "The mutant young therefore sought expression for their religious yearnings among the symbols and mysteries of the non-white world: in Japanese Zen Buddhism, in the legends of the Plains Indians, and in the lamaseries of Tibet."

Some young people began to follow the teachings of the Maharishi Mahesh Yogi, a spiritual leader from India.

Others got "turned on" by L. Ron Hubbard, a former science fiction writer who had founded the Church of Scientology; or Sun Myung Moon, the founder of the "Moonies."

Blast from the Past!

"People started getting into the 'Zen' of things: the Zen of tennis, the Zen of working out, the Zen of motorcycle repair, the Zen of running. I, like many others, started connecting physical activity to the spiritual side. People also started looking at some of the Eastern disciplines like yoga and tai chi, and not only the stretching aspects of these disciplines but the mental aspects. Now they were working the body, the mind, and the spirit."

—American fitness guru Kathy Smith, quoted in Peter Jennings and Todd Brewster's book *The Century*

Still others donned the flowing robes of the India-based Hare Krishna, a group that arrived in the U.S. in 1965 and headed north a short time later. The group's chief tenet of faith was its rejection of material goods and the outside world in favour of communal living and service to the movement. Hare Krishna followers quickly became known for their aggressive recruiting tactics, recalled Swami Hridayananda in a recent interview with *The Los Angeles Times:* "That was the rock 'em, sock 'em Hare Krishna movement, when a small number of zealots lived in the temple and gave everything to the movement. We look back and laugh a lot about ourselves, tackling people at airports and things. Now we're much more concerned about being civilized."

Some young people turned to the occult. According to Alan Edmonds, author of *The Years of Protest 1960-1970,* "In 1968, Ouija boards were outselling Monopoly games, closely followed by the game ESP, and books on reincarnation and psychic phenomena outsold the Bible. One community college in Toronto ran an evening course in witchcraft."

Clearly, a 1965 United Church survey of 1,700 laymen and 347 ministers was right on the money when it concluded that "traditional religious beliefs are breaking down faster than ever."

> ## The Least You Need to Know
>
> ➤ In 1945, 60 percent of Canadians attended church weekly and 82 percent stated that they belonged to a church; by 1990, only 23 percent of Canadians were attending church regularly and just 29 percent claimed to be members of a church.
>
> ➤ The decline in Sunday school enrolment was particularly apparent during the 1960s. By 1970, there were only half as many children attending Sunday school as there had been in 1960.
>
> ➤ In 1965, 83 percent of Roman Catholics attended church regularly. By 1986, this figure had dropped to 43 percent.
>
> ➤ Many young people rejected the established churches or stopped going to church altogether. Some became "Jesus freaks." Others turned to Eastern religions, cults, or the occult.

Part 2
The Seventies

The seventies are the years that everyone loves to hate—a ten-year black hole during which tackiness reigned supreme. We lived in suburban bungalows that featured shag rugs, bold, in-your-face wallpaper patterns, and bathroom fixtures in all of the decade's hottest colours: rust, harvest gold, and avocado green. We tuned in to such high-quality TV fare as The Brady Bunch, The Gong Show, *and* King of Kensington. *We wore platform shoes, bell-bottoms, and homemade fashions made from the latest "stretch and sew" fabrics. And we took to fads like CB radios, streaking, and disco dancing. Yes, boys and girls, it was a scary time indeed...*

Escape to the Suburbs

Step inside the nearest time machine and set the dial to 1975. When the lights stop flashing and the machine stops shaking, you'll find yourself standing in the middle of a suburban neighbourhood, wondering how on earth you're going to tell which wood-panelled station wagon and three-bedroom bungalow belong to your family!

One Size Fits Most

There's no denying it. Uniformity was the name of the game in the suburbs of the 1970s. Despite the builders' best efforts to use different colours of brick to hide the fact that there were, at most, four or five different types of houses on a particular street, it was painfully obvious that there wasn't a whole lot of difference between your house and the house next door. (This wasn't necessarily a bad thing, of course. In fact, it came in quite handy when you were visiting a neighbour's house for the very first time. You never had to ask where the bathroom was. You already knew!)

What the builders couldn't hide—and what became immediately evident to even the most casual observer—was the fact that most of the families living on a particular street were clones of one another, too. The suburbs were almost completely inhabited by white middle-class families. What's more, the families living on a particular street tended to bring home roughly the same amount of money on payday. Whether people were prepared to admit it or not, that was part of the suburbs' appeal: an unwritten guarantee that you'd find yourself surrounded by people who were just like you.

Behind Closed Doors

Wondering what these cookie-cutter houses looked like on the inside?

A typical suburban home was filled with an eclectic mix of materials. Natural products like wood, wicker, bamboo, rope, cork, muslin, burlap, leather, and suede were very popular for home furnishings—but so were plastic, vinyl, and a host of other synthetic products.

Particularly trendy during the decade were wall-sized murals, shag carpeting, peel-and-stick tiles, plants hung in macramé slings, director's chairs, beanbag chairs, inflatable chairs, giant floor pillows, modular "conversation-pit" sofas, waterbeds (some with built-in eight-track tape players!), and what the authors of *Retro Hell: Life in the '70s and '80s, from Afros to Zotz* call "do-it-yourself cheapo furniture": board-and-brick bookcases, crate end tables, and telephone-cable-spool dining tables. (I don't know about you, but I go into sensory overload just thinking about it!)

Blast from the Past!

Think suburban living is a North American phenomenon or a product of twentieth-century life? Think again. People have been singing the praises of life in suburbia since practically the beginning of time. In fact, the King of Persia received a letter that sang the praises of life in suburban Babylon in 539 B.C.: "Our property... is so close to Babylon that we enjoy all the advantages of the city, and yet when we come home we are away from all the noise and dust."

Shop 'Til You Drop

The suburbs were a great place to live if you were 30 years old and had your own car. They weren't quite so terrific if you were a teenager who had to take a 45-minute bus ride in order to reach that teenage mecca, the shopping mall.

It's hard to overestimate the importance of the mall in the lives of suburban teens, circa 1975. It was a much cooler place to hang out than the places that your parents suggested—like the rec room in your basement or, heaven help you, the library. It was also unbelievably cheap. You could spend an entire day at the mall without spending any money—as long as you had the willpower to stay away from Sam the Record Man and you didn't get on the bad side of the walkie-talkie-toting mall security guards whose job it was to chase you away.)

Consider what the editors of *Ben Is Dead* magazine have to say about mall life in the 1970s in their book *Retro Hell: Life in the '70s and '80s, from Afros to Zotz:* "At the center of the adolescent world stood that sacred ground, the mall. No mere village green or marketplace, the mall was an all-encompassing environment where everything you could want to want was found.... Even without money, we still came to pay homage, to stroll, to see and be seen, and perhaps even to fall in love."

Boomer Bytes

The Toronto Eaton Centre opened for business in February of 1977.

Bright Lights, Big City

By the end of the 1970s, high land-servicing costs in the suburbs and the rising cost of gasoline were making people think twice before they made a down payment on a three-bedroom suburban bungalow.

Lorne Braithewaite described the growing appeal of inner-city life in an article that appeared in the April 19, 1980, issue of *The Financial Post:* "The type of people who, after World War II, automatically wanted a three-bedroom home in the suburbs, where they could cut their own grass and visit the community centre, are now heading for high-rise condominiums and other inner-core locations. They're taking these options within walking distance of public transit. Instead of living in the suburbs and having two sizeable cars, they now have one smaller car and rent a bigger one for a couple of weeks whenever they want to take a vacation."

Clearly the mass exodus to suburbia was becoming a thing of the past.

No Name? No Problem!

A revolution in grocery shopping occurred during the 1970s. The man behind the revolution was a rather unlikely hero—a very ordinary-looking grocery store president named Dave Nichol. Dave's claim to fame during the 1970s was the fact that he was the man who put no-name products on the shelves of Loblaw's stores across the country, thereby introducing Canadians to the weird and wonderful world of generic products. (In the 1980s, Dave and his bulldog sidekick would achieve even greater fame via *The Insider's Report*, a Loblaw's publication that did an amazing job of promoting the growing line of high-end grocery products that were being sold under the store's own "President's Choice" label. People treated the *Report* as if it were a newspaper or magazine, carefully reading it from cover to cover. Even newspaper columnist Michele Landsberg sang its praises in *The Toronto Star!*)

The bargain-basement no-name products quickly stole market share away from their pricier brand-name counterparts. Why, after all, would you want to pay top dollar for name-brand baking soda, when you could pick up the no-name equivalent for significantly less?

Within 15 months of being introduced in 1978, the 120 generic products available at that time were accounting for 10 percent of the sales volume in a typical Loblaw's store.

Not all no-name products were successful, however. Some of the first generation of no-name products left something to be desired in the quality department. (I still have flashbacks when I think of the horrible-tasting no-name peanut butter that my parents inflicted on us instead of our beloved Kraft peanut butter—a move that merely encouraged my sisters and me to switch to eating cheese slice sandwiches. Unfortunately, it wasn't long before an even greater horror was inflicted upon us—no-name cheese slices!)

Still, on the whole, no-name products were the right idea for the times. As Deborah Dowling noted in an article that appeared in *The Financial Post* on June 2, 1979, Canadians were quickly becoming a nation of penny-pinchers—at least when it came to day-to-day purchases like grocery items: "Inflation and its pressure on real disposable incomes has made Canadians more value-conscious than at any time since the Great Depression," she wrote. "Yet while generic merchandising seems to be flourishing, there

Boomer Bytes

The Pop Shoppe chain was also able to capitalize on the new-found appeal of generic products. By 1975, the rapidly expanding chain was selling cases of pop for $2.89 at a time when the brand names were going for $5 a case. The chain was also offering consumers more choice in flavours than what they were able to find in a typical grocery store. In addition to such traditional flavours as cola and orange, consumers could fill up the red-and-white plastic Pop Shoppe cases with bottles of grapefruit-flavoured pop!

seems to be no shortage of money or credit for the luxuries, such as boats and travel, that satisfy the Canadian ego."

Death of a Catalogue

While the introduction of generic products to the grocery stores of the nation was a significant development in the retailing world of the 1990s, it seems like a minor development indeed when compared to the death of a Canadian institution—the Eaton's catalogue.

After nearly 100 years of publication (the catalogue had been launched in 1884 at what would eventually become known as the Canadian National Exhibition), Eaton's announced that it was pulling the plug on its catalogue in 1976.

Canadian Business published a eulogy for the catalogue in its March 1976 issue: "By rights, Eaton's last catalogue ought not to be interred in the ground," wrote John A. Edds. "Instead, it should be cremated and its ashes scattered over the length and breadth of Canada. For there is scarcely a square mile of Canada or a segment of Canadian society that hasn't felt the impact of.... Eaton's mail order catalogue."

Here are just a few of the items that were offered for sale in the Spring and Summer 1976 Eaton's catalogue:

Blast from the Past

"Harem floor pillows. Giant pillows for super-lazy lounging or TV viewing. Covered in rust/beige cotton print on one side, rust Orlon acrylic and cotton pile on the other. Button tufted. Filled with shredded plastic foam and cotton. About 40 inches square. Carton of two. $74.95."

—One of the items for sale in the Spring and Summer 1976 Eaton's catalogue

➤ A portable sauna for home or office that featured a "woodgrain pattern vinyl cover" ($59)

➤ A top-of-the-line Hewlett Packard scientific programmable calculator ($989)

➤ An answering machine that featured remote message retrieval ($429.99)

➤ Beanbag chairs in gold, tangerine, brown, or black ($59.98)

➤ A 26-inch console colour TV ($969.95)

➤ A Braun drip-style coffeemaker ($62.95)

➤ A top-of-the-line dishwasher ($539.99)

➤ Nylon shag carpeting in gold, red, blue, green, beige, caramel, and pink ($7 per square yard)

➤ Bathroom fixtures in Aztec gold, avocado, lavender, maritime blue, and antique white ($209 for a toilet; $309 for a tub)

➤ Patch-style wide-leg Lee jeans with matching denim vests and gingham shirts ($22.95 for the jeans, $14.95 for the vest, and $13.95 for the shirt)

➤ A 24-pack of Sheik condoms ($5)

The Least You Need to Know

➤ The suburbs were populated with white middle-class Canadians who earned roughly the same amount of money and who lived in houses with virtually identical floor plans.

➤ Shag carpeting, beanbag chairs, and waterbeds were just a few of the hot decorating trends during the 1970s.

➤ Teenagers who found themselves stranded in suburbia spent their spare time "hanging out at the mall."

➤ The high cost of servicing suburban land and the rising cost of gasoline led some people to think twice before they decided to leave the big city behind and head for the suburbs.

➤ "No-name" products hit the grocery store shelves in 1978. Within 15 months, they had captured 10 percent of the volume of sales in Canadian grocery stores.

➤ The final Eaton's catalogue appeared in 1976, signalling the end to an important chapter in Canadian retail history.

Chapter 11

Long Live the Rec Room

In This Chapter

➤ The rec room revisited

➤ Canadian TV shows

➤ American TV shows

It's no wonder Canadian comedian Mike Myers chose to set his popular *Saturday Night Live* "Wayne's World" sketches in a suburban rec room. That's where all the action was in 1970s suburbia. You see, long, long ago, in the days before 1980s monster homes made main-floor family rooms the norm, families had to head downstairs to watch TV.

While a visitor from another planet might ask why it wasn't possible to put the TV set in the living room upstairs, anyone who grew up in North America knows the answer to that question: the living room wasn't meant to be lived in. It was supposed to be kept spotlessly clean and in museum-like condition so that it could be used to entertain unexpected visitors. (Your parents' visitors, that is. Only a child with a death wish would have considered inviting his own friends to play Dinky cars in the living room.) So while the brightly lit living rooms upstairs remained largely unused, Joe and Jane Canuck and their two kids ended up hanging out in that dark downstairs cave known as the rec room.

Boomer Bytes

A study released in 1975 revealed that, by the time he or she reached the age of 18, a typical child would have spent twice as many hours in front of the TV set as in the classroom.

The rec room was typically decorated with shag or sculptured carpet in one of the decade's hottest colours—rust, harvest gold, or avocado green. The walls were covered in wood panelling (real or fake), which merely added to the cave-like atmosphere. The room was typically furnished with a La-Z-Boy chair, a sofa that had seen better days, and a wooden console television set. (In the middle of February, it became necessary to add something else to the room: a space heater. Hey, it was chilly hanging out below ground level in the middle of a Canadian winter!)

In this chapter, we're going to talk about the TV shows that everyone was watching back in the 1970s. So grab that bowl of popcorn, flop yourself down in your Dad's La-Z-Boy, and get ready to see what was on the tube.

Made in Canada

Two of the most popular Canadian-made television shows during the 1970s were *The Beachcombers,* a drama that focused on the adventures of a scow operator on Canada's West Coast, and *King of Kensington,* a domestically produced sitcom about the adventures of an average guy who lived in Toronto's Kensington Market district, which managed to pull in 1.5 to 1.8 million viewers each week.

The most noteworthy of the Canadian shows produced during the 1970s, however, was *SCTV*—a comedy show that still has a cult-like following nearly 20 years after it went off the air.

Taking its name from the call letters of a fictitious television station, *SCTV* was a television show that did the unthinkable—parody TV. During its years on air (1976 to 1983), it managed to pull in large numbers of viewers from both sides of the border. It also launched the careers of some of the most successful comedians of the time: Andrea Martin, Eugene Levy, John Candy, Joe Flaherty, Catherine O'Hara, Dave Thomas, Rick Moranis, and Martin Short. (All but Martin and Flaherty were Canadians.)

The audience loved it when actors Rick Moranis and Dave Thomas became Bob and Doug McKenzie, co-hosts of a fictitious TV show called *Great White North.* According to Geoff Pevere and Greig Dyment, co-authors of *Mondo Canuck: A Canadian Pop Culture Odyssey, SCTV*'s producers had been asked to come up with an extra two minutes of Canadian content for the Canadian edition of the show—something to keep the folks at the CRTC happy. The result was the McKenzie brothers and *Great White North.*

"A flat with two folding chairs was hauled in, along with a barbecue laden with back bacon, a map of Canada for a backdrop and several cases of Canadian beer in stubby bottles," recall Pevere and Dyment in *Mondo Canuck: A Canadian Pop Culture Odyssey.* "This was to be the set for the so-called McKenzie Brothers: two toque-bearing, parka-wearing, protypically Canuck dimwits whose role was to fill those two distinctly Canadian minutes with some entirely unscripted banter about some distinctly Canadian topic, like how to get a mouse into a beer bottle for a free case, or why doughnut shops have fewer parking spots than tables."

A McKenzie brothers' album, released in the fall of 1981, sold 300,000 copies in less than a month, a feat that put it at the top of the music charts. That November, Canadians from coast to coast were caught up in hosermania. (The favourite insult tossed around by the McKenzie brothers was "you hoser.") Five thousand turned out for a Hoser Day parade through downtown Toronto, dressed in full Bob and Doug regalia: parkas, toques, earmuffs, checkered flannel shirts, and mitts. Unfortunately for Moranis and Thomas, hosermania faded as quickly as it came. The one-and-only McKenzie brothers movie— *Strange Brew*—hardly stayed in theatres long enough for a beer to go flat. Still, as Pevere and Dyment note in their book, the McKenzie brothers phenomenon made it cool to be Canadian: "So what if it came and went faster than a beer on a hot afternoon. For it was a beauty while it lasted, eh?"

Daytime TV

Not thrilled with the quality of shows you can find on daytime TV these days? Count your lucky stars that you're not stuck in the seventies! The shows that aired during the daytime during the decade can be divided into two basic categories: those that were "good for you" and those that were "just plain bad."

Neither category was particularly inspiring. In fact, given the choice between watching daytime TV while you recovered from a head cold or dragging yourself to school where you could hang out with your friends, most self-respecting kids were out the door in a flash.

Here's a list of the shows that Michele Landsberg picked as "the best" and "the worst" on daytime TV in an article that appeared in the November 1974 issue of *Chatelaine:*

The Best

Take 30 (CBC): A news show that "avoids the groveling groupie tone of most talk shows."

Canada AM (CTV): The only Canadian morning talk show.

Coronation Street (CBC): A British import. "The only soap opera that ever cracks a smile."

Kareen's Yoga (CTV): "A soothing half-hour of yoga" in a set filled with soft music and potted palms.

The French Chef (PBS): A cooking show featuring "competent, earthy, and unaffected Julia Child."

Masterpiece Theatre (PBS): A series of "wonderful, British-produced dramas."

The Worst

Juliette and Friends (CBC): A show that "burbles on mindlessly about makeup and interior decorating and showbiz pals of the hosts."

Luncheon Date (CBC): A show that "sics a series of underachieving American singers on us."

Let's Make a Deal (ABC): A show that "plays on human greed and humiliation."

The Newlywed Game (ABC): "Sadistic voyeurism for the daytime Peeping Tom."

As the World Turns (CBS): A soap opera that "still hasn't heard of professional women, blacks, war, poverty, or any other human reality outside of a stereotyped middle-class living-room."

Petticoat Junction (CBC): A U.S. import in which "three girls, all in matching plastic hairdos, simper, wriggle and grovel around any remotely available man."

Truth or Consequences (U.S. network not specified): A game show featuring contestants "who all look like Nixon stalwarts from Iowa."

The Price Is Right (CBS): A game show propelled by "naked greed." (And, no, she wasn't just referring to the scantily clad models on the show!)

And to all the men who might be tempted to feel smug about the inferior quality of "women's television"—the majority of daytime television viewers were, after all, female—Landsberg had this to say: " 'Men's' television, when you think about it, is even sillier. Huge armored oafs charge about a field chasing a pigskin ball. Implausibly smooth and handsome crime-fighters demonstrate their virility by punching, slashing, shooting, and manipulating insane machinery and women with the same indifference. Or, more recently, plump, unhandsome, inarticulate detectives (more like the average male viewer) chase unlikely criminals with tough-guy bravado." Bet that wiped the smug looks off their faces!

Good Sports

Of course, what most guys were tuning in to on the tube were sporting events—and there was plenty worth watching during the 1970s. Over one billion viewers worldwide tuned in to the Montreal Summer Olympic Games in 1976 and 40 million viewers around the globe were on hand to watch the "Battle of the Sexes" between women's tennis champion Billie Jean King and self-confessed male chauvinist pig Bobby Riggs. (King beat him hands down.)

Blast from the Past!

"I'm ready to play, and I'm going to try to win for all the guys around the world who feel as I do that the male is king, the male is supreme," Bobby Riggs told Howard Cosell, in an interview moments before he stepped onto the tennis court. He was defeated by women's tennis champion Billie Jean King, in what was being called "The Battle of the Sexes."

These two events seem almost insignificant, however, when you stop to consider what happened on the ice on September 28, 1972—the day that Team Canada's Paul Henderson scored the winning goal on Vladislav Tretiak in the Canada-Russia hockey series. Employees brought television sets to work and schoolchildren stayed home to watch the final game in the series with the full blessing of their parents. A mind-boggling 12.5 million Canadians saw the game on TV.

In his book *Home Sweet Home*, Mordecai Richler argued that "the moral victory [in the Canada-Russia hockey series] clearly belonged to Russia." After noting that the Russians had deserved to win because of their superior calibre of play, he talked about how the series changed Canadians' feelings about their country: "After the series, nothing was ever the same again in Canada. Beer didn't taste as good. The Rockies seemed smaller, the northern lights dimmer." Sam Orbaum agreed with Richler's take on the situation in a recent article in *The Jerusalem Post:* "When everyone had stopped jumping up and down, hugging strangers, kissing each other, shrieking from euphoric relief and weeping for joy, the dreadful truth crept in: Canada was not undeniably the greatest hockey country on earth."

But the fact that Canada was on top for now was indeed a sweet consolation.

Controversies Both On-Air and Off

Television certainly experienced its fair share of controversies during the 1970s. Three of the perennial hot topics were the way that advertisers were using television to get their advertising messages to children, the way

Blast from the Past!

"The mythology had us believe that [Henderson] combined the best qualities of Gordie Howe, Stompin' Tom Connors and the Fathers of Confederation."

—Geoff Pevere and Greig Dyment, *Mondo Canuck: A Canadian Pop Culture Odyssey*

that women were being depicted on TV, and what types of language and content were and weren't appropriate on television.

Child's Play

Throughout the decade and beyond, there was considerable debate about the tactics that advertisers were using to reach children. Some felt that advertisements aimed at children should be banned altogether. Others disagreed.

The debate wasn't just going on within Canada, of course. The March 19, 1979, issue of *Maclean's* magazine reported that tougher advertising regulations were about to limit how children's advertisers could flog their wares on the U.S. networks: "The snap and crackle of television advertising aimed at young children may be about to go pop," wrote Catherine Fox, who was covering the hearings at the Federal Trade Commission in Washington.

The Commission heard 130 witnesses, including experts who testified that young children were being subjected to an average of 20,000 television commercials each year. By the time the hearings wrapped up, the companies involved in the $600-million-a-year juvenile products industry had racked up some $15 million in legal and public relations fees.

He Says, She Says

There was also considerable debate about what role the networks should play in ensuring that women were depicted in at least a semi-intelligent fashion on the small screen. Morris Wolfe weighed in with his opinion in an article entitled "Television: A propaganda machine for male supremacy" that appeared in the April 1974 issue of *Saturday Night*.

"The CBC might start (and one hopes CTV and Global would follow suit) by establishing some minimum guidelines," he wrote. "Announcers and interviewers, for example, should be told not to refer to females over the age of about fifteen as 'girls' (or 'ladies'); they're women. Interviewers should be told not to ask whether a woman is married, or what her husband's occupation is, unless that information is relevant to the subject at hand. Cameramen and switchers at sports events should be told not to linger on the attractive (or unattractive) women in the audience."

Hot Stuff

Another issue that was much debated both on and off the air was what was—and wasn't—suitable in the eyes of the viewing public.

Blast from the Past!

"The commercials favor the pretty but simple-minded suburban housewife, either being initiated into the mysteries of clean laundry by an officious male voice-over or anxiously waiting for compliments from her husband and children."

—Michele Landsberg, writing in the November 1970 issue of *Chatelaine*

Ottawa television station CJOH learned the hard way that the Canadian public wasn't quite ready to hear the "f-word" on television when it aired an interview in January 1970 in which the dreaded word was used no less than 19 times. The outcry from viewers was immediate and led to the resignations of high-ranking executives in the company that owned CJOH. Journalist Douglas Marshall had this to say in an article that appeared in *Maclean's* magazine in the aftermath of the brouhaha: "Perhaps someday those fundamental Anglo-Saxon expletives that form the bawdy clay of English will be as commonplace on television as the far more obscene detergent commercials. Perhaps. But despite concerted efforts by each new generation of youth, we have not seen the dawning of such an age of acquiescence. The general feeling in the best TV circles is that the basic four-letter words should still be avoided."

While CJOH had unthinkingly crossed that magic line that defined the boundaries of Canadian taste, one man was determined to pole-vault across it time and time again. That man was Moses Znaimer, founder of Citytv, an iconoclastic rebel who was determined to produce television that was fast-paced, unconventional, and in-your-face—in other words, everything that conventional Canadian television was not.

Shortly after it hit the airwaves in 1972, Citytv did the unthinkable: it began airing the notorious *Baby Blue Movies*—a series of soft-porn flicks the likes of which the Canadian viewing public had never seen before.

If Znaimer wanted to put his tiny television station on the map, he'd certainly succeeded.

Blast from the Past!

Some of the best television commercials of the 1970s, according to the Advertising Age Web site:

➤ Coca-Cola's "I'd like to buy the world a Coke" commercial, which featured teenagers singing the refrain and swaying from side to side

➤ Life Cereal's "He likes it" commercial, in which Mikey, who "hates everything," gives the nutritious breakfast cereal his seal of approval

➤ American Express Traveller's cheques "Don't leave home without 'em" commercial, which featured Karl Malden of *Streets of San Francisco* fame.

You can read about the magazine's other favourite commercials from this decade by visiting the *Advertising Age* magazine Web site at http://www.adage.com.

Boomer Bytes

In 1971, the standard length of a commercial dropped from 60 seconds to 30 seconds. By the 1980s, some commercials would be down to just 15 seconds.

Don't Touch That Dial!

Some of the commercials that aired during the 1970s were at least as entertaining as the shows they interrupted.

For starters, there were those unforgettable Kraft Food commercials—commercials that seemed to be designed with the sole purpose of using as many Kraft products as possible! (Before these "Great Recipes From Kraft" commercials hit the airwaves, who knew that you could use marshmallows and peanut butter in the same recipe—or that Miracle Whip could be used as an ingredient in chocolate cake?)

And then there were the *Hinterland Who's Who* one-minute public service announcements prepared by the Canadian Wildlife Service. While these were serious commercials, designed to inform the Canadian viewing public about the fascinating lives of creatures of the wild, they were often the subject of spoofs. And once you'd heard someone do a parody of the commercials, you could never watch them with a straight face again. Still, the commercials must have served their purpose because they remained on the air for more than 30 years.

The American Imports

In February of 1970, *Maclean's* magazine reported that the CRTC was taking drastic steps to stop American TV from flooding into Canada. The CRTC outlawed microwave link-ups carrying American TV stations, which meant that you were only able to watch American TV if you lived close enough to the border to receive U.S. television stations on ordinary cable TV. The magazine's culture critic, Douglas Marshall, had this to say about the CRTC's decision: "Viewers in outlying areas, please do not adjust your sets. We are experiencing difficulties with the reasoning of the Canadian Radio-Television Commission. Critics are working on the problem. Normal service will be resumed as soon as possible."

Blast from the Past!

Yes, Virginia, there was life before wireless remote controls and cable television.

The closest thing to a clicker that could be found in the 1970s rec room was a television converter equipped with an "extra-long cord." This newfangled device allowed you to "change channels [or] switch the set on and off from the comfort of your easy chair!" It was even "softly illuminated for night viewing."

Families that didn't want to pay for cable TV, but who wanted to pick up more channels than just the local CBC affiliate, had little choice but to attach massive TV antennas to towers in their backyards or on the roofs of their houses. The better models were designed to "help block out signals reflected from nearby buildings, walls or hills, minimize ghosts" and block out "snowing" caused by weak signals.

—Source: Spring/Summer 1976 Eaton's Catalogue

Too Little, Too Late

Despite the CRTC's valiant efforts to limit the flow of American programming into Canada, Canadians had long since become hooked on American TV shows, often preferring the glitzy imports to their less slick home-grown counterparts.

The Canadian TV stations that aired them also had grown to love the American imports. A typical import cost $2,000 per half-hour in 1974–75 and could generate revenue of between $20,000 and $24,000. Home-grown shows, on the other hand, cost about $30,000 to make and typically lost money—anywhere from $55 on CTV to $2,050 on the CBC.

Boomer Bytes

A typical half-hour Canadian TV show cost $30,000 to produce—a mere quarter of what was typically spent making a half-hour show in the U.S.

—Source: *The Canadian Encyclopedia*

Here are just a few of the American imports that Canadians loved to tune in to during the 1970s.

Table 11.1 Hit TV Shows That First Hit the Airwaves During the 1970s

1970   *The Mary Tyler Moore Show*

The Odd Couple

The Partridge Family

1971   *All in the Family*

Columbo

1972   *Kung Fu*

M*A*S*H*

The Bob Newhart Show

The Waltons

1973   *Kojak*

1974   *Chico and the Man*

Happy Days

The Rockford Files

The Six Million Dollar Man

1975   *Baretta*

Barney Miller

One Day at a Time

Saturday Night Live

Starsky and Hutch

The Jeffersons

Welcome Back Kotter

Wheel of Fortune

1976   *Charlie's Angels*

Laverne and Shirley

Mary Hartman, Mary Hartman

The Bionic Woman

	The Muppet Show
	The Sonny and Cher Show
1977	*Soap*
	The Love Boat
	Three's Company
1978	*Dallas*
	Fantasy Island
	Mork and Mindy
	Taxi
1979	*Hart to Hart*
	Knot's Landing
	Trapper John, M.D.
1980	*Bosom Buddies*
	Magnum P.I.

Blast from the Past!

The *Schoolhouse Rock* segments that popped up during the Saturday morning cartoons on ABC and were featured "cool" music, designed to teach kids the stuff that they were supposed to be learning in school. Apparently series creator David B. McCall had noticed that his son Davey, who was having trouble learning his multiplication tables, had committed to memory the lyrics of almost every song ever recorded by the Rolling Stones. He decided to teach his son his multiplication tables by setting them to rock music. The strategy worked and he went on to sell the concept to ABC. The segments first aired in 1973 and remained a part of the Saturday morning cartoon line-up for the next 13 years. In response to pressure from baby boomers and Generation X-ers who were eager to take a stroll down memory lane, ABC recently resurrected *Schoolhouse Rock*.

The Brady Bunch

Hard as it may be to believe, given its cult-like following today, *The Brady Bunch* never managed to crack the ranks of the top 20 shows during its five-year run from September 26, 1969, to March 8, 1975. In fact, it didn't really catch on with audiences until after it went into syndication.

Blast from the Past!

"The Brady Bunch provided a better escape from reality than any drug ever ingested by anyone in the Seventies."

—Andrew Edelstein and Kevin McDonough, *The Seventies: From Hot Pants to Hot Tubs.*

Blast from the Past!

"I grew up with 'The Brady Bunch.' My life philosophy is that if it didn't happen on 'The Brady Bunch,' it didn't happen in real life."

—Brady fanatic Maggie Rose, who spent two years looking for a Brady Bunch lunch box before she found one to add to her Brady memorabilia. *Source: Minneapolis Star Tribune.*

However, once the show crossed over into the weird and wonderful land of reruns, it quickly became a favourite with television station program directors and their viewing audiences. According to pop culture expert Andrew Edelstein, the show was frequently plugged into after-school time slots because it was a wholesome product that was available in colour. (Most other family-friendly shows available through syndication at the time were productions like *Leave It to Beaver*, which was only available in black and white.)

Jess Cagle explained the lasting appeal of the show in an article that appeared in *Entertainment Weekly* in 1992: "We are a generation obsessed with the Bradys. We watched them religiously—after school, every day, sometimes twice a day, five days a week, singing that 'Here's the story' theme song, effortlessly memorizing the pilot and 116 subsequent episodes, turning *The Brady Bunch* into one of the most successful syndicated shows ever to be delivered over American airwaves. Now we have come of age. Nostalgia-hungry and shy of the real world, we retreat back to the Brady home, where there's a live-in maid to serve us Kool-Aid and a really cool freestanding staircase designed by our fabulous architect dad."

Charlie's Angels

Another hit television show of the 1970s was *Charlie's Angels*, a detective show that starred a glamorous trio: Farrah Fawcett, Jaclyn Smith, and Kate Jackson.

Fawcett quickly emerged as the favourite with the viewing public, pulling in 20,000 fan letters each week. She inspired the hottest hairstyle of the 1970s (with the possible exception of "the wedge look" made famous by U.S. figure skater Dorothy Hamill)—a fluffy, layered, "big hair" look that required a blow dryer, a curling iron, and lots and lots of hair spray to execute properly. She also managed to sell more than eight million copies of her famous swimsuit poster and earned millions of dollars in royalties for allowing her image to be used on other merchandise, such as T-shirts, lunch pails, dolls, and so on. There was even a *Charlie's Angels* pinball machine!

All in the Family

When *All in the Family* debuted on January 12, 1971, CBS felt obligated to include the following warning: "The program you are about to see is *All in the Family*. It seeks to throw a humorous spotlight on our frailties, prejudices, and concerns. By making them a source of laughter we hope to show, in a mature fashion, just how absurd they are."

It's no wonder the network felt obliged to explain to the North American viewing public what they were about to see. *All in the Family* was, after all, quite unlike any other U.S. TV show that had ever hit the airwaves. The controversial show tackled such sticky issues as racism, the Vietnam War, women's liberation, gay rights, and premarital sex. (The debut episode had Mike—a.k.a. "Meathead"—zipping up his fly as he and Archie's daughter, Gloria, walked downstairs one morning. Clearly this was a show that wasn't going to beat around the bush about anything!)

The show lasted for 13 seasons (although it was reworked into *Archie Bunker's Place* during its final four years on the air). After the credits came down for the final time, Edith and Archie's chairs were moved out of the Bunkers' living-room and into the Smithsonian Institution in Washington.

Saturday Night Live

On October 11, 1975, *Saturday Night Live* hit the airwaves for the very first time. Suddenly, staying at home on a Saturday night was cool. After all, you didn't want to miss out on the hilarious satire of some of the hottest comics of the decade, or the latest

Newsflash

On January 23, 1977, the television mini-series was born. Approximately 130 million viewers tuned in to *Roots*—an eight-night, twelve-hour slavery saga based on a book by Alex Haley. "The televised adaptation of Alex Haley's multigenerational saga about the enslavement of kidnapped Africans and their American assimilation remains to this day the highest-rated series in television history," wrote Salim Muwakkil in an article that appeared in *Newsday* in 1997.

misfortunes of Mr. Bill. (A quick footnote for the uninitiated: Mr. Bill was, in the words of the authors of *Retro Hell: Life in the '70s and '80s, from Afros to Zotz,* "a naive Play-Doh man with a high-pitched whine and a cute dog Spot, trying to make it in this hard cruel world and being the ultimate victim and continuously suffering at the hands of Mr. Hand." Week after week, he was sliced and diced and otherwise maimed by his so-called "friend" Mr. Hand. Holy TV violence, Batman!)

The original cast members of *Saturday Night Live* were, in the words of Andrew Clark, author of *Stand and Deliver: Inside Canadian Comedy,* "a team of anti-television comic minds that had been force-fed television from their days in diapers. They were guerrilla comedians." Included in the cast were Chevy Chase, John Belushi, Gilda Radner, Jane Curtin, and Canadian Dan Aykroyd, whom the show's Canadian-born creator, Lorne Michaels, had met while working at the CBC.

According to Clark, *Saturday Night Live* quickly earned a reputation as the funniest show on the air. "Every kid with comedic aspirations, and who grew up after 1975, has dreamt of performing on SNL," he notes in his book. "Comedians do not crave a spot on SNL because it is the hottest show on the air—SNL goes up and down in popularity. They want it because once you've appeared on SNL, you've touched the thing that inspired you to do comedy in the first place. You've walked through the television screen into your teenage comedian-wannabe fantasy."

The Least You Need to Know

➤ Popular homegrown shows during the seventies included *The Beachcombers, King of Kensington,* and *SCTV.*

➤ There were ongoing debates throughout the seventies about the way advertisers were using television to get their advertising messages across to children, the way women were being depicted on TV, and the language and content that were and weren't appropriate on air.

➤ On September 28, 1972, 12.5 million Canadians watched as Team Canada's Paul Henderson scored the winning goal in the Canada-Russia hockey series. (As a point of comparison, just 10 million Canadians had bothered to tune in when Neil Armstrong took his historic first steps on the moon three years earlier!)

➤ A typical half-hour Canadian TV show cost $30,000 to make—just a quarter of what was typically spent making a half-hour show in the U.S.

➤ Popular American imports during the 1970s included *The Brady Bunch, All in the Family, Charlie's Angels,* and *Saturday Night Live.*

➤ On January 23, 1977, the television mini-series was born. Approximately 130 million North Americans tuned in to *Roots*—an eight-night, twelve-hour slavery saga based on the book by Alex Haley.

Chapter 12

Let's Do the Time Warp Again

In This Chapter

➤ What the best- and worst-dressed Canadians were wearing

➤ The hottest fads of the 1970s

➤ Pet rocks, mood rings, and more

➤ What was playing in the movie theatres and on the radio

➤ What people were reading

It's one of the twentieth century's greatest mysteries: what led millions of North Americans to simultaneously abandon their good taste during the 1970s?

The fashions and fads that seemed so hot during the 1970s seem downright embarrassing today. After all, this was a decade when hot pants, gauchos, platform shoes, and polyester leisure suits were considered cool; when people spent their leisure time playing with CB radios, doing aerobics, watching disaster flicks at the movie theatres, or strutting their stuff under the strobe lights at the nearest disco; and when you had an excellent chance of either giving or receiving a mood ring, a pet rock, or a pair of toe socks. (This was definitely one of those decades when it was better to give than to receive.)

Newsflash!

Between 1972 and 1989, Binney and Smith introduced crayons in a rainbow of fluorescent colors, including Atomic Tangerine, Outrageous Orange, and Screamin' Green.

—Source: History Channel Web site

Blast from the Past!

Can't remember what toe socks looked like? Check out the "Joy of Socks" Web site at http://www.joy-ofsocks.com/joyofsocks/toesocks1.html—you can even find one of the less popular variations on the toe sock—the mitten sock.

Want to know more? Just slip into your earth shoes, click your heels together, and start mumbling, "There's no place like the Seventies." This time, instead of ending up in Kansas, you'll pop up in Canada, circa 1970....

What the Best- and Worst-Dressed Canadians Were Wearing

Wondering what the best- and worst-dressed Canadians were wearing during the 1970s? Here's a crash course in what was considered cool at the time:

➤ *Lycra and spandex:* Disco pants and swimwear were just a few of the items to be manufactured out of the two hot new miracle fabrics, Lycra and spandex. On the upside, the fabrics were capable of drying in virtually no time at all and they came in a variety of eye-popping colours. On the downside, they left little to the imagination—which made them less than flattering to anyone with a "figure flaw" in need of a little camouflage.

➤ *Bright-coloured jogging suits:* A much more body-friendly alternative to spandex workout clothes and skintight jeans, jogging suits quickly became the uniform of both athletes and non-athletes alike. Over time, they morphed into the garment of choice for card-carrying couch potatoes.

➤ *Fake leather and faux furs:* Because it was no longer socially acceptable to wear real leather or real fur, a lot of people started turning to synthetic alternatives. Over time, these synthetic alternatives became even more popular than the originals, both because they were a bit more budget-friendly and because they came in bold colours that Mother Nature had never even imagined. (When was the last time you saw a hot pink mink?)

➤ *Toe socks:* The foot world's equivalent to the glove, toe socks were horribly uncomfortable and unspeakably ugly. They typically were decorated with stripes in a rainbow of different colours, with each toe having a colour of its own. They looked more like something you should be hanging up on Christmas Eve rather than something you should be putting on your body.

➤ *Earth shoes:* Earth shoes made their debut on Earth Day, 1970. Their claim to fame was the fact that they had a "negative heel." (That's just a fancy way of saying that they were designed in such a way that your heel ended up being lower than your toes.) The brainchild of Danish yoga instructor Anne Nalso, the shoes were supposed to "simulate the print of a bare foot in soft earth, with the heel placed lower than the toes to relieve forward pressure and promote better posture." The fact that at least one prominent U.S. podiatrist claimed that 70 percent of wearers developed heel and calf pain within weeks of putting them on scarcely took the shine off this particular fashion fad.

➤ *Platform shoes:* While some folks continued to wear their earth shoes throughout the seventies, the disco crowd switched to platform shoes during the last half of the decade. Platform shoes—which were worn by both sexes—featured heels that were as high as seven inches off the ground. One legendary pair even featured a glass heel filled with water and a live goldfish.

➤ *Hot pants:* Hot pants were scandalously short shorts, made of leather, lace, ranch mink, velvet, satin, denim, and other racy fabrics. Widely considered to be a backlash to the mid-calf "midi" hemline brought out by Paris designers in the aftermath of the miniskirt, hot pants were popular throughout the winter of 1971. (Go figure!)

➤ *Gauchos:* The extreme opposite of hot pants, gauchos were anything but short and sexy. They were basically mid-calf length shorts, featuring an A-frame construction. The authors of *Retro Hell: Life in the '70s and '80s from Afro to Zotz* describe them as "ugly corduroy-pant-like things that were horrendously tacky and unflattering."

➤ *String bikini:* In 1974, the string bikini was popular with the handful of women who had the trim bodies required to carry it off. It consisted of three strategically placed small triangles of cloth that were held together with pieces of string.

➤ *Designer jeans:* Calvin Klein and other brands of designer jeans were the cause of endless conflict between parents and kids during the late 1970s. Parents couldn't understand why anyone would consider paying $50 for a pair of jeans, while kids couldn't imagine going to school in the department store generic brands that their parents seemed to want them to wear. The only way out of this intergenerational fashion war was for the parents to agree to fork over the $100 back-to-school clothing budget and let the kids buy as many or as few pairs of jeans as their budgets allowed. (Guess that explains why the faded look in jeans came into vogue. I mean, if you could only afford one pair of jeans and they got tossed in the washer and the dryer every night before you went to bed, your jeans weren't going to look new for very long.)

➤ *Patches on jeans:* During the 1970s, no self-respecting kid would have been caught dead wearing a new-looking pair of jeans. Jeans that still had that dark blue, just-off-the-store-hanger look were only worn by card-carrying nerds like that group of guys in your math class who attached their calculators to their belts and who carried their pens around in plastic pocket protectors. In order to avoid committing

Blast from the Past!

The jeans fad wasn't just limited to clothing. In 1973, the American Motors Corporation brought out a Gremlin that featured a stitched and studded denim interior.

this ultimate of fashion faux pas, you had to wash, bleach, or otherwise torture your new jeans until they got that much sought-after lived-in look. If you went too far with your efforts to "break in" your jeans, you ended up with holes or tears—a problem that you then solved by sewing on patches in the shape of happy faces, peace symbols, or the Rolling Stones' mouth-and-tongue logo.

➤ *Overalls and painter's pants:* By the late 1970s, bib-style overalls and painter's pants were all the rage with kids, teenagers, and (believe it or not) even a few adults. Part of the appeal was all the pockets. Not only did your painter's pants come with a loop that would supposedly hold your hammer or paintbrush, they also came with a bunch of nifty pockets that could hold your school supplies, your lunch money, and so on.

➤ *"Cool" looks inspired by movies:* Some of the hottest fashion looks of the 1970s were inspired by characters on the big screen. Large numbers of women took to the *Annie Hall* look after seeing the movie of the same name. They started wearing oversized men's shirts, long skirts, and cloddish shoes. Men were also quick to jump on the movie fashion bandwagon. Some started wearing white three-piece suits like the one made famous by John Travolta in *Saturday Night Fever* while others preferred the *Urban Cowboy* look popularized by yet another Travolta flick—a look that required you to team up shoestring ties, fancy cowboy hats with feather bands, glittery silk shirts with mother-of-pearl buttons, jeans, and high-priced boots. (Guys who really got into the *Urban Cowboy* scene also took to riding mechanical bulls in bars. Now there's a fad that really deserved to die!)

➤ *Polyester leisure suits:* While no one other than a second-string lounge lizard would dream of wearing a polyester leisure suit today, there was a time back in the seventies when leisure suits were considered to offer a perfectly respectable alternative to formal business wear. Of course, not everyone took to the pastel-coloured leisure suits. Maitre-d's at the finer restaurants were under strict orders to keep leisure-suit-wearing would-be patrons off the premises.

➤ *Punk-rock look:* The punk-rock look made parents long for the days when their daughters would spend hours in front of the mirror admiring their designer jeans and fussing with their Farrah Fawcett-Majors hairdos. Punkers were into body piercing, dog collars and dog chains, and parading around in black, like their punk-rock idols Sid Vicious and Johnny Rotten of Sex Pistols fame. They were also in the habit of shaving their heads or tinting their Mohawk hairdos in putrid shades that seemed to offer the greatest potential to offend.

Hair Today, Gone Tomorrow

Of course, your fashion image didn't end with your clothing. Not in an era in which millions of North Americans finally had access to the ultimate fashion accessory, a hand-held blow-dryer! For the first time ever, Canadians had an alternative to the conehead-style hair dryers found in hair salons. They went a little crazy as a result, relying on hair mousse and the hot air from the blow-dryer to execute hairdos that simply wouldn't have been possible just a few years earlier.

High school girls took to carrying blow-dryers with them to school so that they could touch up their hairdos after gym class. (After all, it would have been a little depressing to start out the day with a Farrah Fawcett-Majors hairdo, but end the day with your hair plastered to your head!)

Blast from the Past!

In the fall of 1978, toga parties were hot at college campuses. Co-eds, inspired by the hit movie *National Lampoon's Animal House*, dressed up in sheets and muttered the line made famous by John Belushi in the movie: "Toga, toga, toga."

Fads You'd Probably Rather Forget

The 1970s have become famous for some very bad fads—everything from streaking to CB radios to a 1950s nostalgia boom. Here's what you need to know about each of these memorable fads.

Streaking

While streaking didn't catch on in Canada to quite the same extent as it did in the U.S., probably because of the climate, the fad did enjoy its proverbial 15 minutes of fame north of the border, too. The fad started in January of 1974 on U.S. college campuses and soon spread to anywhere there would be a large audience—major sporting events, for example.

It didn't take streakers long to end up with their own theme song. "The Streak," by Ray Stevens, entered the Billboard charts on April 7, 1974, just five days after a streaker disrupted the Academy Awards.

The fad attracted plenty of media attention during the few months that it lasted. Experts were asked to share their thoughts on the whole streaking phenomenon. A University of South Carolina psychology professor told the media that his research had revealed that a typical streaker was "a tall Protestant male weighing 170 pounds with a B grade average, [who] came from a town with a population less than 50,000 and a family where the father in a business or professional man and the mother is a housewife." University of Toronto media guru Marshall McLuhan had weightier thoughts to contribute: "Streaking

Blast from the Past!

Two of the worst songs of the mid–1970s were inspired by CB radios. "Teddy Bear" by Red Sovine, a tearjerker that told the story of a lonely little boy who communicates with truckers by CB radio, and "Convoy" by C.W. McCall, which is about a trucker protest. ("Convoy" became the inspiration for a really bad movie of the same name that starred Kris Kristofferson and Ali McGraw.)

is a put-on, a form of assault," he said. "It's an art form of course. All entertainment has elements of malice and power in it. Streaking has a political point, too. It's a form of activism."

CB Radios

Some say the CB radio fad was sparked by U.S. drivers who were eager to get around the new 55-mile-per-hour speed limit by communicating about the location of speed traps. Others say the fad became popular during the oil crisis, when truckers needed to let one another know which gas stations still had gas. Regardless of what caused the fad, however, it caught on like wildfire. While only a million CB radio licences had been issued in the United States between 1958 and 1973, over two million were issued in 1974 alone. Even Betty Ford, the wife of U.S. President Gerald Ford, got into the act. Her handle? "First Mama."

The Fifties Nostalgia Craze

Another hot fad during the seventies was the fifties nostalgia craze. Movies like *American Graffiti* and *Grease* and television shows like *Happy Days* and *Laverne and Shirley* took viewers back to a saner time. Or at least, that's what they pretended to do.

Newsflash!

The 1973–74 energy crisis forced North American automobile manufacturers to rethink the way they made cars. Gone were the days when bigger was better. With gas prices skyrocketing, auto makers had little choice but to come up with subcompact models like the Ford Pinto (whose habit of blowing up during rear-end collisions had yet to be detected) and the Chevy Vega. Otherwise, they risked losing even more market share to the cheap, dependable, energy-efficient imports. Even existing models ended up being shrunk. The 1975 Cadillac Seville, for example, was 1,000 pounds lighter and 25 inches shorter than its predecessor. (Ironically, it went up in price!)

Fifties-style "sock hops"" and "greaser contests" became popular in elementary and high schools, and some musicians from the 1950s enjoyed a bit of a comeback thanks to the nostalgia craze.

Writer Jeff Greenfield explained the origins of the nostalgia boom in an interview with *Newsweek* in 1972: "The generation that grew up in the Fifties is now equipped to revive itself. We are now old enough to be TV producers and film distributors. In ten years, people will be reminiscing about the '60s." (And in twenty years, the 1970s!)

Body and Soul

The seventies are often referred to as being the "Me generation," a time when it was okay to engage in some heavy-duty navel-gazing. This led some people to focus on their physical health and others to focus on their spiritual well-being.

Those who were interested in taking care of the physical side of things took up running, jogging, or aerobic dance; started eating natural foods like tofu, brown rice, honey, and herbal tea; and went on fad diets, the most popular of which were described in two of the bestselling books of the decade: *The Scarsdale Diet* and *Dr. Atkins' Diet Revolution*.

Say What?

Hot tubs were popular with people who were looking for a way to relax after putting in a hard day at the office. Because these oversized bathtubs were generally large enough to hold six to ten people, it wasn't at all unusual to be invited to a "hot tub party." There were more than 300,000 hot tubs in use by 1979. While some hardy Canadians installed them on their decks and insisted on using them in the middle of January, others wisely chose to keep the hot tubs indoors.

Boomer Bytes

In March of 1975, the CN Tower reached its final height of 1,815 feet, 5 inches tall, making it the tallest freestanding structure in the world. The price tag? A mere $30 million.

Those who were more concerned about taking care of their spiritual needs signed up for classes in transcendental meditation or est, or headed south of the border to visit one of the 2,000 communes that sprung up during the 1970s.

Technology Rules

Of course, the seventies weren't just a decade of touchy-feely stuff. The seventies were also a time when North Americans worshipped technology. In fact, some of the hottest gift items of the decade were high-tech in nature.

In 1972, desk and pocket calculators were all the rage—even if they were prohibitively expensive. You could expect to pay $100 for a calculator that wasn't capable of doing anything flashier than basic arithmetic or $1,000 or more for a scientific calculator that offered a few additional bells and whistles.

In 1975, digital watches were the item at the top of everyone's wish list. Even though they commanded a hefty price—they sold for anywhere from $30 to $3,000—first-generation digital watches weren't particularly useful. You had to push a button in order to read the time—which made looking at your watch while you were driving your car a downright hazardous manoeuvre.

By the end of the decade, the single hottest item was the personal computer. In 1978, *The Financial Post* reported that there were more than 30 different models of personal computers on the market in the U.S., and that these computers ranged in price from $1,000 to $5,000. (Note: The computer itself might only have cost you $1,000, but before you could use it at all, you had to fork over some money for some pricey peripherals: $1,000 for a floppy disk drive—unless, of course, you were willing to settle for a painstakingly slow cassette storage system, which took minutes, rather than mere seconds, to store and retrieve data—$1,000 for a printer; and $800 for the software required to run the machine.)

Boomer Bytes

The digital watch was invented by a Pennsylvania electronics company that was trying to design an electronically timed fuse for military purposes. When the prototypes proved too inaccurate for that application—after all, timing is rather important when you're playing with explosives!—they decided to find another use for the technology that they had developed. The result was the digital watch.

Blast from the Past!

"For a while, it's a good way to keep the kids entertained on a rainy day. But before long, smart kids tend to tire of it—there's only so much you can do with three dots on a screen," wrote Frank Appleton in an article entitled "Games Computers Play," which appeared in *The Financial Post Magazine* in September of 1976. He was talking about Pong—an early video game that was played on a TV set.

The *Financial Post* article concluded that predictions about there being a computer in every home didn't look like they were going to pan out anytime soon. In fact, the paper quoted an expert from Creative Strategies International, a California-based consulting firm, who didn't think that home computers were ever going to prove popular: "No one can think of a use for the microcomputer in the home that can't be done by some other means at a much lower cost," the expert said. "Sure a computer can be used to store recipes, but you can buy a card file and a box for $5 and it will be just as effective. It can also help with personal finances, but you can get the same results with the aid of a calculator. And, of course, the computer offers a great many games but that makes it a very expensive toy. In other words, it's not worth the money to buy a computer for general home use." (Kind of makes you wonder what ever happened to that whiz kid computer consultant!)

Fun and Games—The Sequel

Now it's time to zero in on a few of the more memorable products to hit the store shelves during the 1970s: mood rings, pet rocks, Clackers, and Moon Rocks candy.

Mood Rings

Mood rings were invented by a New York mediation student named Joshua Reynolds. He filled clear quartz stones with liquid crystals that reflected the wearer's body temperature by changing colour. If you were feeling calm and tranquil, the ring turned blue; if you were angry, it turned fiery red; if you were feeling depressed it turned black; and if you were feeling happy, it

Boomer Bytes

More than 20 million mood rings were sold in North America in 1975.

turned purple—at least, that was the theory. A lot of Canadian mood ring wearers learned the hard way that frigid temperatures could cause the ring to remain grey for months at a time!

Pet Rocks

Pet rocks were the brainchild of California advertising executive Gary Dahl. Their key selling point was the fact that, unlike conventional pets, they didn't need to be walked or paper-trained, and they weren't likely to rack up a lot of bills in the pet food or vet bill departments. (Of course, some people did buy food for them: Gary Dahl brought out pet rock food—a chunk of road salt!—after sales of his pet rocks began to skyrocket.)

Pet rocks sold for $5 apiece. They were accompanied with a care-and-training manual that told pet rock owners about all the amazing things their new pets could be taught to do—like play dead.

For whatever reason, pet rocks were a tremendous hit. At the peak of the fad, Dahl was shipping 3,000 to 5,000 pet rocks a day at $5 apiece. (Fortunately, he had a hefty supply of rocks. He had imported 2.5 tonnes of rocks from a beach in Mexico.)

Clackers

When Clackers showed up in the toy stores during the early 1970s, they were an immediate hit with kids—and for good reason. They made a loud, cracking noise that drove grownups crazy!

Clackers basically consisted of two oversized marbles tied to the two ends of a shoelace. You held the shoelace in the middle and jerked your arm up and down, so that the balls would bang against one another.

Unfortunately, the Clackers fad proved to be short-lived. It was discovered that they had a tendency to break apart, shooting hard pieces of plastic at anyone in close range—not a great feature for a toy that was meant to be enjoyed by young children.

Moon Rocks

Moon Rocks were popular during the mid-1970s. They were a type of candy that fizzed and crackled as they sat on your tongue. Kids loved them, but were also a little nervous eating them. There were rumours that if you put too many of them in your mouth at once, something awful would happen to you. Moon Rocks disappeared from the candy shelves shortly after they made their grand debut. (Yikes! Perhaps those rumours were true!)

What Was on the Big Screen

If you were planning a vacation that was going to take you on a plane or to the beach, the last thing you wanted to do the night before your trip was spend time at a movie

Blast from the Past!

"Even though disaster movies are as intellectually limited as primary readers...their current psychological appeal to great numbers of people is intriguing. People used to go to movies to escape their worries: now many of them go to have their anxieties intensified and their worst fears confirmed. We have developed a paranoid, panic-stricken pop-culture. Doom is busting out all over; give us this day our daily dread."

—John Hofsess, "How I Learned to Stop Worrying and Love Disasters," *Maclean's*, January 1975

theatre. If you did, you ran the risk of seeing a movie that would scare you so much that you'd decide to spend your vacation hiding out in your basement.

While *Jaws* (1975) is the best-remembered disaster flick of the 1970s, it actually came smack-dab in the middle of a decade that was full of films of that genre. Other films that managed to scare the film-going public during the 1970s include *Airport* (1970), *The Poseidon Adventure* (1972), *The Towering Inferno* (1974), *Earthquake* (1974), *Airport 1975* (1974), *Airport '77* (1977), and *Airport '79: The Concorde* (1979).

Not all movies were disaster films, however. Other popular films included *Rocky* (1976), *Star Wars* (1977), *Saturday Night Fever* (1977), and a string of Vietnam War films: *Hearts and Minds* (1974), *Coming Home* (1978), *The Deer Hunter* (1978), and *Apocalypse Now* (1979).

While it was by no means a favourite with general viewing audiences, *The Rocky Horror Picture Show* (1973) became a bit of a cult hit, enticing a faithful group of viewers to come out to midnight performances week after week. These diehard fans would dress up like the characters in the movie and throw rice, toilet paper, or playing cards; light candles and turn on flashlights; and shoot water out of squirt guns at the appropriate points of the movie.

Night Fever

The hottest music trend of the 1970s was the disco phenomenon. Suddenly, North Americans began dressing in the tackiest outfits imaginable—think Lycra and three-piece white suits—and heading for the strobe lights on the disco floor. (If you were under age at the time, you had to settle for boogying to "Hot Stuff" at the local roller disco rink.)

Not everyone was thrilled with disco, of course. A Chicago rock DJ sparked the anti-disco movement when he started destroying disco records on the air to protest his station's

conversion from a rock radio station to an all-disco station. He ended up losing his job, but not before he inspired other disc jockeys across North America to stage similar protests.

In Toronto, CITY-FM's morning man Jake Edwards recruited more than 2,000 listeners to join his "Disco Destruction Army" and, under the name Brother Jake and the Incinerators, recorded an anti-disco album with some of his fellow DJs. (One of the songs on the album was called "Disco's in the Garbage.") And in Vancouver, thousands of listeners to Vancouver's CFOX-FM came out to watch a wheelbarrowful of disco albums being destroyed on stage during a rock concert at the Pacific National Exhibition Gardens. Suddenly, it was cool to hate disco!

The anti-disco movement helped to ensure that there would be more music to remember from the 1970s than just those lyrically challenged ditties that you wriggled to on the dance floor.

The Joy of CanCon

In 1971, the Canadian Radio-Television and Telecommunications Commission (CRTC) introduced new regulations which required radio stations to devote at least 30 percent of their airtime to Canadian music. (A song was considered to be "Canadian" if the music or lyrics had been written by a Canadian, the performer was Canadian, or the record was produced in Canada. This sometimes led to ludicrous situations in which bona fide Canadian songs were classified as foreign in the eyes of the CRTC, and vice versa, but overall it was a very good thing for the Canadian recording industry.)

While the regulations were initially criticized by disc jockeys who feared that they were being asked to switch to an "all Anne Murray" format, both the deejays and the Canadian listening public soon discovered that the country had a lot to be proud of musically speaking. Here are just a few examples of the homegrown artists that Canadians were listening to during the 1970s.

Anne Murray

Anne Murray made her musical debut on *Singalong Jubilee*, a popular CBC television show that was shot in Halifax, Nova Scotia. After recording an album with the cast of the show, Murray went on to record her first solo album, *What About Me*, in 1968. The following year, she brought out a second album, *This Is My Way*, which contained her first big hit, "Snowbird." She also enjoyed considerable fame in the U.S., thanks to the

Newsflash!

"Canadian content" regulations were also introduced in the magazine industry in an attempt to give Canadian magazines a fighting chance against the glossy American imports. In 1975, the Liberal government introduced Bill C-58, which eliminated the tax concessions that had been enjoyed by Canadian editions of such foreign-owned publications as *Time* and *Reader's Digest.* In the aftermath of the introduction of this legislation, *Time* pulled the plug on its Canadian edition and *Saturday Night*—one of Canada's oldest and most respected publications—began publishing again. (It had suspended publication the previous year.)

cross-border appeal of such songs as "Love Song" (1974), "You Needed Me (1978), "Could I Have This Dance?" (1980), and "A Little Good News" (1983), all of which received Grammy Awards.

Bachman Turner Overdrive (BTO)

Bachman Turner Overdrive was formed in 1972 by Randy Bachman (formerly of the Guess Who fame). Originally called Brave Belt, the group included bassist Fred Turner and drummer Robbie Bachman (Randy's brother). A third Bachman brother, Tim, joined the band as a guitarist later on. The group's biggest hits were "Taking Care of Business" (1973) and "You Ain't Seen Nothin' Yet" (1974). Randy Bachman left the group in 1975, but the group continued to record without him throughout the remainder of the decade. He rejoined the group to tour in the early 1980s, but by that time the band's popularity had begun to wane.

Rush

Rush released its first album in 1974. That initial self-titled album was soon followed with *2112* (1976) and *Permanent Waves* (1980), both of which were extremely well received in the U.S. The group became known for its unique sound, a blend of fusion jazz and rock 'n' roll. (The group's bio in the Canadian Music Hall of Fame notes: "Musically, Rush has always been an enigma. In a world of three-chord heavy rock, the group's only peers are in the arena of fusion jazz, although its roots are early-to-mid-70's Led Zeppelin and post-psychedelic 'prog-rock.'")

Joni Mitchell

Joni Mitchell was one of the most successful Canadian musical exports during the 1960s and 1970s. In addition to penning songs that other artists made famous—such as "Both Sides Now," which was performed by Judy Collins, and "Woodstock," which became a hit for Crosby, Stills, and Nash—she also enjoyed considerable success as a performer. Her best-known single, "Help Me," hit number seven on the Billboard chart during June of 1974 and soared to number two at home. (The number one hit in Canada at the time was Gordon Lightfoot's "Sundown.") 1974 was definitely the high-water mark of Mitchell's career: she even managed to make the cover of *Time* magazine.

Blast from the Past!

"Joni Mitchell was the consummate 'hippy chick,' Annie Hall meets urban-cowgirl with a haunting beauty that intrigued many famous lovers, from David Crosby, Graham Nash and Stephen Stills, to James Taylor, Jack Nicholson, and Warren Beatty."

—Laura Campbell, "Joni Chic," *The Sunday Telegraph*, February 8, 1998

Buffy Sainte-Marie

During the 1970s, Buffy Sainte-Marie established herself as an international recording star. She was known for writing ballads that focused on human rights issues. She also penned the theme to the hit movie *An Officer and a Gentleman*, "Up Where We Belong," and, along with her young son, Dakota, became a regular on PBS's hit children's show *Sesame Street*.

Blast from the Past!

"The Canadian Radio-Television Commission forced stiffer Canadian content quotas on the country's broadcasters this year, and it has created such a demand for Canadian music that our branch-plant recording industry is suddenly opening its studio doors wide to anyone who can hum "O Canada." It's a nice change: for too many years, the Joni Mitchells and Neil Youngs of this country have followed their careers across the border and then, there being no reason to return, have forgotten the way back."

—John Macfarlane, "What If Anne Murray Were an American?" *Maclean's*, May '71.

Newsflash!

Paul Anka's 1974 hit single "You're Having My Baby" enraged U.S. feminists so much that the National Organization for Women (NOW) awarded Anka their annual "Keep Her in Her Place Award."

Blast from the Past!

"With its cloying, maudlin lyrics and syrupy tone, "Seasons in the Sun" made music fans of the seventies feel like they were attending a funeral. Pointless Records hopes kids today will feel the same way. The record company is reissuing a limited release of the single, which spent three weeks at No. 1 in 1974....The original single, sung by Terry Jacks, retailed for less than $1. The enhanced CD, which includes a CD-ROM multimedia history of the recording of the song, will cost $48. 'This includes an air-sick bag, in case people don't really remember the song,' [a Pointless Records] spokesman said."

—Bill Goodykoontz, "New Craze in Recycling: Old Crazes," *Arizona Republic*, June 10, 1998.

Newsflash!

Fans of Elvis Presley were stunned when the 42-year old, 225-pound King of Rock and Roll was found dead in his home on August 16, 1977.

The Least You Need to Know

➤ Fashion fads of the 1970s included Lycra and spandex swimsuits and disco pants, bright-coloured jogging suits, fake leather and faux furs, toe socks, Earth shoes, platform shoes, hot pants, gauchos, string bikinis, designer jeans, patches on jeans, overalls and painter's pants, "cool" looks inspired by movies like *Annie Hall* and *Saturday Night Fever*, polyester leisure suits, and the punk rock look.

➤ Hot fads included streaking, CB radios, a fifties nostalgia craze, running, and aerobics.

➤ Some of the most popular gift items during the decade were desk and pocket calculators, digital watches, mood rings, and pet rocks.

➤ Schoolchildren enjoyed eating Moon Rocks and playing with Clackers before both items disappeared off the market.

➤ The personal computer was still a novelty item rather than a necessity.

➤ Disaster flicks were big at the box office, as were movies about the Vietnam War.

➤ While disco was the hottest musical trend of the decade, not everyone was into the whole disco scene. Disc jockeys in both Toronto and Vancouver attracted plenty of listener support when they began destroying disco albums.

Chapter 13

Just Watch Me

In This Chapter

➤ Canadians fall out of love with Trudeau

➤ Canada goes metric

➤ Trudeau tries to cover Canada's assets

➤ The oil crisis hits Canadians in the pocketbook. Nixon resigns

➤ The Montreal Summer Olympics come in over budget

At the height of the October Crisis of 1970, Prime Minister Pierre Elliott Trudeau was asked just how far he was prepared to go to quiet the civil unrest in Quebec. His reply? "Just watch me."

That rather flippant comment signalled the end of the honeymoon period for the new PM. While the majority of Canadians supported his decision to handle the crisis by taking the unprecedented step of invoking the War Measures Act when the country was not at war, many were put off by his increasingly arrogant manner. A mere two years after he was swept to power in 1968, the shine was coming off Trudeaumania.

In this chapter, we're going to talk about some of the key challenges that Trudeau faced during the 1970s—everything from the switch to the metric system to economic nationalism to the oil crisis. Then we're going to zero in on one of the other hot

Blast from the Past!

"Pierre and Margaret Trudeau announce that because of Margaret's wishes they shall begin living separate and apart.

"Margaret relinquishes all privileges as the wife of the Prime Minister and wishes to leave the marriage and pursue an independent career.

"Pierre will have custody of their three sons giving Margaret generous access to them.

"Pierre accepts Margaret's decision with regret and both pray that their separation will lead to a better relationship between themselves."

—The official announcement of Pierre and Margaret Trudeau's decision to separate, as reported by *The Globe and Mail*. The announcement was made by the Prime Minister's Office on May 27, 1977. Pierre was 57 and Margaret was 28 at the time.

political stories of the 1970s—the unforeseen costs of hosting the 1976 Summer Olympic Games in Montreal. But before we get into the politics of the seventies, let's start out by looking at what the press was saying about Canada's top politician at the start of the decade.

Fuddle Duddle

Gone were the days when members of the media found themselves being swept up in that 1968 phenomenon known as Trudeaumania. By the early 1970s, the media frequently found themselves in an adversarial relationship with an increasingly remote and sharp-tongued PM.

An editorial in the February 1972 issue of *Maclean's* magazine commented on the Canadian public's disenchantment with Trudeau: "The Prime Minister gives the impression of believing that he and his inner court of advisors...have a monopoly on truth.... Trudeau [needs] to become less of a philosopher-king and more of a compassionate human."

An article in the March 25, 1972, edition of *The Financial Post* noted that the PM was looking "decidedly older than the resilient, sprightly young man who ran off with the Liberal leadership in 1968."

And an article that appeared in the October 1972 issue of *Maclean's* magazine pointed out that "the Prime Minister has been feeling pangs of unrequited love from those he

1960s

The CBC's innovative news and public affairs show "This Hour Has Seven Days" only ran for two years in the mid-'60s but made waves by spoofing the Pope and inviting the Ku Klux Klan on the show and surprising them with a black interviewer.

Mr. Dressup (Ernie Coombs, flanked by puppet sidekicks Casey and Finnegan), was one of the most popular children's television shows in the '60s.

Sylvia and Ian Tyson were two of the most influential folk artists of the '60s; their song, "Four Strong Winds," was an international hit.

Gordon Lightfoot played a key role in the burgeoning Canadian music scene that was centred in Yorkville in the early '60s.

Expo '67 brought the world to Montreal.

Pierre Elliott Trudeau at the height of Trudeaumania in 1968—he had sex appeal, a highly uncharacteristic trait among Canadian politicians.

John and Yoko took time out from their "bed-in" to meet Prime Minister Trudeau.

1970s

René Levesque, leader of the Parti Quebecois, held a press conference to announce that 36 members of his party, and countless more citizens, had been arrested by the police.

The War Measures Act was invoked soon after the kidnapping, by the FLQ, of British diplomat James Cross and Quebec Labour Minister Pierre Laporte.

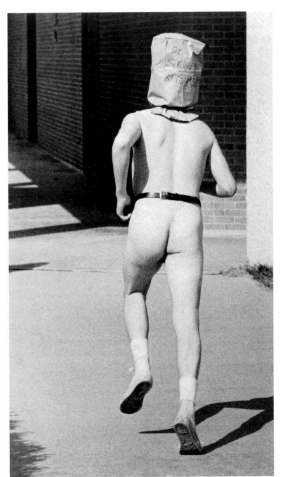 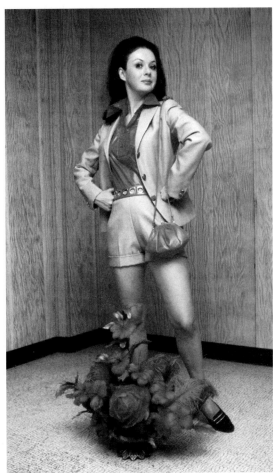

Two fleeting "fashion" trends from the '70s: hot pants and no pants.

A defining moment in hockey history: 12.5 million Canadians were watching when Team Canada's Paul Henderson scored the winning goal against Russia in 1972.

Margaret, Sacha, and Pierre in a playful moment; a year later, Margaret would be partying with the Rolling Stones and hanging out in Studio 54.

Terry Fox, who lost his leg—and ultimately his life—to cancer, inspired the nation with his Marathon of Hope in the early '80s.

At the 1988 Calgary winter Olympics, the Canadian hockey team defeated Czechoslovakia.

The "Shamrock Summit" was a cozy, feel-good affair between the like-minded Prime Minister Brian Mulroney and President Ronald Reagan; they got along so famously that they ended up bursting into a rendition of "When Irish Eyes are Smilin'."

Newsflash!

Canadians' love-hate relationship with the Post Office continued throughout the 1970s. Consider what *Chatelaine* magazine's May 1975 issue had to say about the new mail standards: "Dig out your high school geometry kit for addressing your mail. New Post Office directives forbid writing in the bottom part of the envelope. Why? The postal code must appear no more than 1 3/4 inches and no less than 3/4 inch from the bottom or the envelope faces rejection from new mechanical mail sorters now in Ottawa, Winnipeg, Saskatoon, Edmonton, Calgary, Etobicoke (Toronto), and planned for the rest of the country."

has sought to serve." (The author of this piece, John Gray, then went on to accuse Trudeau of having few political goals other than repatriating the Canadian constitution and working to ensure that Quebec remained a part of Canada. The prime minister, Gray wrote, "is not readily identified with goals or purposes. His own definition of the role of government is to anticipate problems and to avoid crises. That is like saying that the ship of state must stay off the rocks: it says nothing about a destination.")

Still, even those members of the media who had a bone to pick with Trudeau had to admire his style. How many prime ministers would be gutsy enough to mouth an obscenity in the House of Commons and then try to pretend that they'd said "Fuddle duddle"?

The Centimetres Are Coming! The Centimetres Are Coming!

Business and industry leaders had realized for some time that Canada needed to switch to the metric system if it was going to remain competitive in the international marketplace, but Canadians—who had always bought their hamburger by the pound and gasoline by the gallon—weren't so sure that they wanted to learn how to speak the language of kilograms and litres.

But, like it or not, the Canadian government had seen the future and the future was metric. A 1970 White Paper formally stated the federal government's intention to switch to the metric system. Given that 80 percent of the world's trade was being carried out under the metric system—a figure that would jump to 90 percent in 1975 when Britain and its trading colonies started trading in metric—the time had come for Canada to make the switch.

Blast from the Past!

"No longer can a hero of a romantic novel be described as standing six foot in his stocking feet" and "without an ounce of superfluous fat on him." Nor will he be able to thrash a villain "within an inch of his life"—although the villain will no doubt try for his 0.45359 kilograms of flesh. Naturally, a miss will be as good as 1.609 kilometers."

—Maurice de Soissons, writing in the November 1970 issue of *Chatelaine*

In August of 1977, *Maclean's* magazine reported that, by late September, most road signs would contain metric measurements only. (No more zooming down the highway at 60 miles per hour: from now on, you'd be racing along at 100 kilometres per hour.)

The article also noted that the Metric Commission was confident that the switch to metric would be complete by 1980. (The commission, which had a staff of 90 and a $5.5 million budget with which to work its magic, noted that Canadians hadn't dug their heels in to the same extent as their neighbours to the south. In fact, it bragged, a mere 1 percent of the commission's mail contained hostile messages!)

Economic Nationalism

On August 15, 1971, U.S. President Richard Nixon took the U.S. currency off the gold standard and introduced a series of protective measures designed to jump-start the ailing American economy. Canadian politicians were shocked by the suddenness of Nixon's actions: in the past, they'd always received advance warning of any significant shifts in American economic policy.

Trudeau decided to fight fire with fire by introducing his own program of economic nationalism. He created the Canada Development Corporation (to encourage Canadian ownership and management of vital areas of the Canadian economy), the Foreign Investment Review Agency (to screen proposals for takeovers of Canadian businesses), and Petro-Canada (a Crown corporation whose mandate was to develop a Canadian presence in the American-dominated oil industry). Then, in 1980, Trudeau took his program of economic nationalism one step further by introducing the National Energy Program to promote Canadian self-sufficiency in oil.

The Oil Crisis

In 1973, the Oil and Petroleum Exporting Countries (OPEC) declared an embargo on oil exports. Their actions were motivated by anger at Western support of Israel during the Yom Kippur War. The oil embargo had a devastating impact on Western industrial economies. By the time the embargo was lifted in 1975, the price of oil had increased from $3 to $12 a barrel and the Canadian economy was suffering from "stagflation" (a particularly nasty economic ailment that involves both high inflation and high unemployment).

Newsflash!

U.S. President Richard M. Nixon resigned from office on August 9, 1974, after it became common knowledge that he'd been aware of Republican involvement in the break-ins at the Democratic party national headquarters in the Watergate apartment complex in Washington, D.C. Nixon was succeeded by Gerald R. Ford, who subsequently issued a pardon to Nixon for any crimes he might have committed while president. In the aftermath of Watergate, the North American public became increasingly cynical about the workings of government.

One Big Happy Family? Not!

During the 1970s, Canadians in Western Canada, the Atlantic provinces, and Quebec became increasingly vocal about what they believed was wrong with the country.

Westerners were unhappy with the country's new policy of official bilingualism, its decision to switch to the metric system, overly high freight rates, and what they perceived as federal indifference to the plight of farmers. They decided that if they couldn't count on the federal government to help them out, they were going to have to start taking care of themselves. In Alberta, the Conservative government of Peter Lougheed established the Heritage Trust Fund, which was financed by royalties from oil sales and aimed at helping to diversify the resource-oriented economy.

The Atlantic provinces also had their share of grievances. After years of producing record fish harvests, the Atlantic fisheries were starting to run out of fish. Newfoundland Premier Brian Peckford resented Ottawa's involvement in the giant Hibernia oil project (even though the Supreme Court confirmed in 1984 that Ottawa's "meddling" fell well within federal jurisdiction).

And then there were the problems in Quebec—problems that had been simmering for years, but that threatened to boil over by the start of the 1970s. The October Crisis of 1970 had made Canadians acutely aware that "the Quebec problem" wasn't about to go away anytime soon. If anything, it promised to intensify. And with the election of the Parti Québécois in both 1973 and 1976, intensify it did. The Parti Québécois won a legislative majority in 1976 after asking Quebeckers for a mandate to negotiate sovereignty-association with the federal government. Despite his high hopes for a separate Quebec, Parti Québécois leader René Lévesque only managed to convince 40

Newsflash!

Throughout the 1970s, there was a lot of talk about how few women were choosing to pursue careers as federal politicians. Barbara Frum added her two cents' worth to the debate by offering "Insider tips on how to get women elected" in the October 1971 issue of *Chatelaine*. Some of her advice was off-the-wall to say the least. Consider this tip: "A third of all the women who've ever been in Parliament got there on the sympathy vote, as widows. One hard-eyed pro who dismisses the ability of women to get into politics on their own and has been cynically successful running widows on the black crepe ticket, says: 'The only way you'll ever see a hundred women in the House is to provide a hundred rifles to the wives of sitting members, and then teach them how to shoot.'"

Movers and Shakers

Jean Drapeau (1916–1999) was widely considered to be one of the most daring and successful mayors that Canada ever produced. During his 29 years in power in Montreal (during which time he saw seven prime ministers come and go), he helped to bring Expo '67, the 1976 Summer Olympic Games, and the Montreal Expos baseball team to Montreal. There were also some low points, of course: in 1968, all but 47 of Drapeau's 3,780 member police force went on strike, an action that forced Drapeau to call in the Canadian Army to help keep the peace.

percent of the electorate to vote "yes." The rest of Canada breathed a huge sigh of relief. The Quebec problem was under control again—at least for now.

The 1976 Summer Olympic Games

When Montreal Mayor Jean Drapeau began a campaign to drum up interest in a bid for the 1976 Summer Olympic Games, he boldly declared that the Olympics could no more lose money than a man could have a baby.

History would prove him wrong. Drapeau had pegged the cost at $310 million, but the final tally came in at more than four times that: $1.3 billion—and that figure didn't even include the cost of completing the Olympic stadium tower, which wasn't completed until 11 years after the Montreal Olympics were declared officially closed.

You have to give Drapeau credit for trying everything to raise the necessary funds, however. On April 2, 1973, he announced the creation of a lottery to help offset the costs of staging the 1976 Summer Olympics. It was the first government-run lottery in Canada.

The Least You Need to Know

➤ By the early 1970s, Trudeau had earned a reputation for being remote and arrogant. The cool intellectualism that had swept him to power in 1968 was no longer seen as a good thing.

➤ While politicians and business leaders were convinced that the switch to the metric system was going to be good for the country, Jane and Joe Canuck weren't so sure. They found it a chore to have to think in centimetres rather than inches and kilograms rather than pounds.

➤ Trudeau responded to Nixon's program of economic nationalism by introducing some protective policies of his own. During the 1970s, he created the Canada Development Corporation, the Foreign Investment Review Agency, and Petro-Canada.

➤ An oil embargo by OPEC countries caused the price of oil to skyrocket from $3 a barrel in 1973 to $12 a barrel in 1975.

➤ By 1975, the Canadian economy was suffering from "stagflation" (a particularly nasty economic ailment that involves both high inflation and high unemployment).

➤ Western Canadians, the Atlantic Provinces, and Quebec began to be increasingly outspoken about their grievances with the federal government.

➤ U.S. President Richard Nixon resigned from office on August 9, 1974, after it became common knowledge that he'd been aware of Republican involvement in the break-ins at the Democratic Party's national headquarters in the Watergate apartment complex in Washington, D.C.

➤ There was growing concern about how few women were choosing to pursue careers in federal politics.

➤ The 1976 Summer Olympic Games ended up nearly $1 million over budget.

Chapter 14

Harriet Gets a Pay Cheque

In This Chapter

➤ The truth about housework

➤ Canadian attitudes toward working mothers

➤ The pink-collar ghetto

➤ The invention of the microwave oven

➤ Inside the dual-income marriage

North American women had always worked, but until the 1970s most of that work occurred inside the home. And despite what the spin doctors in advertising agencies wanted you to believe, keeping your house clean wasn't necessarily a cakewalk just because you happened to have a bottle of the latest miracle cleanser on hand. As Susan J. Douglas notes in her book *Where the Girls Are: Growing Up Female with the Mass Media,* "Between cleaning, making Jell-O molds, being den mothers, chauffeuring, running the nation's PTAs, and ironing Dad's boxers, housewives...averaged a ninety-nine hour workweek."

That all changed after 1970. For the first time ever, large numbers of women with preschool-aged children began entering the paid labour market.

Blast from the Past!

"Overwhelmingly on TV women are portrayed as household worry warts who concern themselves only on matters such as the cleanliness of their floors or the flavor of their coffee. Their
whole lives are devoted to making men, children, and animals happy and they don't even
seem to be very good at that self-limiting job. In fact, on TV they all look so simple-minded
they rarely get out of the house. They can't even make such teensy-weensy decisions as
which brand of detergent or floor wax to use without some male settling the matter for
them."

—Doris Anderson, "Will *Chatelaine* Have a Male Centrefold?" *Chatelaine*, February 1973

Boomer Bytes

By the end of the 1970s, women
were taking their time getting to
the altar, choosing to marry two
years later on average than women
had done just a decade earlier. They
were also making a conscious effort
to limit the size of their families.
Gone were the days when families
with four or more children were the
norm: the birth rate had dipped to
just 1.7 births per woman.

Hi Ho, Hi Ho, It's Off to Work We Go...

While the thought of vacuuming the same 1,200
square feet of carpeting for the 10,000th time might
have led some women to run screaming out of the
bungalows of suburbia, for most women there was a
more practical reason for re-entering the labour
market: their families needed the money.

A U.S. study conducted in 1976 revealed that the high
rates of inflation that had kicked in during the first
few years of the decade had battered consumer buying
power to the point that it was no longer possible for
many families to enjoy the luxury of relying on a
single income. The study revealed that only 40 percent
of jobs paid well enough to support a family. That
meant that over half of all American families required
two income earners in order to bring home enough
bacon to feed the kids. The situation in Canada was
much the same.

Survey Says...

Unfortunately for those women who entered the workforce during the 1970s, public
attitudes had yet to catch up with economic realities. At the start of the 1970s, more

than three-quarters of Canadians believed that women with young children should not work outside the home.

That attitude was reflected in the shortage of licensed daycare spaces. There were only enough spaces to provide care to 13 percent of the children whose mothers were in the labour force in 1975, and despite ongoing lobbying by feminist activists, this figure would only manage to inch up by another 3 percent over the next seven years.

To make matters worse, many employers agreed that there was no place for women with young children in the workforce. It was assumed that many of these women were on the so-called "mommy track"—that their families would always take precedence over their careers no matter how much lip service they paid to their commitment to their jobs.

Newsflash!

In 1971, the federal government introduced legislation that allowed women on maternity leave to collect 15 weeks of unemployment insurance benefits. The following year, the government brought in changes to the income tax act that allowed working mothers a tax deduction for their childcare expenses.

Consequently, working mothers who wanted to be taken seriously by their employers often had to go to great lengths to prove that they were just as capable as the next guy or gal. Consider what Susan J. Douglas has to say about this problem in her book *Where the Girls Are: Growing Up Female with the Mass Media*: "We were either supposed to act as if children don't hamper our ability to be overachieving workaholics and we can do everything we did before plus raise a baby or two or acquiesce to second-class citizenship, acknowledging that being a mother is so debilitating that we're only capable of having dead-end, place-holding jobs while men, including fathers, and women without kids step on our backs to get the next promotion."

The Pink-Collar Ghetto

As if office politics weren't enough to contend with, the majority of women who re-entered the labour market during the 1970s found themselves trapped in the lowest-paying jobs in the so-called "pink-collar" ghetto. In many cases, they lacked the training and work experience required to land anything better.

To make matters worse, many women shot themselves in the foot, choosing to aim low rather than high when they were scouting around for jobs. As Alison Prentice, Paula Bourne, Gail Cuthbert Brandt, Beth Light, Wendy Mitchinson, and Naomi Black note in their book *Canadian Women: A History*, "The concentration of women in positions that conferred the least control and monetary rewards resulted in large part from the goals they were urged to set for themselves, which persuaded them to view the less authoritative and less remunerative positions as their most appropriate career choices."

Blast from the Past!

"Men may be packing a smaller sandwich in their lunch buckets now that inflation gets the first bite on the family budget, but women workers count themselves lucky to even get a dry crust. Despite their massive post-war move into the paid labor force—about fifty-three percent of all Canadian women work outside the home, and experts think that will rise to seventy percent by the turn of the century—and despite all the drumbeating for equality, women still earn far less than men in the same jobs and are denied the most golden opportunities."

—Michelle Landsberg, *Women and Children First* (1982)

And then there was the reaction of male co-workers to consider. This was something that led more than a few women to settle for the safety of the female-dominated clerical professions rather than trying to land a job in a male-dominated trade. (Most male blue-collar labourers were anything but thrilled at the thought of having to make room on the assembly line for some blowtorch-wielding woman—and they didn't take any pains to keep their opinions to themselves.)

As a result of these three factors, the vast majority of female workers were employed in "pink-collar" jobs during the 1970s. (See Table 14.1.) Just 12 percent of female workers were holding down blue-collar jobs in 1975.

Table: 14.1 The Ten Most Popular Jobs for Women in 1981

1. Secretary, stenographer	6. Nurse
2. Bookkeeper, accounting clerk	7. Elementary or kindergarten teacher
3. Salesperson, clerk	8. General office clerk
4. Teller, cashier	9. Typist, clerk-typist
5. Waitress or hostess	10. Janitor, cleaner

Source: **Canadian Women: A History,** *by Alice Prentice et al*

A Woman's Work Is Never Done

After a hard day holding down a job in a department store or a bank, a 1970s working woman could look forward to putting in a "second shift" on the home front.

It didn't take working women long to discover that there was never enough time to catch up at home. If you took the time to make an elaborate dinner one night, that probably meant that you wouldn't have time to vacuum or do the ironing. And if you spent a lot of time helping your children with their homework, you wouldn't have enough time to sit down and pay your bills. While the women's magazines did their best to provide time management tips and tricks—in 1979, *Chatelaine* magazine even went so far as to hire a time-management expert to provide pointers to a working mother who admitted to being horrendously disorganized on the home front!—at the end of the day, most women recognized that the 1950s housekeeping standards that they had inherited from their mothers were going to have to become a thing of the past.

A Microwave Is a Working Woman's Best Friend

While microwave oven manufacturers liked to emphasize the fact that these new-fangled devices were the very thing that every energy-conscious Canadian family needed, Canadian women were rushing out to buy them for one reason and one reason only: they were tremendous time savers.

That's not to say that Canadian women didn't have a few concerns about these brand new kitchen appliances. After all, microwave ovens used radiation to cook food! That's why Una Abrahamson found it necessary to tackle the safety issue head-on in her "Of Consuming Interest" column in *Chatelaine* magazine in 1975. After admitting that "microwaves in the kitchen sound like 1984 science-fiction," Abrahamson explained that microwave ovens were perfectly safe to use: "Probably the word 'radiation' scares us the

Boomer Bytes

In 1981, for the first time ever, more than half of Canadian married women worked outside the home.

Blast from the Past!

"The first thing you do is to cut out as much as possible of the unnecessary, old-fashioned household clutter and jobs. You can't have everything, and you certainly can't dust everything. According to Conran's Law, housework expands to fill the time available plus half an hour: so it is obviously never finished."

—Shirley Conran, *Superwoman in Action* (1980)

most, but, in fact, microwaves can't pass through metal, i.e., the walls of the oven. The window in the door is also considered solid metal because there's a perforated metal screen in the glass with holes small enough to baffle the microwaves."

Boomer Bytes

Microwave ovens were introduced to the Canadian market in 1972. Six thousand microwaves were sold that year at prices ranging from $450 to $650. By May of 1975, 35,000 Canadian households owned a microwave oven.

—Sources: The *Financial Post, Chatelaine*

Love and Marriage

While microwave cooking helped to relieve some of the pressure on dual-income families, by the end of the decade, the cumulative stress of juggling work and family and rarely if ever finding time for one another was taking its toll on husbands and wives. Men argued that they were doing far more around the house than their fathers had done; women argued that they still weren't doing nearly enough. (Just for the record, syndicated advice columnist Ann Landers tended to side with working women, telling her readers that "[the] husband has an obligation to get off his duff and help with the housework, cooking, marketing, laundry, and the children.")

Fredelle Maynard described the challenge that dual-income couples were facing in an article in the June 1981 issue of *Chatelaine*, titled "New Norm: The Two-Income Couple: Double the Pleasure or Double the Stress?" In the article, she described the difficulties experienced by dual-income couples: "For [dual income] families, the unsolved insoluble problem is time: time to do household jobs, to enjoy the children, to relax. The two

Blast from the Past!

"Work, school, and medical care in America are still organized around the 1950s myth that every household has a full-time mother at home, able to chauffeur children to doctor and dentist appointments in the middle of the day, pick up elementary school children on early dismissal days, and stay home when a child has the flu. Consequently, many parents—especially mothers, who are still expected to take prime childrearing responsibility—are intensely ambivalent about the tradeoffs between work and parenting."

—Stephanie Coontz, *The Way We Never Were: American Families and the Nostalgia Trap*

income couple quickly learns to set priorities and simplify tasks....Survival often depends on doing two things at once: mending while supervising a child's homework, making the weekly shopping trip a family excursion."

"Two-earner families yearned to simplify their lives yet felt they were caught on a treadmill from which neither parent could afford to step off," notes Stephanie Coontz in her book *The Way We Never Were: American Families and the Nostalgia Trap.*

While magazine and newspaper articles repeatedly told working women that they could relieve the stress they were experiencing by cutting back on their working hours or quitting their jobs altogether, these types of "quick fix" solutions failed to acknowledge that many families required both incomes in order to stay afloat and that the dual-income couple was here to stay, like it or not.

Newsflash!

Here are some of the changes *Chatelaine* readers were asking for in December of 1975, according to a consumer opinion poll conducted by the magazine:

1. Reform of the marriage property laws across the country to ensure that in future all property acquired by a couple, except for gifts and inheritances, is owned jointly, both during the marriage and in the event of separation or divorce

2. The introduction of a government pension plan for homemakers

3. Revisions to the country's abortion laws to make abortion an individual decision between a woman and her doctor

4. The prosecution of companies who discriminate against female workers when it comes to jobs, pay, promotion, and credit granting.

5. The introduction of a law that would uphold a married woman's right to half of the matrimonial home in the event of separation or divorce.

6. More government-funded daycare programs

7. Affirmative action laws requiring employers to state their plans for hiring and promoting women.

—Source: "What some women really want," *Chatelaine*, December 1975.

The Least You Need to Know

➤ Housewives averaged a 99-hour work week during the 1950s and 1960s. (It's no wonder they were relieved when Procter and Gamble's Mr. Clean arrived on the scene in 1958. He was the only guy around who was willing to help with the housework!)

➤ By 1976, only 40 percent of jobs paid well enough to support a family.

➤ By the late 1970s, women were choosing to marry two years later on average than women a decade earlier. They were also making a conscious effort to limit the size of their families: the birth rate had dipped to just 1.7 births per woman.

➤ At the start of the 1970s, more than three-quarters of Canadians believed that women with young children should not work outside the home.

➤ In 1973, there were only enough spaces to provide care to 13 percent of the children whose mothers were in the labour force in 1975, and despite ongoing lobbying by feminists, this figure would only manage to inch up another 3 percent over the next seven years.

➤ In 1971, the federal government introduced legislation that allowed women on maternity leave to collect 15 weeks of unemployment insurance benefits. The following year, the government brought in changes to the income tax act that allowed working mothers to deduct childcare expenses from their income taxes.

➤ The vast majority of female workers were employed in "pink-collar" jobs during the 1970s.

➤ In 1981, for the first time ever, more than half of Canadian married women worked outside the home.

➤ By May of 1975, 35,000 Canadian households owned a microwave oven.

➤ By the end of the decade, married couples were finding that the cumulative stress of juggling work and family and struggling to find time for each other was taking its toll.

Part 3

The Eighties

By the time the eighties rolled around, the idealism and energy of the sixties and seventies had fizzled out. Conservative politicians were in power on both sides of the border, "family values" were back in vogue, and Canada's constitutional woes were once again threatening to tear the country apart.

The name of the game was conspicuous consumption. After all, there was no point in carrying a cell phone or driving a flashy sports car unless you could flaunt it in your neighbour's face!

The eighties weren't all bad news, however! They were also the decade in which Canadian artists and sports figures began to attract attention abroad. Thanks to Anne Murray, Bob and Doug McKenzie, and Wayne Gretzky, it was finally becoming cool to be Canadian...

WHEN IRISH EYES ARE SMILING...

Chapter 15

Everything Old Is New Again

In This Chapter

➤ The Brian and Ronnie show

➤ The economic roller-coaster ride

➤ Environmental concerns

➤ Native land claims

When U.S. President Ronald Reagan came to Quebec City in 1985 to meet with Canadian Prime Minister Brian Mulroney, the media started referring to the event as the "Shamrock Summit" in recognition of the two leaders' Irish roots. Mulroney and Reagan got along famously—so famously, in fact, that they ended up bursting into song! Their choice of music? "When Irish Eyes Are Smilin'," of course!

Birds of a Feather

It's not surprising that the two leaders hit it off so well. After all, they had a lot in common. They both believed that cutting taxes and slashing government spending would cure their countries' respective economic woes.

Mulroney had laid his political cards on the table soon after declaring his candidacy for the Conservative Party leadership, and he'd remained true to those beliefs after

Say What?

Both Mulroney and Reagan were firm believers in *supply-side econom-ics*, a theory that states that the economy will thrive if you stimulate the production of goods and ser-vices and keep taxes low. Over time, Reagan's economic policies became known as *Reaganomics*.

sweeping to power in 1984. Here's what he had to say in a 1983 interview with *Maclean's* magazine: "There are no fancy-pants heroes any more with elegant theories and magic wands, just overworked and harassed businessmen, labor leaders and ordinary Canadians who get their hands dirty every day dealing with the pedestrian problems of providing jobs, meeting payrolls, and producing products—only to come home at night to learn on TV that some brave new social artist has invented another government plan that will add to costs, increase paperwork and lessen competitiveness."

Clearly, Mulroney's ideas rang true for a lot of Canadians. On September 4, 1984, Mulroney and the Conservatives won the largest electoral majority in Canadian history, walking away with an unprecedented 211 seats.

Like Mulroney, Reagan too had been given a warm reception by the public when he came to power in 1981. The country was relieved to have the nightmare of the Iran

Newsflash!

On March 30, 1981, a young man named John Hinckley Jr. tried to assassinate President Reagan, in a bizarre attempt to impress American actress Jodie Foster. While Reagan was actually in considerably more danger than the initial news reports had indicated, he managed to make a speedy recovery.

The shock of the assassination attempt helped to boost Reagan's popularity: "His string of one-liners, his self-deprecating wit, his calm in the face of near-tragedy are translating into enormous popularity," Michael Posner wrote in *Maclean's* magazine at the time. "Reagan's approval rating soared 11 points in a *Washington Post*/ABC survey taken one day after the shooting."

Posner also noted that the American public didn't appear to be particularly shocked by the shooting: "It is so much a part of urban existence that what they see on television and what they see on their streets are all of the same piece; the distinctions between murderous reality and what passes for art have been blurred. The attempted Reagan assassination is like an episode from the same old police drama, gone into daytime reruns."

hostage crisis behind it and was eager to indulge in the treat that Reagan was offering them: a heaping serving of good old-fashioned American patriotism. (Iran had held off on releasing the hostages until Reagan was inaugurated as President. It was a final slap in the face for Jimmy Carter, whose presidency had been badly shaken by the crisis.)

As Alan Axelrod notes in his book *The Complete Idiot's Guide to American History,* many Americans welcomed Reagan's "feel-good" style: "Ronald Reagan [was] the most popular president since Ike Eisenhower. Where President Carter took a stern moral tone with the nation, admonishing his fellow Americans to conserve energy, save money, and generally do with a little less, President Reagan congratulated his countrymen on the fact of just being Americans and assured them that all was well—or would be well, just as soon as he "got 'big government off our backs'."

The vast majority of Americans may have been happy to have Reagan in charge, but not all Canadians shared that sentiment. There was tremendous concern that Reagan's "high-noon" mentality would mean a return to the icy tensions of the Cold War that could ultimately spark a war between the two increasingly antagonistic superpowers.

Newsflash!

The Iran–Contra Affair was the biggest scandal to rock the Reagan administration. The U.S. had secretly sold arms to Iran in order to secure the release of hostages who were being held by terrorists in war-torn Lebanon. What's more, a portion of the arms profits had been used to finance the efforts of the Contra rebels who were fighting against the leftist Sandinista government of Nicaragua. These secret dealings were both unconstitutional and illegal. Although Reagan denied any knowledge of these events, he and his successor, George Bush, were severely criticized in special prosecutor Lawrence E. Walsh's report, tabled in 1994.

National Unity Problems Return

Meanwhile, on the other side of the border, Canada was busy dealing with some serious problems of its own. At the top of the list was that perennial favourite: national unity.

The Constitution

During the 1960s and 1970s, several attempts had been made to patriate the Canadian Constitution. On a number of different occasions, the federal and provincial governments came close to reaching an agreement about the formula that would be used to decide future amendments to the Constitution. On each occasion, however, the situation turned into a stalemate when Quebec insisted on greater constitutional powers than the other provinces were prepared to grant it.

Over time, Trudeau grew impatient with the delays. Following the defeat of Quebec separatist forces in the 1980 referendum, Trudeau announced that he planned to ask the British government to place the Constitution in Canada's hands—with or without Quebec's approval. The patriated Constitution was to include both a Charter of Rights and Freedoms and an amending formula. The amending formula would allow Ottawa to call a referendum and take constitutional amendments directly to the people in the event that the governments of Ontario, Quebec, or a majority of western and Atlantic provinces objected to a particular amendment.

The majority of the provinces saw Trudeau's initiative as an attempt to weaken provincial rights. Ontario and New Brunswick were the only two provinces to speak out in favour of the initiative. The rest decided to challenge Trudeau's actions in the courts.

The Supreme Court reached a judgement on the issue in September of 1981, ruling that the "substantial consent" of the provinces (but not full unanimity) was all that was required for the federal government to proceed with its plans for patriation. At this point, nine of the ten premiers decided that if they couldn't beat Trudeau, it certainly made sense to join him. Lévesque—the sole holdout in the group—claimed that he had been betrayed.

The deal that the nine premiers struck with Trudeau resulted in the creation of the Constitution Act. The Constitution Act consisted of the renamed British North America Act (the Act that had brought Canada into being in 1867), an amending formula, and the Charter of Rights and Freedoms.

The amending formula allowed the federal government to change the Constitution, provided it had the approval of both Parliament and two-thirds of the provinces, and that the assenting provinces represented at least 50 percent of Canadians. However, the unanimous consent of all provinces plus both houses of Parliament would be required for changes affecting representation in the House of Commons, the Senate, and the Supreme Court; and for changes regarding the country's designated official languages.

The Constitution Act also offered the provinces a few other bells and whistles. If a province felt that its legislative or proprietary rights were attacked by a particular amendment, it had the right to declare that amendment null and void within its boundaries. The provinces could opt out with full financial compensation from any program established by an amendment that affected educational or cultural matters. As a special concession to Atlantic Canada, one section of the Constitution committed the government to the principle of equalization to "ensure that provincial governments have sufficient revenue to provide reasonably comparable levels of public services at reasonably comparable levels of taxation."

The Charter guaranteed Canadians the right to freedom of speech, association, conscience, and religion, and prohibited discrimination on the basis of colour, sex, or creed. It also enshrined such basic human rights as the right to vote, the right to seek legal counsel, and the right to be protected against arbitrary arrest.

While the Constitution failed to specifically acknowledge the right to self-determination, native Canadians won acknowledgment of aboriginal concerns by securing a guarantee that nothing in the document would affect existing treaty rights or prejudice unsettled land claims. They also obtained a promise from the federal government that a constitutional conference on native rights would be called within one year of the proclamation of the Constitution.

The Constitutional Act was proclaimed on April 17, 1982, by Queen Elizabeth II.

The Meech Lake Accord

Prime Minister Trudeau had managed to work enough magic on the constitutional front to bring Canada's constitution home for the very first time, but the country's unity problems were far from over. Shortly after coming to power in September 1984, Prime Minister Brian Mulroney decided to make an effort to obtain Quebec's approval of the Constitution, even though the province's approval was technically unnecessary.

Quebec Premier Robert Bourassa was characteristically frank about what Quebec wanted: recognition as a distinct society, a veto for constitutional amendments, a greater share in immigration policy, the right to opt out of any new cost-sharing programs without financial penalty, and a requirement that the federal government choose new Supreme Court judges from a list provided by the province.

Mulroney invited the premiers to a First Ministers' Conference at Meech Lake in April of 1987. The premiers tentatively approved a package that met Quebec's key demands and incorporated the concerns of the other provinces. The final agreement was then hammered out during an all-night session in Ottawa on June 3, 1987.

Newsflash!

Opposition to the Meech Lake Accord increased dramatically in English Canada when Quebec Premier Robert Bourassa invoked the notwithstanding clause in the Constitution to nullify a Supreme Court decision regarding the province's controversial new sign law, Bill 178. (The notwithstanding clause allows a province that feels that its legislative or proprietary rights have been attacked by a particular amendment to declare that amendment null and void within its boundaries.) The Supreme Court had ruled that Bill 178 violated the guarantees of freedom of expression provided in the Charter of Rights and Freedoms.

Boomer Bytes

Public opinion polls conducted in 1990 indicated that the majority of Canadians opposed the Meech Lake Accord—even though 70 per cent claimed to know little or nothing about it!

The Meech Lake Accord had to be ratified by both Parliament and the 10 provincial legislatures by June 30, 1990, or else the deal would expire. The controversy started almost immediately. Separatists complained that the distinct society clause didn't go far enough; federalists—including Trudeau—thought it went too far. There were fears that the unanimity requirement for constitutional amendments would prevent reforms from being implemented. There were also concerns that the clause about cost-sharing programs made no mention of national standards.

During the three-year ratification period, the New Brunswick, Newfoundland, and Manitoba governments changed hands. The newly elected governments of Frank McKenna (New Brunswick), Clyde Wells (Newfoundland), and Gary Filmon (Manitoba) were less committed to ensuring that the Meech Lake Accord be passed than their predecessors had been. When Elijah Harper (the sole native member of the Manitoba legislature) used procedural methods to prevent the Accord from passing in Manitoba before the deadline, Filmon decided not to interfere.

Bourassa was furious about the failure of the Meech Lake Accord. He said that Quebec had been humiliated and insisted that his province would never again attend a constitutional conference with the other premiers. (He would change his mind a few

Blast from the Past!

"I'm a big boy, but I was more badly hit than any other prime minister, with the exception of John A. Macdonald. As soon as I came in, the media set itself up as the unofficial opposition.... There was an anti-Conservative and anti-Mulroney bias. They're never going to forgive me for winning two elections, staying on for nine years and walking away with my head held high.

"They must have great unhappiness in their own lives to continue such vendettas into my retirement. Some of them won't be satisfied until I'm six feet under. But who knows? Maybe they'll go before me, and I'll even the score by delivering eulogies at their funerals."

—Former Prime Minister Brian Mulroney reflecting on what it was like to be one of the most hated Prime Ministers in Canadian history, in a 1994 interview with *Maclean's* magazine.

years later, when he agreed to head to Charlottetown to help hammer out the Charlottetown Accord.) His government then passed legislation demanding either a referendum on sovereignty or an offer of constitutional renewal from the rest of Canada.

That wasn't the only fallout from the failure of the Meech Lake Accord. The Bloc Québécois, a federal party that sought an independent Quebec, was formed under the leadership of Lucien Bouchard, a former Conservative cabinet minister who, along with future Quebec Premier Jacques Parizeau, would become the federalists' worst nightmare during the 1990s.

Canada's Economic Woes

The unity crisis wasn't the only problem that the Canadian government found itself grappling with in the 1980s. It also had to deal with the country's economic woes.

Free Trade Agreement

By 1981, the global economy was facing the worst economic slump since the Great Depression. At a loss to know what to do about Canada's sluggish economy, Prime Minister Pierre Elliott Trudeau appointed the Royal Commission on Canada's Economic Union and Development Futures (a.k.a. the Royal Commission on Canada's Future). The commission's report, tabled in 1985, concluded that Canada's economy needed to adapt to global economic change and rapidly evolving technologies. It argued that free trade with the United States was Canada's only hope for continued economic prosperity.

The mere idea of free trade was frightening to many Canadians, who feared that it would lead to job losses and wage cuts and threaten Canada's cultural industries and social programs. It encountered significant resistance from labour unions, feminists, church groups, nationalists, and members of both the New Democratic Party and the Liberal Party. One of the most outspoken critics of free trade was Trudeau himself.

Trudeau didn't stick around to fight the issue in an election, however. He took a long walk one chilly February day in 1984, and decided to announce his retirement. His successor John Turner was unable to lead the Liberals to victory in the election of 1984.

But while Conservative Brian Mulroney didn't say much about free trade during the election of 1984, it didn't take him long to start pursuing the Americans once he assumed control of government. By May of 1986, the two countries were hard at work negotiating the terms of the agreement.

The Americans were characteristically forthright about what they wanted: freedom to invest in Canada, access to Canadian energy and water supplies and other resources, and guaranteed access to the Canadian market for America's service industries. The Canadians were equally sure of what they wanted: elimination of duties and access to the mammoth market to the south.

By the fall of 1987, Canadian and American negotiators had managed to hammer out the details of the treaty. A year of heated debate followed in the House of Commons. When it became clear that the Liberal-dominated Senate was unwilling to ratify the Free Trade Agreement unless the Conservatives received an electoral mandate to pursue such a course of action, Mulroney called Canadians to the polls. The Conservatives returned to power in November of 1988—even through the majority of Canadians voted against them! (They only managed to pick up 43 percent of the popular vote, which indicates that 57 percent of Canadians were unwilling to endorse the Conservative's pro–free trade agenda.)

Getting the Agreement through Parliament was no cakewalk for the Conservatives. The Mulroney government had to invoke closure four times and keep the House in session until 1:48 a.m. on Saturday, December 24—not exactly the usual holiday routine for MPs!

The Agreement passed through the Senate on December 30, 1988, and became law on January 1, 1989. Under its terms, Canada and the United States agreed to eliminate tariffs on primary and manufactured goods over a 10-year period, and to allow for free trade in services as well.

North American Free Trade Agreement

The ink had no sooner dried on the Free Trade Agreement than the Americans announced their intention to negotiate a similar deal with Mexico. Fearing that such a

Newsflash!

Concern about the environment heightened during the 1980s—and for good reason. The country's landfill sites were filling up, the North Atlantic cod fishery was on the brink of extinction, studies were revealing that the ozone layer was being destroyed by chlorofluoro-carbons (CFCs) used in aerosol sprays and other products, tropical rainforests were disappearing at an alarming rate, flooding from the James Bay hydroelectric development was threatening the fragile northern ecosystem of Quebec, and nuclear disasters at both Three Mile Island (1979) and Chernobyl (1986) were leading the public to question the safety of nuclear power. As a result of these growing concerns, Canadians began to practise the three Rs—reduce, reuse, and recycle—and to lobby the federal government to introduce legislation designed to protect the environment.

deal would nullify the effects of the Free Trade Agreement, the Mulroney government asked to be included in the negotiations with Mexico.

Despite massive public opposition (many Canadians argued that Canada should only enter into free trade agreements with countries that had social programs, pollution standards, and collective-bargaining legislation similar to that in effect in Canada), the North American Free Trade Agreement (NAFTA) came into effect on January 1, 1994.

Native Land Claims

Another problem that wouldn't go away during the 1980s was the need to settle native land claims. In 1984, the Inuit of the Mackenzie Delta received a settlement of 242,000 square kilometres of land. Unfortunately, other land claims proceeded much more slowly. At the end of the decade, there were over 500 claims outstanding, and they were being settled at the rate of just three or four per year. At the root of the problem was the federal government's decision to negotiate a maximum of six land claims at a time, a policy that created a tremendous backlog of cases.

Blast from the Past!

"When we have AK–47s, you see, they listen. It's the only way."

—Herby Nicholls, one of the Mohawk involved in the standoff at Oka, quoted in *Maclean's*, July 23, 1990

The painfully slow land claims process sparked native protests across the country, one of the ugliest of which was at Oka, Quebec, in 1990. The issue at stake in the dispute was the town of Oka's decision to construct a golf course on land that the Mohawk regard as sacred.

On March 11, the Mohawk barricaded the main road leading to the golf course. Oka's municipal council obtained an injunction from the Superior Court of Quebec that ordered the natives to remove their barricade by June 30. The Mohawk ignored the court order, demanding the right to negotiate "nation to nation" with the federal government.

On July 11, following a four-month standoff with area Mohawk, members of the Quebec provincial police put the natives on notice that they had four hours to dismantle their roadblock and withdraw. When the deadline passed, 100 police officers stormed the roadblock. Instead of retreating, as the police had predicted they would do, the Mohawk fought back. At the end of the day, Corporal

Boomer Bytes

In 1990, only 43 percent of aboriginal people over the age of 15 had jobs, compared to 61 percent of the rest of Canadians.

Marcel Lemay of the Quebec provincial police lay dead from a gunshot wound.

Nine days after the outbreak of violence, Thomas Siddon, Minister of Indian Affairs, announced that Ottawa had purchased part of the land that was in dispute and that it would negotiate to buy the remainder. The Mohawk would receive the land after the barricades came down. On August 17, at the request of Quebec Premier Robert Bourassa, the Canadian army was sent in to maintain the peace while the terms of surrender were worked out. On the third of October—78 days after it began—the standoff ended.

Stating that "Canada's aboriginal peoples deserve a special place in this country as our first citizens," Prime Minister Brian Mulroney promised that Ottawa would deal with native grievances, improve conditions on reserves, and accelerate the land claims settlement process.

The Least You Need to Know

➤ Both Mulroney and Reagan were firm believers in supply-side economics, a theory that states that the economy will thrive if you stimulate the production of goods and services and keep taxes low.

➤ While Americans were happy to have a flag-waving patriot in power, Canadians were concerned about Reagan's "high noon" mentality, fearing that the escalation in tensions between the U.S. and the USSR could lead to war.

➤ On March 30, 1981, John Hinckley, Jr. attempted to assassinate President Reagan.

➤ The Iran-Contra affair was one of the biggest scandals to rock the Reagan administration.

➤ Throughout the 1980s, the Canadian government was busy dealing with constitutional issues, the Free Trade Agreement, environmental problems, and native land claims.

The Big Crash

It's no wonder that members of the investment community were looking downright squeamish by the time the decade-long roller-coaster ride screeched to a halt in 1990. One moment the economy was spiralling downward with no relief in sight. The next it was shooting upward at dizzying speed. And just when everyone thought the economy was headed upward for good, it took an unbelievably sharp nosedive that left investors wondering if they'd ever find themselves on solid ground again.

In this chapter, we're going to look at the economic highs and lows of the 1980s and some of the more interesting business stories to emerge during the decade—everything from mega-malls to beer bottles to corrupt televangelists. So take your seats, ladies and gentlemen. The ride is about to begin.

Boomer Bytes

While only 9.7 percent of Canadians surveyed by the Conference Board of Canada in mid-1981 indicated that they were planning to buy a new or used car within the next six months and only 3.3 percent indicated that they were planning to buy a house during that time period, a full 58 percent of those surveyed indicated that they were planning to take a vacation in the very near future! (Perhaps this is what is meant by the expression, "When the going gets tough, the tough get going.")

The Recession of 1981–82

The 1980s certainly didn't get off to a particularly strong economic start.

A 1981 Conference Board of Canada study of Canadian's spending habits confirmed what realtors and retailers had already figured out for themselves: consumer confidence was at its lowest point in the 20-year history of the survey.

Canadians certainly had plenty of good reasons for leaving their credit cards in their wallets and thinking twice before they signed up for mortgage and car loans. The country was in the midst of a particularly nasty recession. Industrial productivity was off by 19 percent and the unemployment rate was sitting at 13 percent. Inflation was sky-high and interest rates were going through the roof. (Interest rates reached their peak in May of 1981 when they climbed to an unbelievable 21.5 percent.) A lot of people lost their homes because they could no longer afford to keep up with their mushrooming mortgage payments.

Boomer Bytes

In the early 1980s, nearly one in five Canadians was employed by either a government department or a Crown corporation.

Shop Till You Drop

The only people who seemed to have money to burn during the early 1980s were the Ghermezian brothers. They were in the process of opening the first phase of the $700 million West Edmonton Mall. (The third and final phase would be completed in 1985. It featured virtually every bell and whistle imaginable: a triple-loop roller coaster, a water park, and an indoor ice rink.)

The mall quickly established itself as one of Alberta's

biggest tourist attractions. In fact, one provincial study showed that the West Edmonton Mall was outdrawing Banff National Park!

Not everyone loved the West Edmonton Mall, however. Consider what Vancouver-based retail consultant Ian Thomas had to say about the Ghermezian brothers' famous mall, in an interview with *Canadian Business*: "There's no logic to the mall. No rhyme or reason to it. It was never planned to be the size it is now. The design is not particularly shopper friendly. It's like an amoeba that just grew and grew."

And it was that amoeba-like growth that got the Ghermezian brothers in trouble. Lower-than-anticipated revenues from the property forced them to seek additional financing in 1989. The decade that had started out with a bang for the millionaire brothers was ending with little more than a whimper.

The Official Olympics of Those Who Had Money to Spend

Corporate sponsorship was hot in the 1980s, and one of the hottest sponsorship opportunities of the decade was the 1984 Summer Olympic Games in Los Angeles. An article that appeared in *Maclean's* magazine at the time noted that if entrepreneurship were an Olympic event, Peter Ueberroth, president of the Los Angeles Olympic Organizing Committee, would win the gold medal hands down.

Perhaps learning some lessons from the financially disastrous 1976 Summer Olympic Games in Montreal, Ueberroth and his team managed to keep the 1984 Summer Olympic Games in the black by lining up $120 million in sponsorships from 30 companies, including Coca-Cola, IBM, and American Express. They even managed to convince people to cough up $3,000 each for the honour of carrying the Olympic torch one kilometre in a cross-country relay race to raise money for youth sports programs. Those forking over the cash included American actress Jane Fonda and a member of the Hell's Angels motorcycle gang. (I suppose that made the Hell's Angels the official motorcycle gang of the 1984 Summer Olympic Games.)

The only ones raining on the Americans' sponsorship parade were the Soviets, who decried what they saw as capitalism gone mad. In the end, the Soviets chose not to participate in the McOlympics anyway—although for an entirely different reason. The Soviets decided to sit out the games in retaliation for the Americans' decision to boycott the 1980 Olympic Games in Moscow.

Greed Is Good

The 1980s were a time of corporate acquisitions and mergers. By 1986, 32 wealthy families and nine giant conglomerates controlled over one-third of the non-financial assets of the U.S. Unfortunately, these corporate mergers were frequently accompanied by massive job cuts (or "downsizing," to use a popular euphemism of the time).

The 1980s were also a time when corporations began to pay greater attention to the bottom line. Corporations began "restructuring" in order to become leaner and more profitable. Sometimes this meant automating production. Other times, it meant laying off large numbers of employees and "outsourcing" the work that they had done to less expensive contractors.

It's no wonder that North American workers were feeling a little shell-shocked by all the changes going on around them. Many felt as if the rules of the game had changed overnight. It was no longer enough for a company to make money and provide jobs: its number one priority was to keep the investors happy. Gordon Gecko, the fictional tycoon played by Michael Douglas in the popular movie *Wall Street* (1987) uttered a line that became the motto for corporate tycoons and investment brokers alike in the 1980s: "Greed is good."

The same philosophy carried over into the real estate market. Bidding wars became the norm as frenzied buyers and real estate speculators found themselves scrambling to get their hands on a piece of the hot real estate market. (On March 9, 1987, *The Financial Post* reported that a Toronto property that had listed for $189,900 had sold within days for $201,000.)

Blast from the Past!

"The only emotions that Wall Street understands are fear and greed."

—A Wall Street trader quoted in the October 26, 1987, issue of *The Financial Post*

Newsflash!

While greed was supposedly good during the 1980s, too much greed was...well, bad! One of the most blatant examples of excessive greed was the infamous PTL Club scandal. Headed up by Jim and Tammy Faye Bakker, two American televangelists who knew how to milk the airwaves for money, the PTL (for "praise the Lord") Club was pulling in $1.5 million per month from viewers who wanted to do their part to help Jim and Tammy with the ministry. Things turned ugly for the Bakkers after it was proven that the two of them had been involved in extramarital liaisons and that they'd misused church funds. (The "living salary" that they claimed to draw from church coffers amounted to a boggling $1.6 million in 1987 alone!) In the aftermath of the scandal, a song called "Would Jesus Wear a Rolex on His Television Show?" climbed to the top of the American pop charts. Canadian songwriter Neil Young was similarly inspired: his song "American Dream" is said to be about the Bakkers' fall from glory.

Trouble in Yuppieland

The boom days couldn't last forever, but few were ready when the bubble finally burst. On October 19, 1987 ("Black Monday"), the Dow Jones Industrial Average—a key measure of both stock market performance and the overall health of the U.S. economy—plunged 508 points, nearly twice as far as in the 1929 stock market crash that had ushered in the Great Depression.

Hardest hit by the crash were the so-called yuppies ("Young Urban Professionals")—a group that Joe and Jane Canuck had grown to hate. Between 1987 and 1989, the Canadian luxury car market dropped by 20 percent as the yuppies' stock portfolios went up in smoke. (Victor Doolan, Canadian CEO of BMW, told *The Financial Post* that yuppies had experienced "a change of values" because of the stock market crash, and that they were no longer anywhere near as status-conscious as they had been in the days leading up to Black Monday.)

Newsflash!

As if the stock market crash wasn't enough for the yuppies to deal with, in February of 1990 they were faced with a recall of their beverage of choice, Perrier mineral water. The company was forced to recall a large quantity of its product when traces of benzene were found in some bottles in the U.S.

From Savers to Spenders

In March of 1989, *The Financial Post*'s magazine *Moneywise* reported that Canadians were slowly but surely becoming a nation of spenders. While Canadians had managed to squirrel away 12 to 18 percent of their take-home pay each year before 1985, that figure dropped to just 9 percent after 1985.

To make matters worse, Canadians had racked up record levels of personal debt. By 1989, a typical Canadian was carrying mortgage and consumer debt equal to three-quarters of his or her after-tax income.

Canadian consumers weren't the only ones on a spending spree, however—the federal government was also spending too much money. The federal deficit grew significantly during the 1980s. By 1990, nearly one-third of the government's revenues were being used to service the existing debt. (Back in 1975, only 10 percent of revenues had been required to service the debt.)

Real Men Aren't Afraid to Go Grocery Shopping

The times they were a-changin'..... An article in the March 19, 1990, issue of *Marketing* reported that men—both single and married—were spending more time in grocery stores

than ever before. While 66 percent of grocery shopping was still being done exclusively by female heads of households, 17 percent was being done by male heads of households, 15 percent by both partners together, and 2 percent by someone else entirely.

The article went on to highlight the findings of a 1988 Campbell's Soup study that had indicated that "real men" weren't afraid to grocery shop: "Men who food shop have a more contemporary image of themselves than non-shoppers. They are achievement-oriented and see themselves as up-to-date, liberated, well-organized, ambitious, intelligent, energetic and successful." (The researchers failed to reveal, however, whether those "real men" were ever caught shopping for quiche.)

Cross-Border Shopping Takes Off

Speaking of shopping, the March 31, 1990, issue of *The Financial Post* reported that growing numbers of Canadians were crossing the border to go shopping in the U.S.

Leonard Kubas, president of Kubas Research, explained the increase in cross-border shopping by noting how much money Canadians stood to save: "Consumers find the prices so attractive and the bargains so good, it's worth the drive and one-hour wait at the border."

And there was an added bonus to heading across the border to Buffalo or other U.S. cities—Sunday shopping. For most of the 1980s, Sunday store opening continued to be illegal almost everywhere in Canada.

Crying in Their Beer

Forget mega-mall mania and the stock market crash. The most important business story of the 1980s—at least in the eyes of the beer-loving public—was the disappearance of the traditional stubby beer bottle. For Jane and Joe Canuck, the stubby wasn't just a bottle; it was a Canadian icon that had earned a place of glory alongside the beaver, the Maple Leaf, and the Mounties. (The Disney Corporation hadn't yet bought the rights to the Mounties, so they were still ours.)

According to Dave Preston, a Member of the North American Guild of Beer Writers, the Canadian stubby bottle began disappearing in the early 1980s soon after Carling O'Keefe Breweries introduced Miller High Life (made under licence from the Milwaukee brewing

Newsflash!

Post-it Notes (a.k.a. "sticky notes") were introduced by 3M in 1980. While the technology behind the "repositionable adhesive" had been invented back in 1968, it wasn't until the late 1970s that someone at 3M figured out a use for the adhesive. That's when new product development researcher Art Fry, who was looking for a way to keep his scrap paper book-marks from falling out of his church choir hymnal, came up with the concept for the Post-it Note.

While Fry had a hard time convincing the powers that be at 3M that people would be pre-pared to pay big bucks for bits of scrap paper that promised to stay put, he won the battle in the end. The offices of North America have never been the same....

giant) in a new-style bottle, in 1983. "The bottle still contained 341 ml [equivalent to the 12 ounces held by the stubby] and led the way for other breweries to issue a variety of bottle styles, some with embossed logos and designs, and many with twist-off caps...Labatt soon followed suit and publicized its move with a bottle-shaped card, shipped in the last few cases of Labatt stubbies, stating: 'Blue will be coming to you in a new and distinctive bottle...taller, slimmer, and much more attractive.... This change is a result of lengthy consumer research and effort....'"

Preston also notes that "Apart from giving beer store employees a headache when it came to sorting and returning empties, the new bottle sent breweriana collectors and homebrewers scurrying to gather stubbies before they became extinct a few years later."

It was, after all, the end of an era.

The Least You Need to Know

➤ A 1981 Conference Board of Canada study of Canadians' spending habits revealed that consumer confidence was reaching record lows.

➤ Interest rates climbed to an unbelievable 21.5 percent in May of 1981.

➤ The Ghermezian brothers built a $700 million mega-mall called the West Edmonton Mall. The mall—which featured a triple-loop roller coaster, a water park, an indoor ice rink, and other bells and whistles—quickly became one of the hottest Alberta tourist attractions.

➤ Gordon Gecko, the fictional tycoon played by Michael Douglas in the popular movie *Wall Street* (1987) uttered a line that became the motto for corporate tycoons and investment brokers alike in the 1980s: "Greed is good."

➤ On October 19, 1987 ("Black Monday"), the Dow Jones Industrial Average—a key measure of both stock market performance and the overall health of the U.S. economy—plunged 508 points, nearly twice as far as in the 1929 stock market crash that had ushered in the Great Depression.

➤ Canadians had managed to squirrel away 12 to 18 percent of their take-home pay each year before 1985, but that figure dropped to just 9 percent after 1985.

➤ The federal deficit grew significantly during the 1980s until, by 1990, nearly one-third of the government's revenues were being used to service the existing debt.

➤ By the end of the decade, growing numbers of Canadians were crossing the border to go shopping in the U.S.

➤ The Canadian stubby beer bottle began disappearing in the early 1980s soon after Carling O'Keefe Breweries introduced Miller High Life in a new-style bottle, in 1983.

➤ One of the lasting legacies of the 1980s was the Post-it® Note.

Chapter 17

Brave New World

In This Chapter

➤ The personal computer finally arrives

➤ Cellular phones are all the rage

➤ Canadians take to the answering machine

It was an expression that was repeated time and time again in the late 1980s and early 1990s: "He who has the most toys when he dies wins."

While the expression was meant to be a joke, a lot of people seemed to be taking it seriously. North Americans were in the midst of a spending spree the like of which hadn't been seen since the post–Second World War boom.

Consider what pop culture expert Charles Panati has to say about the decade-long spending spree in his book *Panati's Parade of Fads, Follies, and Manias:* "[Americans] binged on buying—some 62 million microwave ovens, 57 million washers and dryers, 88 million cars and trucks, 105 million color television sets, 63 million VCRs, 31 million cordless phones, and 30 million telephone answering machines. All of this conspicuous consumption in a five-year period mid-decade; and all of these products bought at a time when America had only 91 million households."

Blast from the Past!

You can lead a Canadian to an answering machine, but you can't force him to record an interesting message. While the answering machine became a fixture in many Canadian homes during the 1980s, the greetings that were recorded on these machines were so uninspired that Philips Data Systems—the leading answering machine manufacturer at the time—began providing users of its popular Code-A-Phone answering machine with a 64-page booklet that suggested dozens of humorous messages that businesses could record on their answering machines to discourage callers from hanging up. (Remember, this was in the pre-voice-mail era, when people actually expected a real human being to answer.) The booklet was called "How To Make Your Code-A-Phone Talk Funny."

—Source: *The Financial Post*, November 8, 1980

Newsflash!

In an article in the January 7, 1990, issue of *Maclean's*, communications guru Marshall McLuhan predicted the boom in telecommuting. He noted that the revolution in computer technology would allow both employees and entrepreneurs to set up shop in their own homes.

While similar stats for Canada aren't available, anyone who lived through the decade can confirm that Canadians were also doing their share of buying. Suddenly, big-ticket items like microwave ovens and VCRs were no longer luxuries: in the minds of many Canadians, they had become necessities.

And if you were a yuppie, you had two additional items on your wish list: a personal computer and a cellular phone. These items weren't just practical tools of the business world; they were also status symbols that announced to the world that you'd arrived.

The Personal Computer

In August of 1981, *The Financial Post* reported that business computer manufacturer IBM had decided to enter the home market as well. Its brand new "IBM Personal Computer" was going to go head-to-head with personal computers offered by such companies as Apple, Commodore, and Radio Shack. The price? Anywhere from $2,300 to $9,000, depending on whether you were after the Chevy model or the Cadillac.

Computers were quickly becoming a fact of life for growing numbers of Canadians. In fact, the personal computer was becoming so popular that *Chatelaine* magazine found it necessary to include a "Plain-English Guide to the Personal Computer" in its February 1984 issue, explaining exactly how computers worked and why you might want one.

Have Phone, Will Travel

Information Technology had exciting news for its readers in September of 1983: the cellular phone was on its way.

"It's a workaholic's dream come true: a phone in the briefcase or on the car's dashboard for those unproductive hours on the freeway or other waiting times," raved writer Boyd Neil. "The Aladdin's lamp is cellular radio technology, just around the corner in Canada and maybe one of the biggest growth areas in personal communication products since individual paging systems."

While cellular phones weren't the first mobile phones, they were certainly a vast improvement over the existing types that were already on the market—phones that were plagued by poor reception, roaming limitations, and busy signals. (It's no wonder subscribers to the earliest mobile phone services had difficulty getting a line. In 1984, the Bell Canada mobile phone system in Toronto was only capable of carrying 25 conversations at a time!)

Not surprisingly, given the pent-up demand for such a product, cellular phones became one of the hottest items of the decade—a possession you'd make a point of flashing around if you were wealthy enough to own one. These weren't, after all, a small-ticket item. They cost $2,000 when they made their Canadian debut in 1985—almost as much as a home computer!

Boomer Bytes

Even Barbie got caught up in the personal computer craze. In 1985, the popular doll got her first computer.

Blast from the Past!

Not everyone thought that these high-tech bells and whistles were a good thing. Even Marshall McLuhan was cautioning Canadians about the downside of technological advancement. In a prophetic article entitled "Living at the speed of light" that appeared in the January 7, 1980, issue of *Maclean's*, McLuhan predicted that "In the '80s there will be a general awareness that the technology game is out of control, and that perhaps man was not intended to live at the speed of light."

The Least You Need To Know

➤ Hot-ticket items during the 1980s included microwave ovens, colour television sets, VCRs, cordless phones, telephone answering machines, personal computers, and cellular phones.

➤ In 1981, IBM entered the personal computer market. The initial IBM Personal Computer cost anywhere from $2,300 to $9,000, depending on the number of bells and whistles you wanted.

➤ The cellular phone arrived in Canada in 1985, and quickly became the hottest status symbol going. It was anything but cheap: the first cellular phones cost $2,000.

Chapter 18

Fame and Fortune

In This Chapter

➤ Why Canadians like to bash their heroes

➤ Canada produces its first generation of superstars

➤ CanCon revisited

In December of 1983, Maclean's magazine columnist Charles Gordon made a rather convincing case when he argued that Canadians were guilty of trashing their own heroes. In an article titled "How Canadians mistreat heroes," Gordon described the uniquely Canadian pastime of trashing anyone who happened to stumble into the public eye.

"Canadians used to be great paddlers and great hockey players," he wrote. "Now they are great debunkers. It is a national trait. It's a sad fact that if Christ came back tomorrow, some Canadians would suspect Him of doing it for the endorsements."

Why Canadians Like to Bash Their Heroes

In the remainder of his column, Gordon went on to make a list of all the successful Canadians who'd been slammed by Joe and Jane Canuck in recent years: diplomat Ken Taylor (for enjoying the celebrity life a little too much!), author Pierre Berton (for

Movers and Shakers

If there was one high-profile Canadian (other than Prime Minister Brian Mulroney, of course!) whom the media loved to hate, it was Sondra Gotlieb, wife of Allan Gotlieb, Canada's ambassador to Washington. The Canadian media were almost gleeful when word got out that Gotlieb had slapped the embassy's social secretary Connie Connor across the face at a dinner that she and her husband were hosting at the embassy. *Maclean's* magazine referred to the incident as the "slap that reverberated across North America."

"popularizing" Canadian history—heaven forbid!), ballerina Karen Kain and novelist Margaret Atwood (for being media darlings), and so on.

He noted that Canadians even had a bone to pick with the Great One—Wayne Gretzky. His crime? Being too perfect. "[Canadians] are made uncomfortable by a guy who not only leads the National Hockey League in everything, not only avoids fights and penalties, not only scores but sets up his teammates—not only does all that but is gracious in interviews and seems to be a nice person. Don't you just *hate* a guy like that?"

Gordon wasn't afraid to pinpoint the reasons for all this hero-slamming. He felt that Canadians suffered from a coast-to-coast case of insecurity and argued that beating up their heroes allowed Canadians to "immunize themselves against the disease of envy"— something that they were likely to feel if they compared themselves too closely with their neighbours to the south.

The Winner's Circle

As the decade progressed, Canadians had fewer and fewer reasons to feel envious of the Americans. The Canadians who found their way into the international limelight before 1980 were few and far between—think Paul Anka, Anne Murray, Joni Mitchell, and Neil Young! But that trickle became a flood during the 1980s. Canadians weren't just exporting fish and lumber anymore. They were also exporting their very own superstars. Here are just a few of the Canadians who made names for themselves—and us—during the 1980s:

Art

➤ Canadian painter Robert Bateman, whose finely detailed depictions of wildlife attracted an international audience.

➤ Artists Christopher and Mary Pratt, whose works were described by *Maclean's* magazine as "some of the most resonant images in Canadian art."

➤ Roderick Robbie, the Toronto architect responsible for designing the SkyDome, Toronto's $500 million sports, concert, and convention complex—a facility that couldn't help but show up on the radar screen of any North American sports fan.

➤ Moshe Safdie, the internationally respected Montreal architect responsible for designing the National Gallery of Canada, which opened in Ottawa in 1988.

Newsflash!

The SkyDome opened in June of 1989. Toronto sports fans were particularly enthralled with its retractable roof—a feature that allowed visitors to stay dry if Mother Nature decided to rain on the Toronto Blue Jays' parade.

Literature

➤ Margaret Atwood, author of The *Handmaid's Tale*, a futuristic fantasy about a woman whose sole function is to be a surrogate mother.

➤ Robertson Davies, author of such 1980s bestsellers as *The Rebel Angels*, *What's Bred in the Bone*, and *The Lyre of Orpheus*.

➤ Timothy Findley, author of two of the most critically acclaimed books of the decade: *Famous Last Words* and *The Telling of Lies*.

➤ Northrop Frye, a highly respected Canadian scholar who published *The Great Code* in 1982—a book that *Maclean's* magazine described as "a freewheeling study of biblical narrative and imagery."

➤ Alice Munro, whose collection of short stories about life in a small town, *The Progress of Love*, won the 1986 Governor General's Award for literature.

Blast from the Past!

"Few would seriously argue, anymore, that there is no Canadian literature....Mordecai Richler's well-known jest, 'world-famous in Canada,' ceased to be such a laugh—many Canadians are now world-famous, period. The erstwhile molehill of CanLit has grown to a mountain."

—Margaret Atwood, "Essays on the Millennium/2000: Survival, Then and Now: Canada's premier woman of letters takes a razor-sharp look at the state of Canadian literature," *Maclean's*, July 1, 1999.

➤ Robert Munsch, author of *The Paper Bag Princess*, *Love You Forever*, and other best-selling children's stories of the decade.

Music

➤ Bryan Adams, Canada's hottest pop star during the 1980s.

➤ Liona Boyd, the classical guitarist who also caught the eye of Prime Minister Pierre Elliott Trudeau.

➤ k.d. lang, who created her own brand of "torch-and-twang" country music and took Nashville by storm.

➤ Sharon, Lois, and Bram, who had both a hit television show, *The Elephant Show*, and a series of hit records (including their trademark song "Skinnamarink") during the decade.

Stage

➤ Linda Griffiths, whose one-woman show *Maggie and Pierre* had Canadians rolling in the aisles—albeit at the expense of a former prime minister.

➤ Karen Kain, Canada's very own prima ballerina.

➤ Kate Nelligan, a Canadian actress who wowed New York audiences when she appeared in *Plenty* in 1982.

➤ Eric Peterson, the male lead in the highly successful musical *Billy Bishop Goes to War*.

Big Screen

➤ Dan Aykroyd, the Canadian-born, CBC-bred co-star of *Ghostbusters*, one of the top-grossing comedies of all time.

➤ Jackie Burroughs and Richard Farnsworth, the stars of *The Grey Fox*, one of the first English-Canadian dramas to win international acclaim.

➤ David Cronenberg, Toronto-based director of such twisted but critically acclaimed movies as *Dead Ringers* (a firm about twin gynecologists, of all things) and *The Fly* (which pulled in an impressive $100 million at the box office).

➤ Michael J. Fox, a Canadian actor who had both a hit U.S. TV show (*Family Ties*) and a blockbuster movie (*Back to the Future*) under his belt by the time the decade came to an end.

➤ Norman Jewison, a highly respected Canadian movie director whose *Moonstruck*, a romantic comedy, starred American actors Nicolas Cage and Cher.

Small Screen and Airwaves

➤ Megan Follows, star of *Anne of Green Gables*, a television show based on the best-loved Canadian novel of all time.

➤ Barbara Frum, who moved from the critically acclaimed CBC Radio show *As It Happens* to co-host *The Journal*, the costliest public affairs show the CBC had ever produced.

➤ Peter Gzowski, the easygoing and much-loved radio host of CBC Radio's *Morningside*.

➤ Rick Moranis and Dave Thomas, the "hoser" stars of "Great White North"—one of the most popular segments in the television show that had all of North America talking: *SCTV*.

➤ Linda Schuyler and Kit Hood, the creators of *Degrassi Junior High*, an award-winning television show that was known for its realistic portrayal of pre-teen life.

➤ Moses Znaimer, the Citytv co-founder whose unique style of television programming captured the attention of broadcasters around the world.

Science

➤ Marc Garneau, a naval commander from Quebec City who earned the distinction of being the first Canadian in space when he participated in the 1984 Challenger mission.

➤ John Polanyi, the University of Toronto chemistry professor who received a Nobel Prize for his research on molecular changes during chemical reactions.

Business

➤ Scott Abbott and Chris Haney, the inventors of Trivial Pursuit, a phenomenally successful game that took the world by storm.

➤ Robert Campeau, a savvy Canadian financier who set a record for the largest U.S. takeover by a Canadian when he forked over $10.9 billion to purchase Federated Department Stores of Cincinnati.

➤ Garth Drabinsky, who put together North America's second-largest cinema empire under the Cineplex Odeon name.

➤ Eskander, Raphael, Nader, and Baham Ghermezian (a.k.a. "the Amazing Ghermezians"), four brothers who build the gigantic West Edmonton Mall in the early 1980s.

Newsflash!

One homegrown success story that Canadians couldn't ignore during the 1980s was the enormous popularity of Trivial Pursuit. The game sold millions of copies in 27 different counties, making Canadian-born inventors Scott Abbott and Chris Haney millionaires along the way. The peak year for sales was 1984, when 20 million copies were sold in the U.S. alone. By the end of the decade, Trivial Pursuit had become the most popular game in the world.

➤ Frank King, the millionaire oilman behind Calgary's bid for the 1988 Winter Olympic Games, which earned a $46 million profit for the city.

➤ Harrison McCain, an entrepreneur who was credited by *Maclean's* magazine with having "parlayed a single french-fry into a multinational giant, with sales exceeding $1 billion."

➤ Jim Pattison, director of a merchandising and manufacturing empire and the one-dollar-a-year chairman of Vancouver's highly successful Expo '86—an event that pulled in 22 million people from around the world.

➤ Paul, Albert, and Ralph Reichmann (a.k.a. "the Reichmann brothers"), a family that managed to build a $7.6 billion empire whose holdings included oil and gas reserves as well as spectacular property developments, such as the $7 billion Canary Wharf property in London, England.

➤ Peter Pocklington, a meat-packing entrepreneur and would-be politician who also happened to own one of the most successful Canadian hockey teams of the 1980s, the Edmonton Oilers.

➤ Alfred Sung, the Toronto fashion designer who became famous around the world for his classic, sophisticated styles.

Sports

➤ Carling Bassett, Canada's darling on the tennis courts.

➤ Alex Baumann, the Canadian swimmer who won two gold medals and one silver at the 1984 Summer Olympic Games in Los Angeles.

➤ Gaetan Boucher, the speedskater who brought home two gold medals and a bronze from the 1984 Winter Olympics in Sarajevo.

➤ Laurie Graham, Canada's most successful female skier of the decade, renowned for being both a fearless downhill racer and the winner of six World Cup races.

➤ Wayne Gretzky, a hockey player who earned the name the "Great One" for being a class act both on and off the ice.

➤ Ben Johnson—the fastest man in the world in 1988 until he was stripped of his Olympic Gold medal when it was revealed that he had used illegal steroids.

➤ Elizabeth Manley, the figure skater who skated her way to a silver medal at the 1988 Winter Games in Calgary, stealing the crowds' hearts along the way.

➤ Brian Orser, the figure skater who won the hearts of Canadians at the 1988 Winter Games in Calgary when he took a silver medal in the so-called "battle of the Brians." (He was battling American skater Brian Boitano.)

➤ Steve Podborski, who made skiing history by becoming, in 1982, the first North American to win the prestigious World Cup title.

Blast from the Past!

"The pressure on athletes to win at any price was overwhelming. Those who reached the Olympics carried with them the knowledge that they were surrogate warriors in the rivalry of nations and that only medals counted in the tallies kept by press and public. It was winners, not good sportsmen, who attracted the lavish courtship of commercial sponsors. In a decade that seemed to value little else, the scent of fame and fortune held a powerful allure. As a young man of scant education and few skills, Ben Johnson was barely employable; as the fastest man in the world, he was worth $10 million in commercial-endorsement contracts."

—Kevin Doyle and Ann Johnston, *The 1980s: Maclean's Chronicles the Decade.*

CanCon Revisited

Although Canadians were finally making it to the ranks of superstardom, not everyone thought that this was necessarily a good thing.

Bob Bossin, of the Canadian folk music group Stringband, argued in the August 31, 1981, issue of *Maclean's* magazine that these so-called Canadian superstars were really just clones of their American counterparts: "Other countries produce distinguished movies, distinctive music and their own cars. We make American cars, American music and movies like *The Kidnapping of the President.*"

Bossin went on to argue that Canadian performers who showed any type of creativity were being shut out of the performing arts by broadcasters who wanted them to conform to the standards being set by the Americans: "Performers who are in fact remarkable embodiments of northern originality are passed off as failed versions of American cultural clichés. They are not in style—that is, the all-American style so admired by the eastern media. Producers and programmers, editors and entertainment writers, stare so fixedly at the southern sky that they miss the northern lights altogether."

He concluded his piece by noting that Canadians in other parts of Canada weren't as guilty of falling into this trap as Canadians in southern Ontario—"perhaps...because the magnetic pole of New York is weakened by distance."

Blast from the Past!

"We still tend to ape American forms. We are too quick to adjust to what they have done and accept their standards as our standards, their styles as our styles."

—CRTC chairman John Meisel, in an interview with *Maclean's* magazine in 1980

The Least You Need to Know

➤ Canada finally "came of age" during the 1980s, producing large numbers of homegrown superstars in fields ranging from sports to the arts to business.

➤ The board game Trivial Pursuit sold millions of copies in 27 different languages, making Canadian-born inventors Scott Abbott and Chris Haney millionaires along the way. The peak year for sales was 1984, when 20 million copies were sold in the U.S. alone.

➤ Not all of the attention that Canadian superstars attracted was positive. When Ben Johnson tested positive for steroid use and was stripped of his gold medal at the 1988 Summer Olympic Games, many Canadians felt that he had tarnished the country's reputation.

the '80s Bunch

Family Ties

In This Chapter

➤ The cult of overwork

➤ Canadian working women sing the daycare blues

➤ The backlash against feminism

➤ How Canadians felt about the economy, their political leaders, and the family.

If you wanted to get ahead in the corporate world in the 1980s, you had to be prepared to clock extra hours. Lots and lots of extra hours. The quickest way to commit career suicide was to be caught dashing out the door at 5:00 p.m. when your colleagues were still hard at work at their desks.

The Cult of Overwork

"Throughout the '80s, it was considered almost chic to be on a treadmill," noted journalist Lesley Barsky in an article in the May 1990 issue of *Chatelaine*. "A bulging Filofax had a perverse cachet, as if the more appointments you penciled in, the more status you deserved."

Unfortunately, not all workers were able to put in the number of hours that many employers were expecting. It was one thing, after all, to burn the candle at both ends if you were a free-wheeling single guy in your early 20s. It was quite another if you were a 30-year-old single mother whose preschoolers were being cared for at a daycare centre that closed its doors at 5:30 sharp.

The Daycare Blues

And daycare was, after all, one of the biggest headaches that Canadian families faced during the 1980s. At the start of the decade, there were just 87,000 licensed childcare spaces available for the 721,000 Canadian children who needed them. And even if you could afford to have a nanny come into your home to take care of your children—an option for only a few high-income families—there was no guarantee that you'd end up with Mary Poppins. There were, after all, plenty of the "nannies from hell" who were the subject of a feature-length article by Shona McKay in the December 1990 issue of *The Financial Post*.

Catch-22 Meets Nine-to-Five

A lot of working mothers began to feel that they were caught between a rock and a hard place. If they turned off their computers at 5:00 p.m. to pick up their kids at daycare, their co-workers whispered that they had clearly opted for "the mommy track" rather than "the career track." On the other hand, if they put in long hours at the office, those very same colleagues would be the first to accuse them of being bad mothers.

The problem, according to Alan Mirabelli of the Vanier Institute of the Family, was that Canadian society had yet to fully acknowledge the fact that most Canadian households required two paycheques if they were to have any hope of maintaining the same standard of living that they had enjoyed during the 1950s. "We're still working in rearview mirror mode," he told a reporter from *Maclean's* magazine.

As if that wasn't bad enough, many women found themselves struggling to break through the glass ceiling—an invisible barrier that kept women in the pink-collar ghetto, unable to land positions in upper management.

Some women decided to stick around and fight. Others decided to cash in their chips and go into business on their own. By the end of the 1980s, three times as many businesses were being started by women as by men.

The New Woman in Mr. Clean's Life

It seemed that the only folks in the business world who had clued in to the fact that working women had become a force to be reckoned with were the marketers.

Leonard Kubas, president of the Retail Marketing Association of Canada, told a group of marketers in 1981 that companies needed to target advertising messages at a new type of woman—a woman who held down a job from nine to five. What's more, they needed to recognize that working women were interested in top-quality products that would save them time, not in bargain-basement money savers that wouldn't do the job nearly as well: "The most precious commodity working women possess is time, not money," he noted.

Boomer Bytes

A 1985 *Chatelaine* survey revealed that 83 percent of Canadian women did more housework than the men in their lives did.

I'm Not a Feminist, But...

At some point during the late 1970s or early 1980s, "feminist" became a bad word. Women who felt that they needed to speak out about a women's issue began to preface their comments with the words "I'm not a feminist, but..."

Bronwyn Drainie commented on this phenomenon in an article that appeared in the September 1986 issue of *Chatelaine*. "The heady days of revolutionary fervor are gone," she wrote. "And many women in their mid-20s to mid-30s, who take their advances in status for granted, are a little embarrassed by what they perceive to be the strident rhetoric of their older sisters."

The Pornography Debate Heats Up

Of course, not all feminists were big on rhetoric. Some preferred direct action. In the 1980s, radical elements within the women's movement were engaging in tactics that the movement had never resorted to before—like firebombing! In November of 1982, a radical feminist group known as the Wimmin's Fire Brigade firebombed three Red Hot Video outlets in British Columbia to protest the chain's sale of materials that the Wimmin's Fire Brigade considered degrading to women.

The pornography issue was on the front burner for much of the first half of the decade. In January 1982, thousands of women protested a decision by First Choice Canadian Communications—a cable television company—to carry programming from the Playboy Channel in the U.S. And in September of 1983, Margaret Atwood wrote about the differences between erotica and pornography in an article that appeared in *Chatelaine*.

"It would be naive to think of violent pornography as just harmless entertainment," she wrote. "It's also an educational tool and a powerful propaganda device. What happens when boy educated on porn meets girl brought up on Harlequin romances? The clash of expectations can be heard around the block. She wants him to get down on his knees with a ring, he wants her to get down on all fours with a ring in her nose. Can this marriage be saved?"

Boomer Bytes

In 1990, a *Maclean's*/Decima Research poll revealed that 69 percent of Canadians no longer saw any meaningful differences between the three mainstream political parties.

Survey Says...

During the 1980s and early 1990s, Maclean's magazine and Decima Research conducted a series of polls to find out what Joe and Jane Canuck had to say about the Canadian economy, the country's leaders, and the state of the Canadian family. Here are the highlights of what they discovered:

➤ Canadians' confidence in the health of the country's economy took a beating during the 1980s. In 1984, 79 percent of Canadians were confident about the country's economic future. By the end of the decade, that number had dropped to just 69 percent.

➤ Canadians also lost their faith in their country's leaders. In 1984, half of Canadians felt confident that the government would solve the country's economic problems. By 1989, only one quarter felt that way.

➤ A poll taken in the early 1990s revealed that while 63 percent of Canadians felt that the family in general was in a state of crisis, 61 percent reported that their own family life was very happy. In fact, as journalist Mary Nemeth noted at the time, "Three-quarters of all respondents said that their families are full of love; 61 percent said they had happy childhoods; 83 percent of parents said that having children has made them happier still." What's more, even though growing numbers of Canadians were opting for divorce, one-third still believed enough in the institution of marriage to make that walk down the aisle again.

Blast from the Past!

"The traditional family...conjures up postwar images of serenity, of stability, of white picket fences and cheerful children greeting daddy at the door, of mothers spending long, unhurried days coaxing and teaching tender young souls.... Nowadays, it seems, the only young families who can afford the white picket fence are too hurried to enjoy leisurely hours within its perimeter. And it could just as well be a father, or a single mother, running to the door of someone's house to pick the kids up from daycare."

—Mary Nemeth, writing in *Maclean's* magazine in 1994

The Least You Need to Know

➤ The 1980s were the age of overwork—a time when it was trendy to be a borderline workaholic!

➤ Daycare spaces continued to be in short supply. At the start of the decade, there were just 87,000 licensed childcare spaces available for the 721,000 Canadian children who needed them.

➤ In 1981, 68 percent of Canadians believed that women with children were generally considered to be less serious about their careers than their male colleagues.

➤ A 1985 *Chatelaine* survey revealed that 83 percent of Canadian women did more housework than the men in their lives.

➤ Feminism became a bad word during the 1980s. Young women in particular became reluctant to identify themselves as feminists.

➤ Canadians lost confidence in their country's economy and political leaders during the 1980s.

➤ A poll taken in the early 1990s revealed that while 63 percent of Canadians felt that the family in general was in a state of crisis, 61 percent reported that their own family life was very happy.

Chapter 20

The Good, the Bad, and the Ugly

In This Chapter

➤ 1980s fads

➤ The decade's hottest toys

➤ What Canadians were wearing

➤ What was coming across the airwaves

Think the seventies had a monopoly on bad taste? Then how do you explain such eighties fads as deely boppers—those glitter-coated antennae that people used to like to wear at parties—or those bright yellow "Baby on Board" signs that popped up on the rear windows of half the cars on the road?

Much as some folks might like to pretend that silly fads and ugly fashions died with the 1970s, the fact of the matter is that seventies bad taste carried over well into the 1980s. (It was kind of like having a bad hangover except that instead of waking up with a splitting headache, you woke up and discovered that you had a set of neon-pink deely boppers on your head.)

Bad Fads

While deely boppers and "Baby on Board" signs were perhaps the epitome of 1980s bad taste, there were plenty of other fads that earned themselves a place in the Bad Fads Hall of Fame. Let's look at a few of the decade's more prominent inductees:

Rubik's Cube

There were two types of people in the world in 1980: those who knew how to solve the Rubik's cube and those who didn't. Those who knew how to solve the cube delighted in doing so right before your eyes in just a matter of minutes. (One whiz kid in the States set a record for unscrambling the cube in 28 seconds flat.) Those who *didn't* know how to solve the puzzle either ignored the Rubik's cube craze altogether or peeled the stickers off the cube when no one was looking and pretended that they had solved the puzzle. (Of course, everyone knew if you cheated by peeling the stickers off the cube. No matter how hard you tried, you could never get the stickers to line up neatly again.)

Just in case you were so traumatized by your inability to solve the Rubik's cube that you have permanently repressed your memory of it, let me remind you what it looked like. It was a cube with three rows and three columns on each side; each side of the cube was a different colour. All of the rows and columns moved, so it was possible to scramble the cube so that all of the colours got mixed up. There were 43,252,003,274,489,856,000 different ways to scramble the cube.

The cube was the brainchild of Professor Erno Rubik, an architecture professor at the Budapest School of Commercial Art in Hungary. He invented the cube in 1974 in order to teach his students about the properties of three-dimensional objects.

Toward the end of the 1970s, Ideal Toys got wind of Rubik's invention and licensed U.S. rights. The product hit the market in 1980, selling 4.5 million cubes that first year. By 1980, over 100 million Rubik's cubes had been sold worldwide.

North Americans became obsessed with the cube. Some people developed wrist tendinitis from spending too much time trying to solve it, and at least one woman mentioned the Rubik's cube in her divorce petition! At the height of the craze, there were no fewer than 50 books about the Rubik's cube available, with titles ranging from *101 Uses for a Dead Cube* to *How to Live with a Cubaholic*.

Feeling nostalgic about the Rubik's cube? Don't

despair. You can relive the agony and ecstasy of the whole Rubik's experience by trying the online Rubik's cube that you'll find listed in the Web site directory at the end of this book. (Pssst... You won't even have to peel the stickers off the squares to solve this particular Rubik's cube. When you reach the point of utter despair, you simply hit a button and the computer solves the puzzle for you. Imagine how much happier the eighties would have been if that option had been available to the millions of people who never did manage to solve the darned thing.)

Couch Potatoes

The term "couch potato" was coined in the late 1970s to describe people—men in particular—whose idea of a workout was sitting on the couch and reaching for the remote.

During the 1980s, the shame associated with being a couch potato momentarily disappeared. People rushed out to buy couch potato dolls and books like *The Couch Potato Handbook*. At one point, it even looked as if couch potatoes across North America were going to congregate in Chicago for their very own convention, complete with TV dinners. (In the end, however, the event had to be cancelled: no one seemed willing to get off the couch long enough to organize it.)

Lip-Synching

It was a rare high school that didn't stage at least one lip-synching contest at some point during the 1980s. After all, where else could you get such cheap entertainment? Kids would get up and mouth the lyrics to hit songs while pretending to be their favourite rock stars. Some even chose to accompany themselves on air guitars (imaginary musical instruments)!

Lip-synching lost its shine at the end of the decade, when the musical group Milli Vanilli was stripped of its Grammy Award after it was revealed that some of the group's hit songs had been lip-synched.

Home Renovations

While teenagers were busy lip-synching, adults were busy renovating the homes that they'd purchased for sky-high prices during the real estate boom. That led to an entirely new sideline for many builders: fixing up home renovation disasters caused by do-it-yourselfers who had far more enthusiasm than know-how.

"People who try to renovate on their own mean that I am at no loss for work," Toronto carpenter Peter Kornas told *The Financial Post* magazine in June 1987. "I would say I spend 20 to 30 percent of my time fixing up other people's sloppy jobs."

Toronto consulting engineer Bob Dunlop was even more frank. He stressed that couples needed to factor in a hidden cost—"divorce dust"—before taking the crowbar to the drywall.

Say What?

Cabbage Patch Kids were pudgy-faced dolls that came with adoption papers. They were the hottest toy on the market during the mid-1980s. During the peak year for sales—1985—more than $600 million worth of Cabbage Patch Kids were sold in North America.

The Decade's Hottest Toys

The three hottest toys of the 1980s were Cabbage Patch Kids, Smurfs, and Teenage Mutant Ninja Turtles.

Cabbage Patch Kids mania hit North America in late 1983. It seemed that every little girl had a Cabbage Patch Kid on her wish list that year, and there weren't nearly enough dolls to go around. The result was pandemonium in the toy stores. One woman even ended up with a broken leg.

The Smurfs were two-inch figurines made out of moulded plastic. There were 98 different male Smurfs—with names such as Brainy, Greedy, and Jokey—and one female Smurf named Smurfette. The Smurfs were so popular that they got their own TV cartoon and their image was soon splashed all over lunch boxes, knapsacks, and other kiddy paraphernalia.

The Teenage Mutant Ninja Turtles was the name of both a high-action cartoon show and a line of hideously ugly toys boasting such unlikely names as Michelangelo and Raphael. Some parents refused to let their children tune in to the cartoon because it seemed to exist solely to create demand for the toys (which it did extremely well!). Others were reluctant to let their kids watch the show because the Turtles were constantly shouting things like "Kowabunga, dude!" and then clobbering their enemies on the head.

On the Dance Floor

The dance crazes of the 1980s weren't like anything that had come before. Some, like rap and breakdancing, involved athletic manoeuvres and gyrations. Others, like slam

Blast from the Past!

One of the hottest new trends in orthodontics during the 1980s was braces for adults. While only 5 percent of orthodontic patients during the 1970s were adults, by the 1980s, they made up one-third of the patients in a typical orthodontic practice. The principal reason for seeking out orthodontic treatment was cosmetic. Orthodontists claimed to be able to work small miracles—particularly on chins. Consider what one dentist told *Maclean's* magazine in 1981: "If we had gotten our hands on Joe Clark, he would have won the election."

dancing, seemed more an act of aggression than anything that resembled fun. And then there was the "moonwalk" made famous by pop star Michael Jackson—a smooth backward motion in which the dancer's feet slid across the floor in a Jell-O–like fashion.

By far the most controversial dance of the 1980s was the lambada—a Brazilian form of bump-and-grind that involved a lot of highly provocative grinding on the part of the two dance partners. (The dance was so erotic that two French record producers described it as "a good alternative to sex in the age of AIDS.")

What Canadians Were Wearing

Thanks to the influence of American television, music videos, and films, Canadians found themselves indulging in the same fashion fads as their neighbours to the south. Here's a quick guide to what was considered hot in North America during the 1980s:

The Flashdance look: This was a look made famous by actress Jennifer Beals in the hit movie *Flashdance*. It basically consisted of a short-sleeved sweatshirt worn over a tank top, tight-fitting pants, and leg warmers.

The Madonna look: Pop star Madonna scandalized the older generation but fascinated teenage girls by wearing underwear as clothing. Fishnet stockings and pencil-sharp pointy brassieres became the trademark look for both the Material Girl herself and all the Madonna wannabes.

High-tech running shoes: Wannabe athletes convinced their parents to cough up the cash for $200 pairs of running shoes that featured shock-proof heels, air-cushioned soles, and other bells and whistles.

The glove: When singer Michael Jackson wore a single white sequined glove to the Grammy Awards in 1984, he sparked one of the eighties' most bizarre fashion trends. (Those who really got into the Michael Jackson look also wore shiny red leather jackets and practised Jackson's trademark "moonwalk.")

The Musical Grab Bag

The eighties produced some great music. It also produced some of the worst music of the entire century! This was, after all, the decade when Debbie Gibson, George Michael, and Duran Duran ruled the airwaves.

The only good news about the 1980s was the fact

Blast from the Past!

"In the late eighties, hair color exploded. Madonna let her roots show, supermodel Linda Evangelista went from blond to red to brown (within a few weeks), and Cyndi Lauper vibrated with Crazy Color. From then on, the pretense of naturalness was dead."

—Julie Logan, "Beauty Report: Dos by the Decade: Did we or didn't we?" *In Style*, October 1, 1998

that Canadians were finally getting their share of the spotlight—possibly because the Americans were so taken by the musical talents of such performers as Bryan Adams and Alannah Myles that they actually managed to forget that the stars were Canadian!

Newsflash!

John Lennon was shot and killed on December 8, 1980, by a crazed fan, Mark Chapman.

Boomer Bytes

Michael Jackson's *Thriller* album became the bestselling LP of all time, spending 37 weeks at the top of Billboard's album chart and selling more than 40 million copies worldwide.

Newsflash!

According to Geoff Pevere and Greig Dymond, co-authors of *Mondo Canuck: A Canadian Pop Culture Odyssey*, the most important pop culture development of the 1980s was the launching of Moses Znaimer's MuchMusic in 1984. Calling itself "the Nation's Music Station," MuchMusic provided Canadian bands with unprecedented exposure and "did more to promote and develop a national pop-star system than any development in Canadian music since CanCon."

The Least You Need To Know

➤ Over 100 million Rubik's Cubes were sold worldwide between 1980 and 1990.

➤ Other hot fads during the 1980s included deely boppers, Baby on Board signs, the couch potato craze, lip synching, and home renovations.

➤ The hottest toys of the decade were Cabbage Patch Kids, Smurfs, and Teenage Mutant Ninja Turtles.

➤ 1980s dance crazes included rap, breakdancing, slamdancing, the "moonwalk," and the lambada.

➤ Fashion fads included the Flashdance look, the Madonna look, high-tech running shoes, and the glove.

THE CANADA...
SHE LOVE ME...
SHE LOVE ME NOT...

Chapter 21

Only in Canada

In This Chapter

➤ All the news that's fit to print

➤ The great censorship debate

➤ The reign of Peter the Great

Canadians continued to engage in some heavy-duty cultural navel-gazing during the 1980s.

They wondered how Canadian magazines could possibly hold their own against the slicker and better-financed American imports. They worried about the fact that independent newspapers were being swallowed up by giant conglomerates for whom publishing was merely an interesting sideline. They wondered if there would be anything left of Canadian book publishing within a few years.

Fortunately, during their darkest hours—those days when it seemed like *Chatelaine* was being left in the dust by *Cosmo* and that people were more interested in reading a Danielle Steele novel than picking up a copy of Mordecai Richler's latest book— Canadians could tune in to *Morningside* and hear that all was right in the world. (Or at least from the 49th parallel up.)

Boomer Bytes

In 1981, 75 percent of Canadians reported that they read magazines on a regular basis.

All the News That's Fit to Print

Canadians certainly had good reason to be worried about the health of the Canadian publishing industry during the 1980s. After years of being in precarious health, it seemed to be taking a turn for the worse.

Magazine Wars

The Canadian magazine industry was fighting for its life against the glossy consumer magazines that made their way across the border and into Canadian homes. In 1984, 65 percent of paid-circulation magazines in Canada were published outside the country. The real, ugly truth, however, was that more than half of the Canadian-produced magazines that were finding their way to Canadian coffee tables were hybrid publications like *Time, Reader's Digest,* and *TV Guide:* magazines that masqueraded as Canadian publications, but that actually contained significant amounts of American content.

Newspaper Woes

The Canadian newspaper industry was on equally shaky ground. By the late 1980s, after two decades of consolidation in the industry, only eight Canadian cities were still being served by two or more separately owned newspapers. Even worse, growing numbers of newspapers were being bought up by large conglomerates whose holdings were concentrated in areas other than publishing. ("Will that be a newspaper chain along with your real estate empire, sir?")

There was sufficient concern about the state of the newspaper industry for the federal government to appoint both a Senate committee and a royal commission to look into the problem: the Senate Special Committee on Mass Media (1969–70), chaired by Senator Keith Davey, and the Royal Commission on Newspapers (1981), chaired by Tom Kent. The two groups came up with some excellent recommendations—the Davey Commission recommended the establishment of a Press Ownership Review Board and the Kent Commission recommended that legislation be introduced to prohibit the same company from owning both newspapers and radio or TV stations in the same market—but none of their recommendations ever became law.

As if the magazine and newspaper problems weren't enough for the publishing industry to contend with, the Canadian book world was also going through a rough time. By 1985, 60 percent of book sales were going to foreign-controlled publishers and distributors, despite the fact that homegrown publishers were bringing out more than 4,000 new titles each year.

Boomer Bytes

Here are some numbers worth noting re: the health of the Canadian newspaper industry, circa 1986:

The total circulation of all 100 Canadian dailies was 5.5 million.

Eighty percent of adult Canadians reported that they read a daily newspaper at least three or four times a week.

Seventy-four percent of newspapers in Canada were owned by chains, with 59 percent of the country's newspapers being divvied up between the Southam (32.8 percent) and Thomson (25.9 percent) chains.

The Great Censorship Debate

It's ironic: while some publishers were doing their best to get people to buy books, the federal government seemed determined to make it more difficult than ever for certain types of books to make it into the hands of Canadians.

During the 1980s, Little Sister's Book and Art Emporium—a Vancouver gay and lesbian bookshop—challenged the ways in which Canadian customs officers routinely inspected materials to determine whether they were suitable for Canadians. The bookstore claimed that the materials it was importing were often unfairly held up at the border, simply because customs officials knew that the goods were destined for a gay and lesbian bookstore.

Bookstore owners weren't the only people affected by the long arm of the Canadian censor, however. In the early 1990s, censors in Saskatchewan decided that it was their duty to protect the people of the province from what it described as unacceptable scenes of sadomasochism in *Exit to Eden,* a comedy starring those two hard-core porn artists (not!), Dan Aykroyd and Rosie O'Donnell.

Never mind the fact that Chicago film critic Roger Ebert had described those very same sex scenes as "lifeless, listless charades" that ranked as "practically family entertainment." Or that model Iman, who had a part in the film, declared, "This is not an S and M movie. This is S and M lite." The Saskatchewan censors knew what was best for the people of the province, right?

Well, maybe.

In the end, after making fools of themselves (and the rest of Canadians), the censors agreed to allow the movie to be shown in Saskatchewan.

Canadian-born Dan Aykroyd wasn't particularly surprised or upset by the controversy, commenting only that it was "great publicity for the film."

The Reign of Peter the Great

As hard as it may be to believe today, *Morningside,* the CBC's flagship radio show during the 1980s and 1990s did, in fact, exist before Peter Gzowksi came on board. In those long-forgotten days before the king of the Canadian airwaves ascended to the throne of morning radio in 1982, *Morningside* was hosted by none other than Don ("Charlie Farquharson") Harron.

Morningside under Gzowski quickly earned a reputation—deserved or not—for being the miracle glue that held Canada together. By the early 1990s, it had become the hottest ticket to fame for any flag-waving Canadian with a book to push, a record to promote, or a story to tell. If anyone could save Confederation, it was Peter Gzowski. Or at least that's what many Canadians believed at the time.

According to former CBC Chairman Patrick Watson, shows like *Morningside* hit a nerve with Canadians who cared about the country. These listeners tuned in to CBC Radio to get their daily dose of "song and story, information and comedy, nonsense and faith, conversation and performance, aspiration and fear, accountability and challenge, that speak to us out of our shared experience as a nation."

Blast from the Past!

Not everyone thought that *Morningside* was a sure-fire cure for what ailed the country. Consider what Geoff Pevere and Greig Dymond had to say about the show in their 1996 book *Mondo Canuck: A Canadian Pop Culture Odyssey:* "If *Morningside,* which is listened to by less than 15 percent of the entire nation each day, is all the glue we've got, we might as well be trying to bind the *Titanic* with Bondfast."

The Least You Need to Know

➤ In 1984, 65 percent of paid-circulation magazines in Canada were published outside the country.

➤ In 1986, the total circulation of all 100 Canadian dailies was 5.5 million, and 80 percent of adult Canadians reported that they read a daily newspaper at least three or four times a week.

➤ By the mid-1980s, 74 percent of newspapers in Canada were owned by chains, with 59 percent of the country's newspapers being divvied up between the Southam (32.8 percent) and Thomson (25.9 percent) chains.

➤ By 1985, 60 percent of book sales were going to foreign-controlled publishers and distributors, despite the fact that homegrown publishers were bringing out more than 4,000 new titles each year.

➤ During the 1980s, Little Sister's Book and Art Emporium, a gay and lesbian bookstore in Vancouver, B.C., accused Canada Customs of unfairly censoring material that was imported by the store.

➤ Peter Gzowski joined *Morningside* in 1982. During his years behind the mike, the show was widely regarded as the most influential show on Canadian radio.

Chapter 22

The World According to CNN

In This Chapter

➤ The dawn of the instant news era

➤ The sexiest anchors on Canadian TV

➤ The TV cameras hit Parliament Hill

➤ *Reach for the Top* goes off the air

➤ *Fashion Television* makes its debut

➤ Canadians finally win at sitcom roulette

The 1980s were the decade in which instant news was born. CNN created the phenomenon shortly after its 1980 debut, and CBC Newsworld gave instant news a uniquely Canadian twist after it hit the airwaves in 1989.

The appeal of instant news was obvious: why wait for coverage in tomorrow morning's paper or tonight's late-evening newscast, when you could get details of a breaking news story while it was happening? Never mind the fact that you had to sit through hours of ho-hum coverage while the news you'd already heard was repeated over and over to fill air time. That was a small price to pay for being "right there" as a story broke. Or at least that's what the networks kept telling us.

Blast from the Past!

"Television is our first true robot, a machine with a human likeness. It has an adjustable complexion and glows in the dark. We huddle around it as if it were the ancestral fire; changing channels, a modern form of stoking."

—Percussionist Brian Borealis of the Toronto-based rock-and-roll band the Nukes, writing in *Maclean's* magazine in December of 1980.

Of course, Newsworld's debut wasn't the only exciting development in the world of Canadian TV during the 1980s. Let's take a look at some of the other big stories that happened during the decade.

Hunk TV

The biggest story of the decade—from a pop culture perspective, at least!—has to be the magazine article that none of us ever thought we'd live to see: a full-length feature in *Chatelaine* magazine on the sexiest anchormen on Canadian TV.

The article, written by Allan Gould, featured a full-page head shot of Keith Morrison, the 36-year-old co-host of CBC's *The Journal*—an anchor whom *Toronto Sun* editor Barbara Amiel once described as "he of the chiseled profile, stunningly deep-set eyes and blond Robert Redford looks." Morrison admitted in the piece that being this good-looking could, in fact, be a liability for a male anchor: "There have been occasions in my career when I felt my work wasn't taken seriously because of my looks."

Other "hunks" featured in the piece included the CBC's Peter Kent and Knowlton Nash; CTV's Harvey Kirck, Lloyd Robertson and Richard Brown; and ABC's Peter Jennings. (If only *Playgirl* had been aware of all this talent when it was looking for candidates for its "Men of Canada" issue a few years earlier!)

MPTV

If the women of Canada couldn't stand the excitement of watching the country's handsome male anchors,

Newsflash!

Ex-television anchor Christine Craft hit the newspaper headlines when she successfully sued a Kansas City, Missouri, television station for demoting her from anchor to reporter because, in her boss's words, she was "too old, too unattractive, and not deferential enough to men." She was 36 at the time.

they could bring their heart rate down considerably by tuning in to the proceedings on Parliament Hill.

One of lasting legacies of the Trudeau era (other than the word "fuddle duddle"!) was the introduction of TV cameras to the House of Commons. For the first time, Canadians were able to tune in to the workings of government—the good, the bad, and the ugly.

Charles Gordon described the Canadian viewing public's initial reaction to "MP" TV in an article that ran in *Maclean's* magazine during the early 1980s: "When television first came to the House of Commons, the political parties began getting messages from their media consultants: the thumping of desks was disturbing people in their living rooms and frightening the parakeet. Soon, desk thumping had gone the way of the balanced budget, and members of Parliament were clapping their hands, like members of the studio audience."

Gordon predicted that television was not yet through changing the way the political game was played. "Soon, arguing and heckling will go the way of desk thumping, and that will be too bad, since vigorous debate is what Parliament is all about. It is not television's idea of what Parliament is all about, however."

CBC Dumps *Reach for the Top*

The unthinkable happened in 1985. After more than 30 years of stumping the smartest high school students in the country, CBC's *Reach for the Top* went off the air.

CBC brass decided that the time had come to pull the plug on the show when audience surveys revealed that it had long since lost the very audience it was supposed to be attracting: teenagers. The program—which was extremely popular during the 1960s and 1970s—was decidedly unhip by the 1980s

Boomer Bytes

One hundred and six million North American viewers tuned in to watch the *M*A*S*H* finale in 1983.

Still, its passing did not go unnoticed: the CBC received no fewer than 800 letters protesting the decision to cut the show, and one member of Parliament stood up in the House of Commons to demand that the CBC do something to save this "all-Canadian young people's show." (Unfortunately, the MP didn't quite have his facts straight: during its dying days, the show was far more popular with the geriatric crowd than anyone under 20!)

Fashion Television Hits the Airwaves

Citytv's *Fashion Television* (FT) premiered in 1986. Known for its daring coverage of the fashion industry (think sheer fabrics and peekaboo styles!) and its irreverent host, Jeanne

Beker (the former host of another gutsy Citytv show, *The New Music*), the show had managed to attract a following of 100 million viewers in 120 countries by the time its tenth birthday rolled around.

Boomer Bytes

Seeing Things was broadcast in 40 different countries. It aired on many PBS stations in the U.S. in 1983, becoming a cult hit with hoser wannabes south of the border.

According to an article that appeared in *Maclean's* magazine in 1996, the show attracted a particularly loyal following amongst Canadian prison inmates. "I'm sure that if you were in prison and there were a lot of sexy girls on TV, you'd watch that show—especially if it's up against *60 Minutes*," explained the show's co-creator, Jay Levine.

Canada Finally Wins at Sitcom Roulette

It's a question that has puzzled pop culture historians for years: why has it proved next to impossible for

Blast from the Past!

Here are some of the more memorable TV commercials that aired during the 1980s, according to Advertising Age magazine:

➤ Chrysler's "If you can find a better car, buy it" campaign, featuring company president Lee Iacocca

➤ Wendy's "Where's the beef?" commercial, featuring a crusty old lady named Clara Peller

➤ Kodak's "Daddy's little girl" commercials, which encouraged teary fathers everywhere to capture those Kodak moments while they could

➤ Apple Macintosh's "1984" commercial, which suggested that Big Brother and IBM were one and the same. The commercial aired during the 1984 Superbowl, and helped to launch the so-called Macintosh revolution.

➤ Pepsi-Cola's "Choice of a new generation" campaign, featuring pop music icon Michael Jackson

➤ California Raisins "I heard it through the grapevine" ads, featuring Claymation animation technology.

You can read about the magzine's other favourite commercials from this decade by visiting the *Advertising Age* magazine Web site at www.adage.com.

Canada—the country that gave the world *SCTV,* Lorne Michaels of *Saturday Night Live* fame, and other comedy legends—to produce a decent sitcom?

Between the early 1950s and the early 1980s, Canada took no less than a dozen cracks at the can. Each time, the results were appalling. (I mean, *King of Kensington* was considered to be a *successful* comedy, for Pete's sake!)

Fortunately, the comedy fairy must have waved her magic wand when Louis Del Grande came up with the concept for *Seeing Things,* a hit Canadian sitcom that attracted a loyal audience of 1.3 million viewers. The show featured Del Grande as Lou Ciccone, a bumbling newspaper reporter who happened to have clairvoyant powers.

It's easy to figure out why Canadians loved the show: not only was it funny and laced with irony, it also made an art out of taking potshots at the Americans (a winning formula for any Canadian TV show!). *Maclean's* television critic Brian D. Johnson explained the show's unique appeal in an article that ran in the magazine in January 1986: "With in-jokes about *The Journal,* Montreal's Olympic Stadium, and Toronto's WASP establishment, Del Grande makes its Canadian setting highly obvious. In fact, he goes out of his way to paint American television and pop stars as poisonous. While filming one episode, the costume crew gave Ciccone's son, Jason, a Bruce Springsteen T-shirt. Del Grande turned the incident into an on-screen joke by telling him: 'Go put on a T-shirt with a Canadian hero. Enough of this cultural imperialism.'"

Funny as the line was, the joke was actually on Canadian viewers: Del Grande was born and bred in New Jersey!

Yesterday Once More

It's true what they say: you can't go home again. Much as you might like to hop inside a flower-painted Volkswagen Beetle and take an express trip back to the 1960s, or slip into your best disco wear and relive the night life of the late 1970s or early 1980s, it simply can't be done. What you can do, however, is have fun remembering the best and worst that those decades had to offer—everything from colour television to pet rocks to deely boppers!

In this book, we've looked at the most significant social, political, economic, and cultural events of the sixties, seventies, and eighties—the good, the bad, and the ugly. Hope you've enjoyed the ride!

> **The Least You Need to Know**
>
> ➤ In December of 1983, *Chatelaine* ran an article titled "A Who's Who of Canada's Sexiest Anchormen."
>
> ➤ In 1985, the CBC decided that the time had come to pull the plug on *Reach for the Top*.
>
> ➤ *Fashion Television* debuted in 1986. It attracted millions of viewers from around the world—including a loyal following in Canadian prisons!
>
> ➤ *Seeing Things* was one of Canada's first successful comedies. It was broadcast in 40 different countries.

Glossary: A Guide to the Essential Lingo of the '60s, '70s and '80s

Aerobics A popular 1970s fitness activity that involved working out while listening to disco-type music. The typical attire—made famous by both actress Jane Fonda and actress/singer Olivia Newton John—consisted of a spandex workout suit, leg warmers, and a headband.

Agent Orange A pesticide that was used to defoliate the jungles during the Vietnam War.

Air guitar This terms refers to an imaginary guitar that is played by wannabe musicians who have more enthusiasm than equipment. The term was first coined in 1983.

ATM The fancy name for a bank machine. The ATM was invented in the U.S. in 1977, but it didn't come into common use in Canada until the 1980s. In the early years, you could only use your own bank's ATMs, something that could cause a major crisis if you were low on cash and you weren't able to find the right type of ATM.

Awesome The eighties way of saying "cool."

Baby on Board Miniature traffic caution signs that overprotective parents attached to their cars during the late 1980s.

Baby boom A period of high birth rates that lasted from the early 1950s to about 1965 in Canada.

Bad Another eighties way of saying "cool."

Biological clock A woman's awareness that she'd better start her family soon if she wants to have children. The expression came into vogue in 1978.

Black light A light bulb that makes clothes that have been washed in phosphates glow in an eerie fashion in a dark room. The effect is particularly dramatic on white clothes. Black lights were considered cool during the 1960s and 1970s.

Black power An expression used by militant black leaders who were growing impatient with the slow pace of civil rights reform in the U.S. in the 1960s.

Blended family What you got when you "blended" members of one or more separate family units into a single family unit (e.g. if two single parents who each have children marry). The most famous blended family on TV was *The Brady Bunch*. The term was first used in 1977.

Boom box A large radio or cassette deck that was typically played at top volume. The term was first used in 1976.

Branch plant syndrome When large multinational corporations opened up branch plants in Canada, but continued to make all important decision at the foreign head office.

Break dancing A form of street dancing that required elaborate gymnastic moves. The term became popular in 1976.

Burnout Physical or emotional exhaustion caused by too much work, too much information, and/or too much stress. The term became popular in 1980.

Cabbage Patch Kids A pudgy-faced doll that had parents duking it out in the toy store aisles during the early 1990s.

Camcorder A small, hand-held video camera. Camcorders were all the rage during the 1980s.

CanCon Short for "Canadian content." Refers to federal government requirements concerning the amount of Canadian content on TV or radio.

Channel surfing The "sport" enjoyed by couch potatoes. Channel surfing involves flipping from channel to channel using a remote control. The term was first coined in the early 1990s.

Cocooning The decision to stay at home and watch TV rather than dine out and catch a movie. The term was made famous by futurist Faith Popcorn in the late 1980s.

Consciousness-raising groups Organized discussion groups in which participants were encouraged to share their feelings and "vent." Consciousness-raising groups were particularly popular with women during the 1970s.

Cool Something or someone very hip. A popular expression from the 1960s onward. The word "cool" has always been, well, *cool*.

Couch potato Someone whose idea of a workout involves lifting the remote control off the coffee table. The term was first coined in 1979.

Credibility gap Growing mistrust by citizens of their government or others in authority. A much-used expression during the 1960s.

Culture shock A feeling of confusion and alienation that comes from sudden cultural change. People started talking about culture shock during the 1970s.

Day-Glo clothing Clothing containing fluorescent dye or resin that glows in ordinary daylight. Day-Glo clothing was hot during the 1960s.

Deely boppers Glitter-coated antennae people wore at parties during the 1980s. It will be up to anthropologists to explain why the deely bopper phenomenon occurred.

Designer jeans High-priced jeans with labels bearing the name of Calvin Klein, Jordache, and other 1970s designers. A prepubescent Brooke Shields sent shock waves through the advertising world when she slipped into a pair of designer jeans and purred, "Nothing comes between me and my Calvins. Nothing!" The term came into vogue during the late 1970s.

DINK Double income, no kids. (The people everyone loved to hate during the 1980s.)

Disco The hottest music trend of the 1970s music with mindless lyrics but a pulsating beat. Disco dancing involved wearing tacky Lycra and spandex "disco wear" (or three-piece white suits, if you'd managed to catch a bad case of Saturday Night Fever) and then gyrating under the strobe lights on the disco dance floor.

Disco Destruction Army A mercy mission led by kind-hearted radio deejays at Toronto's CHUM Radio around 1980. It involved the physical destruction of disco record albums.

Domestic partner Politically correct seventies-speak for the person you were living with. A synonym for "significant other." Both terms came into vogue in 1977. During the 1980s, they would be replaced with POSSLQ.

Domino theory The American government's belief that you had to prevent communism from becoming rooted in any particular country in order to prevent it from spreading to neighbouring countries. The domino theory was one of the key justifications for the Vietnam War.

Downsizing A corporate euphemism for job cuts. The term came into vogue during the early 1990s.

Draft The U.S. government's conscription of civilians to serve in the military. Young men who fled to Canada to avoid the draft during the Vietnam War were known as "draft dodgers."

Dweeb Someone who was extremely uncool. The eighties word for "nerd."

Earth shoes Funky 1970s shoes that were designed in such a way that your heel ended up being lower than your toes. They got their name because they made their grand debut on Earth Day. (Just imagine what an awful name they would have been saddled with if they'd made their debut on Groundhog Day.)

Earth tones A euphemism for downright ugly shades of gold, green, and brown. Earth tones were popular during the 1970s.

Ego-shopping Buying something because you want to own it, not because you need it. The term caught on in the late 1980s when yuppies were busy wearing the numbers off their credit cards.

Elephant pants Pants that flare out below the knee so dramatically that they're almost large enough to wrap around an elephant's ankle. Elephant pants were popular during the late 1960s.

Fanny pack A nylon pouch that was strapped around the waist and that could hold such essentials as your wallet, your cellular phone, and your keys. Even men wore fanny packs when they were at their peak of popularity (around 1987).

Feminine mystique Unhappy housewife syndrome as described by American journalist Betty Friedan in her1963 bestseller *The Feminine Mystique.*

Fuddle duddle What Prime Minister Pierre Elliott Trudeau claimed he was saying in the House of Commons when he was accused of uttering an obscenity in 1971.

GI Joe A soldier action figure. GI Joes were a popular toy during the 1960s until Dr. Spock (the pediatrician, not Mr. Spock, the *Star Trek* dude) spoke out against them.

Gag me with a spoon Valley Girl–speak for "yuck." A term that had a blissfully short life during the early 1980s.

Gauchos Midcalf-length shorts that looked like a cross between regular shorts and elephant pants. Gauchos were the extreme opposite of hot pants.

Gay power The rallying cry of the homosexual community.

Generic products No-name products that claimed to be every bit as good as their brand name equivalents. Dave Nichol of Loblaw's was responsible for getting Canadians hooked on generic products during the 1970s.

Go-go boots White leather midcalf boots that were worn by nightclub cage dancers and women who thought they were hot stuff during the 1960s. Go-go boots were immortalized by Nancy Sinatra's song "These Boots Are Made For Walkin'."

Going ballistic An expression that meant that someone was going off the deep end. The term became popular in 1984.

Granny glasses Half-frame eyeglasses that were popular during the late 1960s.

Granny dresses Dowdy, ankle-length dresses that were popular for a brief period during the late 1960s. Granny dresses were believed to be a backlash against the mini-skirt.

Great White North A satirical "CanCon" segment on the hot 1970s and 1980s comedy show *SCTV.* The segments featured Bob and Doug McKenzie, two beer-drinking hosers.

Groovy Another word for "cool." A popular expression during the 1960s and early 1970s, but a decidedly uncool expression after that point. Anyone who used the word "groovy" after 1975 was viewed as a burnt-out hippie.

Gross Something repulsive. A popular expression during the 1970s.

Hacker A computer geek. The term became popular around 1976.

Haight-Ashbury A San Francisco community popular with drug users in the 1960s.

Hair mousse Shaving cream–like foam that you applied to your hair in order to add volume. Hair mousse was extremely popular around 1984.

Hamburger Helper An instant casserole mix that allowed budget-conscious homemakers to get the maximum amount of mileage out of a pound of hamburger. Hamburger Helper was particularly popular during the early 1970s when meat prices skyrocketed.

Happy face A grinning yellow smile that showed up on buttons, TV shirts, and other seventies paraphernalia.

Have a cow To get overly excited about something. Popular in the late 1980s.

Heritage Trust Fund An Alberta fund that was financed with royalties from oil sales during the 1970s. The purpose of the fund was to help to diversify the province's resource oriented economy.

Hippies A term coined in the mid-sixties to describe young people with long hair, beards, and other unconventional clothing, who belonged to the counterculture.

Hoser An insult made famous by Bob and Doug McKenzie of *Great White North* fame during the early 1980s.

Hot tub An oversized bathtub, big enough to entertain your friends in.

Hot pants Scandalously short shorts made of leather, lace, ranch mink, velvet, satin, denim, and other racy fabrics. Hot pants were popular during the early 1970s.

Hot Something or someone that's very, very "cool." Also something that has been stolen, as in "I think that stereo's hot."

House music Heavily repetitive disco-style music.

Infomercial Television commercials that almost sounded like real TV shows. *Almost.* Infomercials became increasingly popular after 1983. By the late 1980s, when home shopping channels were all the rage, it was possible to tune in to a network that offered 24 hour a day content-free programming!

Insider's Report A flyer that Loblaw's put out to promote the chain's high-end "President's Choice" grocery products. *The Insider's Report* was first published during the 1980s.

Jackie Kennedy look Clothing, accessories, and hairstyles that attempted to mimic the super-chic look of Jacqueline Kennedy, wife of John F. Kennedy. The look was particularly popular in 1961, the year that the Kennedys moved into the White House.

Jesus freaks Hippies who turned to Christianity. Formally known as members of "The Jesus People movement," Jesus freaks captured the public's attention from about 1969 to 1974. After that, they disappeared from sight.

Karaoke Getting up in a bar and singing Top 40 hits after you've had one too many beers. The fad—which came to North America via Japan—was particularly popular in 1988.

Lame A person, place, or thing that was totally uninspiring. The term became popular in the late 1980s.

Lava lamp A tall, skinny lamp which was filled with semi-solid wax that bubbled away as it was heated with a coil. Lava lamps were considered to be the height of cool during the 1960s. (Of course, everyone was stoned at that time, so they didn't exactly have Martha Stewart–like decorating sense.) Also known as Lava Lites.

Macramé A popular 1970s craft that involved tying a series of knots to make wall-hangings, potholders, vests, and other items.

Mall chick A girl who lived at the mall. The term became popular during the 1980s.

Mall rat A teenager who spent a great deal of time hanging out at the mall. The term was coined in 1981.

Me generation A time when it was okay to engage in some heavy-duty navel-gazing because you were supposed to be the centre of your own universe.

Media event An occasion manufactured to give journalists the necessary photo opportunities and sound bites (quotable quotes). The expression was invented in 1976.

Midlife crisis That awful realization that you're not getting any younger. The term became popular in 1974, following the publication of Gail Sheehy's book *Passages*.

Mommy track The notion that you can't "have it all"—that women who choose to have families will be seen as less committed to their jobs as women who choose to pass on motherhood. The term became popular in 1987.

Monokini A bikini without the top. A 1960s thing.

Mood ring A ring with a clear quartz stone that was filled with liquid crystals, and that supposedly changed colours to reflected the wearer's mood. If you were feeling calm and tranquil, the ring turned blue. If you were angry, it turned purple. Or at least that was the theory. A lot of Canadian mood ring wearers learned the hard way that frigid temperatures could cause the ring to stay grey for months at a time! Mood rings were popular around 1975.

Moral majority Members of the religious right. The term was coined in 1979 to refer to Jerry Falwell and his followers.

Munsinger affair Canada's first major parliamentary sex scandal, which involved the associate minister of National Defence and a German prostitute. The scandal caused waves during the early 1960s.

Muzak Mind-numbingly bland music that was played in elevators and over the public address systems in department stores.

Nerd Someone who was extremely uncool. This term would be replaced by *dweeb* during the 1980s.

Networking The art of making business contacts. The term became popular in 1986.

New wave The kind of heavily synthesized music performed by groups like Gary Numan and Blondie during the early 1980s.

Noname products See "Generic products."

Not! A nifty linguistic device that allowed you to make an untrue statement and then immediately contradict yourself. Example "Disco is cool. *Not!*" First used during the "Wayne's World" segments of *Saturday Night Live* in the 1980s.

Ookpik An owl-like furry toy that Canada shared with the world during the 1960s.

Outing The act of forcing someone to admit that he or she is a homosexual by threatening to go public with the news. The term started being used around 1990.

Painter's pants Pants with a loop that was supposed to hold your hammer or paint brush; and a bunch of nifty pockets for school supplies, lunch money, and so on. Painter's pants were popular around 1976.

Pencil you in Late 1980s yuppie-speak for setting up an appointment. Example "I'll pencil you in for lunch on Friday."

Personal computer The 1980s term for computers in the home. Before that the prevalent term was microcomputer.

Personal trainer A fitness coach who works with clients on a one-to-one basis. Celebrities started using the services of personal trainers in 1975. They soon became the *de rigueur* fitness accessory for the rich and not-so-famous, too.

Pet rocks A 1975 fad that was the brainchild of California advertising executive Gary Dahl. Their key selling point was the fact that, unlike conventional pets, they didn't need to be walked or paper-trained, and they weren't likely to rack up a lot of bills in the pet food or vet bill departments.

Phat Yet another '80s way to say "cool." (Just how many words did one decade need for "cool"?)

Platform shoes Clunky shoes that featured heels that went as high as seven inches off the ground. The hottest thing in footwear during the mid-1970s.

Politically correct Saying anything that was potentially controversial in the blandest, least offensive way possible—even if the meaning ended up getting lost along the way. The term was first used in the 1960s (at which point it was considered a *good* thing!), but didn't become part of daily conversation until the 1980s.

Polyester leisure suit An alternative to the more formal business suit. Usually manufactured out of pastel-coloured polyester. Trendy in the mid-1970s.

Pong An early video game played on a TV set. It resembled a game of ping pong, except that it wasn't quite that exciting. Pong was popular in the 1970s—when there weren't any other electronic games!

Population explosion The belief that birth rates were skyrocketing and the world would soon be overpopulated. The population explosion was a big concern around 1970.

POSSLQ Stood for "persons of opposite sex sharing living quarters." A more polite way of saying "live in" during the 1980s.

Power breakfast A business networking session that was held over breakfast. Power breakfasts promised to be the key to corporate success in the 1980s.

Preppie A yuppie in training. Someone who wouldn't dream of stepping out of the house unless he or she was wearing a Lacoste shirt (complete with alligator insignia), neat-looking cotton pants, a cloth belt, and deck shoes. Preppies were ostracized by non-preppies during the early 1980s.

Psychedelic drugs Illegal drugs which produce vivid, colourful hallucinations.

Pumping iron Weight lifting. The term came into vogue in 1977, following the release of *Pumping Iron*, a documentary about Mr. Universe himself, Arnold Schwarzenegger.

Punk rock look A look that involved body piercing, shaving your hair into a Mohawk, wearing dog collars and dog chains, and parading around in black clothing like Sid Vicious and Johnny Rotten of Sex Pistols fame. The aim was to offend, and punk rockers usually succeeded. Punk rock was popular in the late 1970s.

Quality time The belief that it's not how much time you spend with your children, but rather the quality of the time that counts. The term was coined in 1977, just as large number of women with young children began re-entering the paid labour force.

Quiet Revolution The period from 1960 to 1968 when Quebec went through a process of rapid modernization.

Rad Very, very cool. An eighties term.

Reaganomics U.S. President Reagan's economic policies. (See also "supply-side economics.")

Restructuring A euphemism for downsizing. Definitely eighties-speak!

Rubik's cube A puzzle. A plastic handheld cube made up of smaller cubes covered with coloured stickers. The idea was to manipulate the small cubes so that each side of the larger cube displayed only one colour. Rubik's cubes were very popular during the early 1980s.

Second shift The shift on the home front that a working woman puts in after she's worked from nine to five.

Sexual revolution The liberalization of sexual morality.

Share To make a personal revelation to members of a support group. Example: "I have something to share with the group." The term came into vogue in about 1978 when people were busy rushing off to their consciousness-raising groups.

Significant other Politically correct seventies-speak for the person you were living with. A synonym for domestic partner. Both terms came into vogue in 1977. In the 1980s, the terms would be replaced with the more cryptic POSSLQ.

Slam dancing A form of dancing that involved slamming your body into someone else's. An early '80s phenomenon.

Solar panels Glass panels that were installed in your home to capture the heat of the sun. Popular during the 1970s.

Sound bite A catchy phrase uttered in front of the TV cameras. The term came into vogue during the 1980s.

Space cadet Someone who was so clued out that they seemed to have gone to another planet. A popular 1980s insult.

Spaz Someone totally uncoordinated. Another 1980s insult.

Spazzing Getting overly excited about something. A much-used expression during the 1980s.

Spin doctor A public relations professional who seeks to alter the public's perception of an event by providing the right presentation. A 1980s term.

String bikini Three small, strategically placed triangles of cloth that were held on a woman's body with pieces of string. Women who were particularly brave actually attempted to swim in the things. String bikinis were popular during the early 1970s.

Summer of Love The 1967 gathering at Haight-Ashbury.

Sunscreen The politically correct 1980s term for suntan lotion.

Superball A small, hard, rubber ball manufactured by WhamO, which bounces very high. A popular toy during the 1960s.

Superhypermost Janis Joplin's description of life on drugs.

Supply-side economics A 1980s theory that states that the economy will thrive if you stimulate the production of goods and services and keep taxes low. See "Reaganomics."

Surrogate mother A woman who carries a fertilized egg in her uterus on behalf of another woman. The term became popular during the 1980s.

Test-tube baby A baby who is conceived outside the mother's body. The term was used after the birth in 1978 of Louise Brown, the world's first test-tube baby.

Thalidomide A sleep-inducing drug used in the early 1960s that was found to produce skeletal defects in developing babies.

Tie-dyed look Random, coloured patterns on fabric that were created by dyeing or bleaching scrunched/rolled up fabric so that only some of the fabric was affected by the colour change.

Toe socks Gloves that you wore on your feet. Horribly uncomfortable and unspeakably ugly.

Trivial Pursuit The hottest board game of the 1980s—and a Canadian invention no less!

Troll dolls Ugly little dolls that high school girls and college women carried around for luck during the 1960s.

Trophy wife A woman who is prized for her youth and good looks by a husband who is old enough to be her father. The term came into vogue in 1984.

Trudeaumania The Canadian public's enthusiastic support of Pierre Elliott Trudeau during the election of 1968.

Tubular Valley Girl–speak for something totally cool. Undeniably eighties!

Turn on, tune in, drop out The catchphrase of drug guru and ex-Harvard professor Timothy Leary. Leary encouraged people to get in touch with "the universe within," connect with the world around them; and take a break from work, school, or whatever prevents getting in touch with themselves. Definitely a sixties term.

Twister A party game in which players twist into pretzel-like contortions to follow game moves on a large, multicolour polkadot plastic sheet that is placed on the floor. A sixties thing.

User-friendly Something that is easy to use. The term was popularized by the computer industry after 1982.

Valley girl A spoiled teenage girl living in California's San Fernando Valley. The term was popularized in the 1982 song *Valley Girl*, performed by Frank Zappa's daughter Moon Unit Zappa. Over time, the term was used to describe any vacuous pampered princess, regardless of where she lived.

Veg To do nothing; to make like a vegetable. People were into vegging during the eighties.

Virtual reality A computer-generated version of reality. The term was first used in 1989.

Walkman The brand name for Sony's brand of personal stereo. The term became popular after 1979.

Wannabe Someone who wants to be someone or something else. The term became popular in 1985.

Watergate The scandal that led to U.S. President Nixon's resignation in August of 1974.

Woodstock An outdoor musical concert that ran from August 15 to 17, 1969, on a farmer's field near the hamlet of Woodstock in New York State. People who came of age during the 1960s are frequently referred to as "the Woodstock generation" because the weekend of peace and love symbolized all that was good about the 1960s.

Timeline: 1960 to 1990

1960

Only in Canada...

– A Gallup poll reveals that 95 percent of Canadians are happy with their lives.

– University of Western Ontario sociologist William Mann reports that there is no sexual revolution on Canadian campuses: only 13 percent of female students and 35 percent of male students have ever had sex.

Fads and Trends

– The first oral contraceptive hits the U.S. market on August 18.

– More than 90 percent of Canadians are able to tune in to one or more of the 59 TV stations broadcasting in Canada.

– Two-thirds of Canadian households have one car and 10 percent have two or more cars.

– Drinks are packaged in aluminum cans in the U.S.

– Felt-tipped pens hit the market.

– *The Financial Post* tells male executives that they're likely to get better suits if they let their wives do the choosing.

Politics and Economics

– *The Financial Post* asks if MPs are overpaid at $10,000 per year.

– Nearly 75 percent of foreign investment in Canada comes from a single source: the United States.

- The Liberal Party comes to power in Quebec on June 22, signalling the start of the Quiet Revolution.
- In the U.S. presidential campaign, Kennedy ends up defeating Richard Nixon by a mere 113,000 votes out of the 68,800,000 that were cast.
- A U.S. reconnaissance airplane is shot down over the U.S.S.R.

Entertainment and Sports

- A Montreal bookseller is convicted of peddling obscene material for selling D.H. Lawrence's critically acclaimed novel *Lady Chatterley's Lover*.
- The hottest movies in the theatres are *Psycho*, *Exodus*, and The *Apartment*.
- *The Apartment* walks away with Best Picture honours at the Academy Awards.
- North Americans are reading *Born Free* and *The Rise and Fall of the Third Reich*.

Science and Technology

- U.S. launches the first weather satellite to monitor global cloud cover.
- The caesarean rate in Canada is 5 percent. By the late 1980s, it will have risen to about 25 percent.

Etc.

- Princess Margaret marries.
- Prince Andrew is born.

1961

Only in Canada...

- Canadians spend $60 million on their gardens and $200 million on sporting gear.
- Canadians buy five million packs of playing cards.
- One-third to one-half of the residents of Canadian suburbs are children.
- Average weekly wages range from a low of $57.03 in Prince Edward Island to a high of $85.20 in Ontario.

Fads and Trends

- The electric toothbrush is invented.
- Procter and Gamble invents the world's first disposable diaper, which is marketed under the brand name Pampers.
- The Twist is the hottest dance craze.

Politics and Economics

- Republican Dwight D. Eisenhower is defeated by Democrat John F. Kennedy, who becomes the 35th President of the United States.
- Cuba is invaded at the Bay of Pigs by rebels trained and supplied by the U.S.
- The Berlin Wall divides the city on August 13.

Entertainment and Sports

- *West Side Story* wins Best Picture honours at the Academy Awards
- The hottest movies in the theatres are *Breakfast at Tiffany's*, *One-eyed Jacks*, *Guns of Navarone*, *West Side Story*, *Judgment at Nuremberg*, *Splendor in the Grass*, and *The Parent Trap*.
- Canada's first private broadcaster, CTV, is licensed.
- People are reading *The Agony and The Ecstasy*, *Black Like Me*, *To Kill a Mockingbird*, and *Catch-22*.
- The Chicago Blackhawks win the Stanley Cup.

Science and Technology

- IBM introduces the Selectric typewriter.
- The U.S. sends a chimpanzee into space.
- Astronaut Alan Shepard becomes the first American in space.
- Soviet cosmonaut Yuri Gagarin orbits the Earth.
- The perinatal mortality rate in Canada is 28 per thousand. By 1992, this figure will have dropped to 7 per thousand.
- Thalidomide is approved for use in Canada on April 1.

Etc.

- Lego comes to Canada.
- Mattel brings Barbie's boyfriend Ken to life.

1962

Only in Canada...

- *Maclean's* predicts that by the year 2000, Canadians will have twice as many leisure hours as working hours.
- Canadians are spending a billion dollars a year on liquor.
- The last hanging takes place in Canada at Toronto's Don Jail on December 11 when Ronald Turpin and Arthur Lucas are executed for murder.

Fads and Trends

- A Harvard University psychology instructor named Timothy Leary experiments with LSD for the first time.
- *The Financial Post* describes an exciting new innovation in infant wear: the sleeper!
- The Mashed Potato is the hottest dance craze.
- Frisbees hit the Canadian market.

Politics and Economics

- The Canadian dollar is worth 92.5 cents U.S.
- Wal-Mart opens for business in the U.S.

– Over 16,000 U.S. troops are called in to help ensure the safety of the first black student to enroll at the University of Mississippi.

– The Cuban missile crisis lasts from October 22 to 28. During this time, Canadians wonder if they're going to be caught in a war between the two superpowers.

Entertainment and Sports

– *Lawrence of Arabia* is voted Best Picture at the Academy Awards.

– The hottest movies in the theatres are *The Miracle Worker, The Manchurian Candidate,* and *How the West Was Won.*

– People are reading *One Flew over the Cuckoo's Nest, Sex and the Single Girl, Silent Spring, Ship of Fools,* and *Happiness is a Warm Puppy.*

– Johnny Carson becomes host of *The Tonight Show.*

– The Toronto Maple Leafs win the Stanley Cup.

Science and Technology

– September 29th, Canada launches Alouette I—the first of four Canadian satellites to be launched under an agreement signed with the U.S. National Aeronautics and Space Administration (NASA).

– The federal government begins forcibly removing thalidomide from pharmacies across the country in April.

– The Canadian Bankers Association publishes its first standards and specifications for the magnetic encoding of cheques.

– Marshall McLuhan writes *The Gutenberg Galaxy,* a book which describes the cultural transformations caused by print technology.

– *Saturday Night* magazine warns that by 2026, there wouldn't even be enough standing room on the surface of the earth for all the planet's inhabitants.

Etc.

– Movie star Marilyn Monroe commits suicide at 36.

1963

Only in Canada...

– Pierre Berton scandalizes the readers of *Maclean's* magazine by speaking out in favour of premarital sex.

– *Maclean's* reports that one Canadian student in three doesn't get beyond grade eight and that seven out of ten don't finish high school.

– *Chatelaine* runs an article on the effects of nuclear war on children.

Fads and Trends

– High school girls and college women start carrying around troll dolls as good luck charms.

Politics and Economics

– Liberal Lester B. Pearson takes over as Prime Minister from Progressive Conservative John G. Diefenbaker.
– Martin Luther King Jr. organizes the massive March on Washington, where he gives his famous "I have a dream" speech.
– Police in Birmingham, Alabama, arrest 1,000 civil rights protesters on May 6.
– U.S. President John F. Kennedy is assassinated in Dallas on November 22. Following JFK's assassination, Vice President Lyndon B. Johnson begins his six years as U.S. President.
– The U.S., U.S.S.R., and Great Britain sign a nuclear test ban treaty.

Entertainment and Sports

– Lorne Greene records an album, which is panned by *Maclean's* magazine.
– The hottest movies in the theatres are *The Birds, Lawrence of Arabia, Dr. No,* and *Cleopatra.*
– *Tom Jones* walks away with Best Picture honours at the Academy Awards.
– Betty Friedan's book *The Feminine Mystique* is published.
– People are also reading *Travels with Charley, Seven Days in May,* and *The American Way of Death.*
– The Toronto Maple Leafs win the Stanley Cup.
– The first metal tennis racket is patented in the U.S.

Science and Technology

– The world's first female astronaut, Russian Valentina Tereshkova, makes a three-day space flight.
– *The Financial Post* reports that 24 of the top 30 universities in Canada have installed computers.
– Touch-tone telephones and cassette tape recorders debut in the U.S.

Etc.

– A Roper poll indicates that 36 percent of Americans believe that TV is a more reliable source of news than newspapers. Only 24 percent believe that newspapers are more reliable.
– Lever Brothers airs a Wisk detergent advertisement that features a black boy and a white boy at play.
– Weight Watchers International is incorporated.

1964

Only in Canada...

– A Gallup Poll reveals that nearly half of Canadians are concerned about the amount of American investment in Canada.
– Canada's Ookpik owl achieves international fame.

Fads and Trends

– The topless bikini (or "monokini") is invented.

– The miniskirt and the "mod" look are in fashion.

– Paris designers introduce the "see-through dress." Chandler's on Toronto's Bloor Street manages to sell 2,000 of the dresses.

– GI Joe invades the toy store shelves. Over 2 million GI Joes are sold in North America within a year.

– The Swim and the Watusi are the hottest dance crazes.

Politics and Economics

– 31 percent of Canadian workers are women.

– The federal government begins to issue Social Insurance Numbers (SINs) to Canadians.

  Martin Luther King Jr. receives the Nobel Peace Prize for his civil rights work.

Entertainment and Sports

– *My Fair Lady* wins Best Picture honours at the Academy Awards.

– The hottest movies in the theatres are *Tom Jones, Zorba the Greek,* and *Dr. Strangelove.*

– *This Hour Has Seven Days* debuts on the CBC television network on October 4.

– 73 million North Americans tune in to watch the Beatles appear on *The Ed Sullivan Show.*

– People are reading *John Lennon in His Own Write, The Spy Who Came in from the Cold,* and *A Moveable Feast.*

– Marshall McLuhan writes *Understanding Media*—a book that brings him international fame.

– The Toronto Maple Leafs win the Stanley Cup.

– Instant replays are used for the first time in sports broadcasting.

– Cassius Marcellus Clay (who will later become known as Muhammad Ali) tells reporters that he is "the greatest" and then goes on to defeat world heavyweight champ Sonny Liston.

– Olympic Games held in Tokyo.

Etc.

– Elizabeth Taylor and Richard Burton wed.

1965

Only in Canada...

– The University of British Columbia is starting to provide its students with information about birth control.

– A Quebec City law prohibiting women from displaying their thighs in public is still being enforced. Women are giving written warnings that tell them to "cover your thighs or risk a fine of $100 or three months in jail."

– A United Church survey of 1,700 laymen and 347 ministers concludes that "traditional religious beliefs are breaking down faster than ever."

Fads & Trends

– Chatty Cathy is the doll that every little girl wants to own.

– The hottest new toys are GI Joe and the Superball

– Twister is invented.

– Thirty million dollars worth of skateboards are sold in the U.S.

– Lava lamps are hot.

Politics & Economics

– Canada's new flag, the Maple Leaf, is officially proclaimed on February 15.

– The country's gross national product soars past the $50 billion mark for the first time ever.

– Pierre Elliott Trudeau joins the federal Liberal Party.

– Anti-Vietnam protestors burn their draft cards as a symbol of their opposition to the war. In Canada, peace activists carry signs that read "End Canadian Complicity."

Entertainment & Sports

– Pierre Berton sends shock waves through church circles when he writes *The Comfortable Pew: A Critical Look at the Church in the New Age.*

– People are reading *The Source, The Autobiography of Malcolm X,* and *Dune.*

– The hottest movies in the theatres are *My Fair Lady, Dr. Zhivago,* and *The Pawnbroker.*

– *The Sound of Music* walks away with Best Picture honours at the Academy Awards.

– The Beatles' *Help!* becomes the world's first music video.

– Ninety-six percent of NBC's nighttime schedule is being broadcast in colour.

– The Montreal Canadiens win the Stanley Cup.

Science & Technology

– An airplane flies around the world over both poles for the first time ever.

– Consumer advocate Ralph Nader writes *Unsafe at Any Speed,* an indictment of the poor safety standards of the automotive industry.

Etc.

– A malfunctioning relay switch in Ontario blacks out 30 million in Canada and the U.S.

– The Canada–U.S. Automotive Products Agreement creates a single North America–wide market for cars, trucks, buses, tires, and automobile parts.

– Black activist Malcolm X is assassinated.

– The Hare Krishna arrive in the U.S.

1966

Only in Canada

– Eighty-six percent of Canadians have a clothes washer, but only 25 percent have a clothes dryer. Just 23 percent have a freezer and 3 percent a dishwasher.

- "Colour television is a nice gimmick, a very nice gimmick indeed, but it isn't that much of an improvement over black and white," writes Peter Gzowski in *Maclean's* magazine.
- In August, *The Globe and Mail* observes that Canada is experiencing "a curious mood of rebellion, of irresponsibility, of resentment" and that "Canadians are doubting all former stable things."
- *The Financial Post* predicts that "perhaps as many as one third of all the cars in Canada" will have air-conditioners in the future.
- Canada has a greater percentage of its population under the age of 15 than any other Western nation.
- There are five million school-aged children in Canada—twice as many as there were in 1952.
- Canada gets its first topless dancers at a bar called the Cat's Whisker in Vancouver.

Fads & Trends
- The miniskirt arrives from Great Britain.

Politics & Economics
- The price of silver increases dramatically, which means that coins containing silver are actually worth more than their face value. The Royal Mint decides to cut the percentage of silver in coins to just 50 percent.
- Prime Minister Lester B. Pearson establishes the Royal Commission on the Status of Women.

Entertainment & Sports
- CBC's first colour broadcast occurs on October 1, 1966.
- People are reading *In Cold Blood* and Masters and Johnson's *Human Sexual Response*.
- Marshall McLuhan writes *War and Peace in the Global Village*.
- The hottest movie in the theatres is *The Sound of Music*.
- *A Man for All Seasons* walks away with Best Picture honours at the Academy Awards.
- Nancy Sinatra's hit single "These Boots Are Made for Walkin'" helps to move truckloads of white leather go-go boots.
- *This Hour Has Seven Days* goes off the air.
- A study sponsored by the National Association of Broadcasters reveals that 63 percent of those surveyed would prefer commercial-free television.
- The Montreal Canadiens win the Stanley Cup.

Science & Technology
- The chemical structure of DNA is discovered.

Etc.
- Indira Gandhi becomes Prime Minister of India.

1967

Only in Canada...

– Canada's national anthem—*O Canada*—is approved by Parliament.

– Canada celebrates its 100th birthday. The country embarks on a year-long celebration, the highlight of which is Expo '67 in Montreal, which attracts 50 million visitors.

– *Maclean's* magazine reports that fathers are welcome in the delivery room at St. Joseph's Hospital in Hamilton, Ontario.

– A poll published in *Maclean's* magazine reveals that Canadians are as divided about the Vietnam War as their neighbours to the south.

– Canadian hippies hang out in Toronto's Yorkville Village.

– Illicit drug use becomes increasingly popular with young Canadians, many of whom make the trek to Haight-Ashbury, San Francisco, so that they can be part of the so-called Summer of Love.

Fads & Trends

– Day-Glo paint colours are hot.

– Hot Wheels are invented.

– A British model named Twiggy redefines what it means to be thin.

Politics & Economics

– Canada celebrates its Centennial.

– Pierre Elliott Trudeau becomes the federal minister of justice.

– The Royal Commission on the Status of Women is formally established.

– The Six-Day War breaks out in the Middle East.

– The Royal Bank is the first chartered bank involved in sponsoring the launch of a new mutual fund. The fund is called Royfund.

Entertainment & Sports

– People are reading *The Confessions of Nat Turner, Death of a President,* and *The New Industrial State.*

– Vancouver Sun columnist Simma Holt (later a Liberal MP) writes *Sex and the Teenage Revolution,* a book that is peppered with colourful firsthand accounts of sex, drugs, alcohol abuse, crime, and broken families.

– The hottest movies in the theatres are *Cool Hand Luke, The Graduate,* and *Bonnie and Clyde.*

– *In the Heat of the Night* (directed by Canadian Norman Jewison) walks away with Best Picture honours at the Academy Awards.

– Gordon Lightfoot's *Canadian Railroad Trilogy* is first heard on the CBC on January 1.

– *Mr. Dressup* hits the airwaves.

– The Toronto Maple Leafs win the Stanley Cup.

– Mickey Mantle of the New York Yankees hits his 500th career home run.

– Muhammad Ali refuses to enlist in the Vietnam War for religious reasons.

Etc.

– The National Library opens in Ottawa.

1968

Only in Canada...

– CBC TV gives a Penman's underwear commercial the thumbs down, ruling that "No treatment could make a men's underwear commercial acceptable at the present time."

Fads & Trends

– Ouija boards are outselling Monopoly games.

– Hot, psychedelic Day-Glo colours are all the rage.

– Nehru jackets are very popular.

– Waterbeds and jacuzzis are introduced.

Politics & Economics

– Liberal Pierre Elliott Trudeau becomes the country's prime minister.

– The federal government changes section 208 of the Criminal Code, which outlawed abortions except when the procedure was necessary in order to save a woman's life. A woman can now obtain an abortion if she can prove to a hospital abortion committee that an unwanted pregnancy is damaging her mental health.

– The Watkins Task Force releases a report titled *Foreign Ownership and the Structure of Canadian Industry*. The report recommends the creation of a special agency to deal with multinational corporations.

– The Tet offensive in February signals a turning point in the Vietnam War. The American public is no longer behind the war.

– On May 16th, an American infantry company led by Lieutenant William L. Calley marches into the South Vietnamese hamlet of My Lai, slaughtering 347 unarmed civilians—mainly old men, women, and children. The American public doesn't learn of the attrocities for another year and a half.

– Four Canadian chartered banks launch Chargex, a nationally recognized credit card that gives consumers the freedom to charge their purchases regardless of where they decide to shop.

Entertainment & Sports

– People are reading *Airport*, *Soul on Ice*, and *Myra Breckinridge*.

– *Oliver!* wins Best Picture honours at the Academy Awards.

– The hottest movies in the theatres are *The Good, the Bad, and the Ugly*; *2001*; and *Yellow Submarine*.

– The Canadian Radio-Television Commission (CRTC) is created under new broadcast legislation.

– The Montreal Canadiens win the Stanley Cup.

Science & Technology

– A single silicon chip can hold 256 bits of RAM—more RAM than a room-sized computer had been able to hold just a few years earlier.

Etc.

– Pediatrician and author Dr. Spock is convicted of aiding draft dodgers and is sentenced to two years in jail, but doesn't end up serving any time.

– Martin Luther King, Jr., is assassinated in Memphis, Tennessee, on April 4.

– Senator Robert Kennedy announces his candidacy for the Democratic presidential nomination but is assassinated immediately after giving his victory speech in the California Democratic primary.

1969

Only in Canada...

– *Chatelaine* asks a matchmaker to help identify the traits that would make up the perfect mate for the newly elected PM.

– *The Financial Post* reports that a national postal code system is in the works for Canada.

– Montreal Mayor Jean Drapeau is forced to call in the Canadian army to help keep the peace when all but 47 of the city's 3,780-member police force go on strike.

Fads & Trends

– The Jesus People movement begins. Within five years, it has all but disappeared.

Politics & Economics

– Revenue Canada rules that turkeys that are given to employees at Christmas time must be reported on the individual T4 slips as gifts. Bah, humbug!

– The Official Languages Act is passed.

– The divorce laws are changed to include the grounds of cruelty, desertion, and simple "marital breakdown."

– After making his now-famous statement that the state has no business in the bedrooms of the nation, Prime Minister Pierre Elliott Trudeau ushers in legislative changes that remove some of the restrictions against homosexual relationships between consenting adults.

– After Johnson's term, Republican Richard M. Nixon is elected U.S. President.

– The Bank of Montreal becomes the first Canadian bank to offer a discount to senior citizens.

– Ford is selling 23 models of cars in Canada, one-third of which are huge luxury vehicles.

– The total credit debt in Canada has jumped from $223 per person in 1960 to $515 per person.

Entertainment & Sports

– People are reading *Portnoy's Complaint, The Peter Principle, The Godfather,* and *Slaughterhouse Five.*

– The hottest movies in the theatres are *Oliver!, Midnight Cowboy,* and *Butch Cassidy and the Sundance Kid.*

– *Midnight Cowboy* wins Best Picture honours at the Academy Awards.

– *The Brady Bunch* goes on the air.

– The Public Broadcasting Service is launched in the U.S. One of its first programs is a highly acclaimed children's show called *Sesame Street.*

– The Woodstock rock concert attracts 400,000 young people to a farm in upstate New York. The concert runs from August 15 to August 17.

– The Montreal Canadiens win the Stanley Cup.

Science & Technology

– Astronauts Neil Armstrong and Edwin E. Aldrin, Jr., become the first human beings to walk on the moon on July 20. Canadian Prime Minister Pierre Elliot Trudeau has this to say: "Man has reached out and touched the tranquil moon. May that high achievement allow man to rediscover the earth and find peace."

– Neiman-Marcus is advertising a "kitchen computer" in its Christmas catalogue. The price? An eye-popping $10,600!

– There are 225 million telephones in use around the world.

Etc.

– Beatle John Lennon goes to Ottawa to meet with Trudeau.

– The world's population reaches 3.5 billion.

– Charles Manson and some of his followers are indicted for the murder of actress Sharon Tate and four others.

1970

Only in Canada...

– CRTC vice-chairman Harry Boyle tells *Maclean's* magazine that Canadian broadcasters had "goddamn better" improve the quality of Canadian programming "or else there'll be no broadcasting system."

– Ottawa television station CJOH airs an interview in January in which the dreaded "f-word" is used no fewer than 19 times. They learn the hard way that the Canadian public isn't quite ready to hear it.

– There are only half as many Canadian children attending Sunday school as there were in 1960.

Fads & Trends

– Midcalf-length dresses, coats, and skirts are in fashion.

– There are 231 million television sets in use around the world.

Politics & Economics

– A mere two years after Trudeau was swept to power, the shine is coming off Trudeaumania.
– A White Paper formally states the federal government's intention to switch to the metric system.
– Students protesting the Vietnam War are shot and killed by the U.S. National Guard at Kent State University and Jackson State University in Mississippi.
– Trudeau recognizes the People's Republic of China.
– The October Crisis in Quebec leads Trudeau to invoke the War Measures Act.

Entertainment & Sports

– *Patton* walks away with Best Picture honours at the Academy Awards.
– The top-rated show on American TV is *Rowan and Martin's Laugh In*.
– "Bridge over Troubled Water" is at the top of the charts in the U.S.
– Rock star Elton John makes his North American debut on August 25.
– The first New York Marathon is held.
– The Boston Bruins win the Stanley Cup.

Science & Technology

– The first Earth Day is held on April 22.

Etc.

– *Maclean's* columnist Walter Stewart accuses Canada of being "the butcher's helper" in Vietnam. He's angry about the behind-the-scenes role that Canada is playing in the war.
– *Chatelaine* publishes an article titled "We Lived with a Computer," which describes a family's firsthand experiences with a home computer.
– More than three-quarters of Canadians believe that working women with young children should not work outside the home.

1971

Only in Canada...

– *Chatelaine* magazine publishes Barbara Frum's list of "insider tips" on how to get women elected to Parliament. One of the tips is "Marry a man who's already there and become his widow."
– Reliable Toys—a Canadian-owned toy manufacturer—runs a series of print advertisements explaining why it doesn't use television to advertise its products to children: "Instead of spending millions building up your child's hopes with TV commericals and then letting them down, we spend our time and money making toys that kids love."

Fads & Trends

– Hot pants (short shorts for women) are popular throughout the winter months. (Go figure!)

Politics & Economics

- Canada and the People's Republic of China exchange diplomatic envoys.
- The Trudeau government creates the position of Secretary of State for Multiculturalism.
- The federal government introduces legislation that allows women on maternity leave to collect 15 weeks of unemployment insurance benefits.
- Between 100 and 200 gay activists go to Parliament Hill in Ottawa to draw attention to "the demands and grievances of homosexual citizens."
- On August 15th, U.S. President Richard Nixon takes the U.S. currency off the gold standard and introduces a series of protective measures designed to jump-start the ailing American economy. Trudeau decides to fight fire with fire and introduces his own program of economic nationalism.
- Two-thirds of Americans want their government to pull out of the war in Vietnam.

Entertainment & Sports

- TVOntario launches *Polka Dot Door,* a half-hour children's program that features an oversized puppet named Polkaroo. Polkaroo is mocked by adults until a better victim comes along, a purple dinosaur named Barney.
- The Canadian Radio and Television Commission forces stiffer Canadian-content quotas on the country's broadcasters.
- *The French Connection* walks away with Best Picture honours at the Academy Awards.
- The top-rated show on American TV is *Marcus Welby, M.D.*
- *The Ed Sullivan Show* goes off the air after a legendary 23-year run.
- The publisher of *Prevention* magazine drops dead on *The Dick Cavett Show* after boasting, "I am so healthy, I expect to live on and on."
- On January 12, *All in the Family* debuts.
- Television commercials go from a standard length of 60 seconds to a standard length of 30 seconds.
- Cigarette advertisements are banned from U.S. television.
- "Joy to the World" is at the top of the charts in the U.S.
- Rockers Led Zeppelin record their now-classic song "Stairway to Heaven."
- The Montreal Canadiens win the Stanley Cup.

Etc.

- Trudeau marries Margaret Sinclair, the daughter of a former Liberal cabinet minister.

1972

Only in Canada...

- Microwave ovens are introduced to the Canadian market. Six thousand are sold within a year at prices ranging from $450 to $650.
- CityTV airs the notorious *Baby Blue Movies*—a series of soft-porn flicks the likes of which the Canadian viewing public has never seen before.

Politics & Economics

- The federal government brings in changes to the income tax act that allow working mothers to deduct childcare expenses from their income taxes.
- *The Financial Post* magazine reports that the pressures of office are starting to show in Trudeau's langage and appearance.
- Police arrest five men who are attempting to break into and wiretap the Democratic Party offices on June 17. This signals the beginning of the Watergate scandal, which will eventually force President Richard Nixon from power.

Entertainment & Sports

- Margaret Atwood writes *Survival: A Thematic Guide to Canadian Literature*. It sells 30,000 copies in its first year.
- *Ms. Magazine* publishes its premier issue.
- *The Godfather* walks away with Best Picture honours at the Academy Awards.
- Moses Znaimer and his partners co-found Citytv in Toronto.
- The top-rated show on American TV is *All in the Family*.
- "The First Time Ever I Saw Your Face" is at the top of the charts in the U.S.
- David Bowie, then married with a child, announces that he is gay. One month later, he launches his androgynous Ziggy Stardust character.
- On September 28, Team Canada's Paul Henderson scores the winning goal on Vladislav Tretiak in the CanadaRussia hockey series.
- Four hundred and fifty million viewers worldwide tune in to the Munich Olympics on TV. The coverage alternates between footage of Olympic events and updates on the kidnapping of Israeli athletes by Palestinian terrorists.
- The Boston Bruins win the Stanley Cup.

Science & Technology

- The Royal Bank becomes the first Canadian financial institution to use automatic tellers (called "Banquettes").
- Pulsar introduces the $2,100 Pulsar Time Computer—an 18-carat gold digital watch. When the batteries die after four months, the watches have to be shipped back to the factory to be "recharged."
- Desk and pocket calculators are all the rage—even though they are prohibitively expensive. Prices range from $100 to $1,000.

Etc.

- Sherbrooke, Quebec, becomes the battlefield for a bloody feud between members of two rival motorcycle gangs.

1973

Only in Canada...

- *Chatelaine* magazine announces that it won't be following in the footsteps of

Cosmopolitan magazine by publishing a nude male centrefold.

– *Time Canada* runs an article that reveals that William Lyon Mackenzie King, who served as Prime Minister of Canada for a total of 23 years between 1921 and 1948, believed that he was able to communicate with his dead mother through his beloved dog, Pat.

Fads & Trends

– American Motors Corporation brings out a Gremlin that features a stitched and studded denim interior.

Politics & Economics

– Irene Murdoch is denied a half interest in the Alberta farm that she and her husband had built together over the course of their 25-year marriage, because the judge decides that her work is the fulfilment of her wifely duties and has no cash value. The case sparks an outcry and leads to family law reform in every Canadian province.

– Montreal Mayor Jean Drapeau announces the creation of a lottery to help offset the costs of staging the 1976 Summer Olympics.

– The Paris Peace Accords are signed, bringing an end to the Vietnam War.

– The *Roe vs. Wade* decision in the U.S. strikes down all restrictions on abortion.

– *Chatelaine* reports that a homemaker's unpaid contributions to the family amount to about $8,600 per year.

– OPEC countries raise oil prices by 70 percent, causing a period of rampant inflation around the world.

Entertainment & Sports

– *The Sting* walks away with Best Picture honours at the Academy Awards.

– *The Rocky Horror Picture Show* hits the theatres.

– "Killing Me Softly with His Song" is at the top of the charts in the U.S.

– The top-rated show on American TV is still *All in the Family.*

– *Variety* magazine reports that Americans overwhelmingly consider TV commericals to be a small price to pay in exchange for the privilege of watching free programming.

– The big three U.S. networks devote almost 300 hours of coverage to the Senate Watergate Hearings and, along the way, wave goodbye to $10 million in lost ad revenues and air time.

– Three-minute *Schoolhouse Rock* commercials begin airing on ABC during the Saturday morning cartoon slot.

– The Montreal Canadiens win the Stanley Cup.

– Women's tennis champ Billy Jean King and self-confessed male chauvinist pig Bobby Riggs face off in "The Battles of the Sexes." King beats Riggs hands down.

Science & Technology

– Supermarket bar codes are first used in the U.S.

– Canada becomes the first country in the world to employ satellites for domestic communications.

1974

Only in Canada...

— Morris Wolfe describes television as "a propaganda machine for male supremacy" in a hard-hitting article in Saturday Night. He urges broadcasters to tell their announcers not to refer to females over the age of 15 as "girls" and to refrain from asking if a woman is married or what her husband's occupation is unless it's relevant to the interview.

Fads & Trends

– In January, the streaking fad starts on U.S. college campuses and it is only a matter of time before Canadians get in on the act, too.

– The string bikini is popular with the handful of women who have the figures to carry it off.

– CB radios are hot.

– A black model appears on the cover of *Vogue* magazine for the very first time.

Politics & Economics

– Vice President Gerald R. Ford becomes U.S. President as Nixon resigns in the wake of the Watergate scandal.

Entertainment & Sports

– Paul Anka's hit single "You're Having My Baby" enrages U.S. feminists so much that the National Organization for Women (NOW) awards Anka their annual "Keep Her In Her Place Award".

– *The Godfather, Part II,* walks away with Best Picture honours at the Academy Awards.

– The Global Network comes on the air in January.

– The top-rated show on American TV is still *All in the Family.*

– "The Way We Were" is at the top of the charts in the U.S.

– The Philadelphia Flyers win the Stanley Cup.

Science & Technology

– The two-year energy crisis forces American automobile manufacturers to rethink the way they make cars.

Etc.

– Patty Hearst, the granddaughter of publishing magnate William Randolph Hearst, is kidnapped by members of the Symbionese Liberation Army.

1975

Only in Canada...

– Thirty-five thousand Canadian households own a microwave oven.

Fads & Trends

– Pet rocks and mood rings are the hottest new fads.

– Customized vans and digital watches are cool.

– The Hustle is the latest dance craze.

– A study by the U.S.-based Council on Children, Media, and Merchandising reveals that about half of advertisements airing during children's shows are for food products (primarily sugared cereals, cookies, candies, and soft drinks) and 30 percent are for toys.

Politics & Economics

– Trudeau introduces wage and price controls to help stem inflation.

– About 10 percent of the government's revenues are required to service the debt.

– Just 12 percent of female workers hold down blue collar jobs.

– There are only enough spaces to provide care to 13 percent of the children whose mothers are in the labour force.

Entertainment & Sports

– Bachman Turner Overdrive's *Not Fragile* is named Album of the Year at the Juno Awards.

– Paul McCartney's *Band on the Run* picks up Bestselling Album honours (Foreign or Domestic) at the Juno Awards.

– "Love Will Keep Us Together" is at the top of the charts in the U.S.

– *Jaws*, the most famous disaster flick of the 1970s, hits the movie theatres just in time for summer.

– *One Flew over the Cuckoo's Nest* walks away with Best Picture honours at the Academy Awards.

– On October 11 *Saturday Night Live* hits the airwaves for the first time.

– The top-rated show on American TV is still *All in the Family*.

– Infamous sportscaster Howard Cosell gets his own variety show on ABC.

– A study reveals that, by the time he or she reaches age 18, a typical child will have spent twice as many hours in front of the TV set as in the classroom.

– A typical import TV show costs $2,000 per half-hour and can generate revenue of between $20,000 and $24,000. Homegrown shows, on the other hand, cost about $30,000 to make and typically lose money—anywhere from $55 on CTV to $2,050 on the CBC.

– A California TV station violates a federal ban on television commercials that feature contraceptives by airing an ad for Trojan condoms.

– The Philadelphia Flyers win the Stanley Cup.

Science & Technology

– In March, the CN Tower reaches its final height of 1,815 feet, 5 inches, making it the tallest freestanding structure in the world.

Etc.

– Canadians resent new postal regulations, which require that the postal code be situated at least 3/4 inches but no more than 1 3/4 inches from the bottom of the envelope. (See why the country had to go metric?)

1976

Only in Canada...

- The CN Tower celebrates its grand opening.
- Eaton's pulls the plug on its mail order catalogue.

Politics & Economics

- The Parti Québécois wins a legislative majority after asking Quebeckers for a mandate to negotiate sovereignty-association with the federal government.
- Only 40 percent of jobs in Canada pay well enough to support a family.
- The average family income for a Canadian household is twice what it was in 1971, but due to the effects of double-digit inflation, they are actually only 23 percent higher in terms of spending power.

Entertainment & Sports

- Bachman Turner Overdrive's *Four Wheel Drive* is named Album of the Year at the Juno Awards.
- Elton John's *Greatest Hits* picks up Bestselling Album honours (Foreign or Domestic) at the Juno Awards.
- "Tonight's the Night" is at the top of the charts in the U.S.
- *SCTV* makes its debut.
- *Rocky* walks away with Best Picture honours at the Academy Awards.
- The top-rated show on American TV is still *All in the Family.*
- *SCTV* goes on the air.
- The Montreal Canadiens win the Stanley Cup.
- Over one billion viewers worldwide tune in to the Montreal Summer Olympic Games.
- Maclean's magazine reports that the security bill alone for the Summer Olympic Games in Montreal is likely to top $100 million.
- The final tally for the 1976 Summer Olympic Games, which Montreal Mayor Jean Drapeau had pegged at $310 million, comes in at more than four times that much: $1.3 billion.

Etc.

- The U.S. celebrates its bicentennial.
- Twenty-nine people die and 151 become ill after attending a Legionnaires' convention. The mysterious illness that kills them becomes known as Legionnaires' disease.
- Coke has 26.2 percent of the U.S. pop market; Pepsi has 17.4 percent.

1977

Only in Canada...

- Movie star Brigitte Bardot travels to Newfoundland to protest the seal hunt. She describes the baby seal as "an adorable bundle of wool."

Fads & Trends

– Clogs are popular footwear for both men and women.

– Volkswagen announces its plans to discontinue the Beetle.

– There are two million vans on the road in the U.S., with an additional 570,000 being sold each year.

Politics & Economics

– Democrat Jimmy Carter is elected President of the United States. He takes over from Republican Gerald Ford.

Entertainment & Sports

– The rock group Heart causes a stir when it picks up a Group of the Year Award at the Junos, but tells a U.S. magazine that they've always been an American act.

– André Gagnon's *Neiges* is named Album of the Year at the Juno Awards.

– Peter Frampton's *Frampton Comes Alive* picks up Bestselling Album honours (Foreign or Domestic) at the Juno Awards.

– Fans of Elvis Presley are heartbroken when the 42-year-old, 225-pound King of Rock and Roll is found dead in his home on August 16. A decade after his death, some fans will still be denying that Elvis is really dead.

– "You Light Up My Life" is at the top of the charts in the U.S.

– *Saturday Night Fever* and *Star Wars* hit the theatres.

– *Annie Hall* walks away with Best Picture honours at the Academy Awards.

– The top-rated show on American TV is *Happy Days*.

– One hundred and thirty million viewers tune in to watch *Roots*.

– The Montreal Canadiens win the Stanley Cup.

Science & Technology

– The first automated teller machine (ATM) opens in a bank lobby in Dayton, Ohio.

– The first liquid crystal display (LCD) digital watch appears on the market.

Etc.

– Pierre and Margaret Trudeau announce their separation.

– A massive blackout in New York City leaves nine million people without electricity for between four and twenty-five hours. The subsequent vandalism, looting, and other criminal activity results in the arrest of 3,700 people.

– A KLM Royal Dutch Airlines Boeing 747 crashes into a Pan American World Airways Boeing 747 on an airport runway in the Canary Islands; 570 people die.

1978

Only in Canada...

– Generic products hit the grocery store shelves.

Fads & Trends

– Toga parties are hot on college campuses. The fad is inspired by the hit movie *Animal House.*

Entertainment & Sports

– Dan Hill's *Longer Fuse* is named Album of the Year at the Juno Awards.
– Fleetwood Mac's *Rumours* picks up Bestselling Album honours (Foreign or Domestic) at the Juno Awards.
– *The Deer Hunter* walks away with Best Picture honours at the Academy Awards.
– "Night Fever" is at the top of the charts in the U.S.
– The top-rated show on American TV is *Laverne and Shirley.*
– Ninety-eight percent of American households have television sets.
– Beta home video machines hit the market. Over time, they're driven off the market by the technologically inferior VHS video machines.
– The Montreal Canadiens win the Stanley Cup.

Science & Technology

– Ultrasound technology provides an alternative to X-rays.
– *The Financial Post* reports that there are more than 30 different models of personal computers on the market in the U.S., and that they range in price from $1,000 to $5,000.

Etc.

– A jetliner and a single-engine plane collide in midair over San Dieg;. 144 people die.
– There are now 4.4 billion people in the world.

1979

Only in Canada...

– Philips Data Systems tries to inspire Canadians to make their answering machine messages a little more creative by including a booklet entitled "How to Make Your Code-A-Phone Talk Funny" with its answering machines.

Fads & Trends

– Trivial Pursuit—the brainchild of Canadian inventor—stakes the world by storm.
– The term "couch potato" is used for the first time, but it doesn't really catch on until after the publication of *The Official Couch Potato Handbook* in 1983.
– Three hundred thousand hot tubs are in use in North America.

Politics & Economics

– Trudeaumania wavers and Progressive Conservative Joe Clark is elected prime minister.
– Iran holds 52 Americans captive in the U.S. embassy in Tehran. For the next year and a half, U.S. TV spots tell Americans to "remember the hostages" and large numbers of Americans tie yellow ribbons to trees as a symbol of remembrance.

Entertainment & Sports

– Canadian Lynn Johnston's comic strip "For Better or for Worse" is picked up by large numbers of Canadian and American newspapers. Within two years, she has a following of 50 million daily readers from around the world.

– Burton Cummings' *Dream of a Child* is named Album of the Year at the Juno Awards.

– The Bee Gees' *Saturday Night Fever* picks up Bestselling Album honours (Foreign or Domestic) at the Juno Awards.

– "My Sharona" is at the top of the charts in the U.S.

– *Apocalypse Now* hits the theatres.

– *Kramer vs. Kramer* walks away with Best Picture honours at the Academy Awards.

– The investors behind *Porky's,* perhaps the most infamous sexploitation film ever made, walk away with a 100 percent tax write-off courtesy of the Canadian government.

– Chicago rock deejay Steve Dahl is fired after he is caught destroying disco records on the air. (His station had just switched to an all-disco format.)

– There are 300 million television sets in use worldwide.

– A *TV Guide* poll reveals that 44 percent of Americans are unhappy with what they're seeing on TV.

– The top-rated show on American TV is *Laverne and Shirley.*

– The Montreal Canadiens win the Stanley Cup.

Science & Technology

– Sony introduces the world's first portable stereo, the Walkman.

Etc.

– Canadian ballerina Karen Kain starts dating Lee Majors, TV's *Six Million Dollar Man.*

– There is an accident at the Three Mile Island nuclear plant in the U.S.

– The first Starbucks coffee shop opens for business in Pike Place, Seattle.

1980

Only in Canada...

– On April 12, Terry Fox begins his Marathon of Hope, a cross-Canada run to raise money for cancer research. The run ends at Thunder Bay on September 1 when cancer is discovered in his lungs.

– The Canadian Union of Postal Workers goes on strike for six weeks.

Fads & Trends

– Rubik's Cubes and preppy clothing are in vogue.

– Rollerblade inline skates and Post-It Notes ® are invented.

Politics & Economics

– Canada's national anthem, *O Canada,* is officially adopted under the National Anthem Act.

- Trudeau returns to power after a vote of nonconfidence topples the newly elected Conservative government of Joe Clark.
- Parti Québécois leader René Lévesque fails in his bid to convince Quebeckers to vote yes in the referendum on sovereignty-association. Only 40 percent of Quebeckers support the idea.
- Trudeau introduces the National Energy Program.
- A state of emergency is declared in the U.S. as thousands of Cuban refugees enter Florida.
- Six U.S. embassy officials, posing as Canadians, escape from Iran. The Canadians involved in the rescue are heroes in the eyes of the world.

Entertainment & Sports

- Anne Murray's *New Kind of Feeling* is named Album of the Year at the Juno Awards.
- Supertramp's *Breakfast in America* picks up Bestselling Album honours (Foreign or Domestic) at the Juno Awards.
- The top-rated show on American TV is *60 Minutes*.
- Television mogul Ted Turner launches North America's first 24-hour-a-day news channel, the Cable News Network (CNN).
- The "Who Shot J.R." episode of Dallas pulls in 83.6 million viewers.
- *Ordinary People* walks away with Best Picture honours at the Academy Awards.
- Major league baseball teams go on strike for seven weeks.
- U.S. Olympic Committee decides to boycott the Moscow Games.
- The New York Islanders win the Stanley Cup.

Science & Technology

- Tampons are linked to toxic shock syndrome.

Etc.

- Mount St. Helens volcano erupts in Washington State; 36 people die.
- Former Beatle John Lennon is shot dead by a crazed fan, Mark David Chapman on December 8.
- Labour unrest in Poland leads to a massive strike involving 200,000 workers.

1981

Only in Canada...

- For the first time ever, more than half of Canadian married women are working outside the home.
- *Chatelaine* runs an article entitled "New Norm: The Two–Income Couple – Double the Pleasure or Double the Stress?"

Fads & Trends

- Pac Man is the most popular video game in the video arcades.

Politics & Economics

– In September, the Supreme Court rules that the "substantial consent" of the provinces (not full unanimity) is all that is required for the federal government to proceed with its plans for patriation.

– The Democrats are defeated by the Republicans, with Ronald Reagan becoming the 40th U.S. president.

– Americans wear yellow ribbons and TV stations remind viewers to "remember the hostages" who are being held in Iran.

– Iran releases the 52 American hostages that it has been holding in the U.S. embassy in Tehran for 444 days (since November of 1979). The hostage release occurs in January, just as newly elected U.S. president Ronald Reagan is taking over from outgoing President Jimmy Carter—a final slap in the face for Carter, whose election chances were badly harmed by his inability to resolve the hostage crisis.

– *Maclean's* magazine describes outgoing President Jimmy Carter as "a decent man" and expresses concerns about incoming President Ronald Reagan's "high noon mentality."

– On March 30, a young man named John Hinckley Jr. attempts to assassinate President Reagan in a bizarre attempt to impress American actress Jodie Foster.

– Martial law is declared in Poland.

– In May, interest rates climb to an unbelievable 21.5 percent.

– A Conference Board of Canada study confirms consumer confidence is at its lowest point in the 20-year history of the survey.

– The bank rate rises to 21 percent and the prime lending rate to 22.75 percent.

– The global economy is facing the worst economic slump since the Great Depression.

Entertainment & Sports

– The first phase of the West Edmonton Mall is completed.

– The McKenzie Brothers' album, released in the fall, sells 300,000 copies in less than a month. Five thousand "hosers" turn out for a Hoser Day parade through downtown Toronto, dressed in full Bob and Doug regalia: parkas, toques, earmuffs, checkered flannel shirts, and mitts.

– Anne Murray's *Greatest Hits* is named Album of the Year at the Juno Awards.

– Pink Floyd's *The Wall* picks up Bestselling Album honours (Foreign or Domestic) at the Juno Awards.

– The 24-hour music video channel MTV airs in the U.S. with "Video Killed the Radio Star" by the Buggles as its first song.

– The top-rated show on American TV is *Dallas*.

– *Chariots of Fire* walks away with Best Picture honours at the Academy Awards.

– The New York Islanders win the Stanley Cup.

Science & Technology

– IBM introduces the IBM Personal Computer.

– The U.S. Food and Drug Administration approves aspartame for consumer use.

Etc.

– Prince Charles marries Lady Diana Spencer.

– U.S. President Ronald Reagan fires 12,000 striking air traffic controllers.

– *The Washington Post* returns its Pulitzer Prize after it is revealed that reporter Janet Cooke made up her story about a child on heroin.

– Egyptian leader Anwar Sadat is assassinated at a military parade.

1982

Only in Canada...

– Fifty-three percent of Canadian women work outside the home.

Fads & Trends

– Reese's Pieces get a sales boost because they are *E.T.'s* favourite candy.

– Jane Fonda puts out the first of what will be a string of celebrity workout videos.

Politics & Economics

– The British House of Commons passes the Canada Act of 1982, ending British legislative jurisdiction over Canada. Queen Elizabeth II signs the Canadian constitution into law on April 17.

– Canada experiences a severe recession.

Entertainment & Sports

– Loverboy's *Loverboy* is named Album of the Year at the Juno Awards.

– John Lennon's *Double Fantasy* picks up Bestselling Album honours (Foreign or Domestic) at the Juno Awards.

– This year's hit movie is *E.T.*

– *Late Night with David Letterman* debuts on TV.

– The top-rated show on American TV is *Dallas*.

– *Gandhi* walks away with Best Picture honours at the Academy Awards.

– The New York Islanders win the Stanley Cup.

Science & Technology

– American Barney Clark of Seattle receives the world's first artificial heart. He dies three months later.

Etc.

– The Vietnam War Memorial is dedicated in Washington, D.C. The memorial features the names of the 60,000 soldiers who were killed or who went missing during the war, including those Canadians who volunteered for service.

– Thousands of Canadian women protest First Choice Canadian Communication Corp.'s decision to carry Playboy Channel features.

- Eight people die after taking Tylenol that has been deliberately contaminated. The product disappears from the store shelves while new tamper-proof packaging is designed.
- A Boeing 737 crashes into the Potomac River in Washington, D.C., killing 78.
- Polish activist Lech Walesa is released from government detention and martial law is suspended in that country.
- Argentina and Britain go to war over the Falkland Islands.

1983

Only in Canada...

- Carling O'Keefe Breweries introduces Miller High Life in a new style bottle, abandoning the traditional Canadian "stubby" beer bottle along the way. Labatt soons follows suit, leaving beer bottle collectors scrambling to get their hands on some stubbies before they are gone forever.
- *Playgirl* magazine announces its plans to publish a special "Men of Canada" edition.

Fads & Trends

- Vanessa Williams becomes the first black Miss America.
- Torn sweatshirts become a *de rigueur* fashion item after Jennifer Beals makes them famous in the hit movie *Flashdance*.
- Cabbage Patch Kids mania hits North America—which leads to chaos at the toy stores.

Politics & Economics

- U.S. President Ronald Reagan describes the U.S.S.R. as the "Evil Empire" and proposes a revolutionary new antimissile defense system nicknamed "Star Wars."
- U.S. troops invade Grenada.
- First Lady Nancy Reagan launches the "Just Say No" drug education program.
- U.S. President Ronald Reagan openly backs the Contra rebels against the Marxist Sandinista government of Nicaragua.
- Jesse Jackson becomes the first black man to address the Alabama legislature.

Entertainment & Sports

- Loverboy's *Get Lucky* is named Album of the Year at the Juno Awards.
- Men at Work's *Business As Usual* picks up Bestselling Album honours (Foreign or Domestic) at the Juno Awards.
- The top-selling video of the year is *Jane Fonda's Workout Video*. It holds the number one spot for four years.
- The final episode of *M*A*S*H** attracts 106 million viewers.
- The top-rated show on American TV is *60 Minutes*.
- *Terms of Endearment* walks away with Best Picture honours at the Academy Awards.
- The New York Islanders win the Stanley Cup.

Science & Technology

– A joint Canadian-American study fails to agree on the causes and effects of acid rain.

– The Bell mobile phone system in Toronto can only handle 25 phone calls at a time.

– Apple Computers become the first computers to use a mouse.

Etc.

– Canadian abortion crusader Dr. Henry Morgentaler opens abortion clinics in Toronto and Winnipeg.

– A two-year drought in Ethiopia results in a wide-spread famine.

– A Soviet missile brings down a Korean Air Lines Boeing 747, killing 269 people.

1984

Only in Canada...

– Seventy-nine percent of Canadians are optimistic about the country's future.

– Half of Canadians feel confident that the government will solve the country's economic problems.

Fads & Trends

– Madonna demonstrates new uses for underwear.

– Stonewashed jeans are popular.

– Twenty million copies of Trivial Pursuit are sold in the U.S. during the year.

– Cabbage Patch Dolls continue to be North America's hottest toy.

Politics & Economics

– Prime Minister Pierre Elliott Trudeau announces his resignation. He is succeeded by John Turner. Turner is subsequently defeated by Conservative Brian Mulroney, whose party wins the largest electoral majority in Canadian history, walking away with an unprecedented 211 seats.

– The Inuit of the Mackenzie Delta receive a settlement of 242,000 square kilometres of land.

– Jeanne Sauvé becomes Canada's first woman governor general.

– The Canadian unemployment rate is 11.9 percent.

Entertainment & Sports

– Bryan Adams' *Cuts Like a Knife* is named Album of the Year at the Juno Awards.

– The Police's *Synchronicity* picks up Bestselling Album honours (Foreign or Domestic) at the Juno Awards.

– Moses Znaimer launches MuchMusic, "the Nation's Music Station".

– The top-rated show on American TV is *Dallas*.

– At the top of the bestseller list for most of the year is George Orwell's *1984*.

- *Amadeus* walks away with Best Picture honours at the Academy Awards.
- The Edmonton Oilers win the Stanley Cup.
- The Soviets announce their intention to boycott the Summer Olympic Games in Los Angeles.

Science & Technology

- Astronaut Marc Garneau becomes the first Canadian in space.
- *Chatelaine* publishes a plain-English guide to the personal computer.
- The Bell Canada mobile phone system in Toronto is capable of handling 25 phone calls at a time.

Etc.

- Trudeau's divorce becomes final. He is granted custody of the couple's three young sons.
- The Pope visits Canada. He is transported around in a specially equipped security vehicle that is dubbed "the Popemobile."
- A toxic gas leak in the Union Carbide Plant in Bhopal, India, kills 2,500 people and injures thousands more.
- A gunman kills 20 people and wounds 16 others at a McDonald's restaurant in San Ysidro, California, before being shot dead himself.
- Bishop Desmond Tutu of South Africa wins the Nobel Peace Prize.

1985

Only in Canada...

- A *Chatelaine* survey reveals that 83 percent of Canadian women are doing more homework than the men in their lives.

Fads & Trends

- Nintendo introduces its video game system.
- Men start adopting the *Miami Vice* look made famous by American TV hunks Don Johnson and Philip Michael Thomas.
- Coca-Cola puts out a new formula but demand for the original is strong so they bring it back and sales are ten times higher than the new formula.
- A Campbell's Soup study reveals that men who do the grocery shopping are "achievement-oriented and see themselves as considerate, up-to-date, liberated, well-organized, ambitious, intelligent, energetic, and successful." (But not modest.)

Politics & Economics

- Many of the sections of the Indian Act that unfairly discriminate against native women are removed.
- During the "Shamrock Summit" in Quebec City, Prime Minister Mulroney and U.S. President Reagan agree their countries will support each other in Star Wars research and free trade.

– Canadian Fisheries Minister John Fraser resigns in the wake of the "tainted tuna" scandal.

– Canada's divorce laws are liberalized again.

– The Parti Québécois is defeated by the Quebec provincial Liberals led by Robert Bourassa.

– U.S. President Ronald Reagan orders a trade embargo with Nicaragua.

– Canadians managed to squirrel away 12 percent to 18 percent of their take-home pay each year before 1985, but that figure has now dropped to just 9 percent.

Entertainment and Sports

– The third and final phase of the Ghermezian brothers' West Edmonton Mall is complete. The Mall features a triple-loop rollercoaster, a water park, and an indoor ice rink.

– Bryan Adams' *Reckless* is named Album of the Year at the Juno Awards.

– Bruce Springsteen's *Born to Run* picks up Bestselling Album honours (Foreign or Domestic) at the Juno Awards.

– *Out of Africa* walks away with Best Picture honours at the Academy Awards.

– The top-rated show on American TV is *Dynasty*.

– The Edmonton Oilers win the Stanley Cup.

Science and Technology

– The *Titanic* is discovered south of Newfoundland, in waters over 10,000 feet deep.

– Barbie gets her first computer.

Etc.

– Steve Fonyo ends his cross-Canada run to raise money for cancer research.

– Live Aid concerts raise $95 million for Ethiopian famine relief.

– An Air India Jet en route from Canada to Ireland explodes, killing 329 people, most of them Canadians of Indian origin.

– An air crash in Gander, Newfoundland, kills 248 American soldiers and eight crew members.

– A tornado in Barrie, Ontario, kills 12 people.

1986

Only in Canada...

– Only 43 percent of Canadian Roman Catholics are attending church regularly—a significant drop from 83 percent in 1965.

– *Chatelaine* refuses to publish a Perry Ellis fragrance advertisement that contains an obscenity.

Fads & Trends

– Cordless small appliances take the Canadian marketplace by storm.

Politics & Economics

– Canada receives a United Nations award for being a haven for refugees.

– Canada and other Commonwealth countries adopt economic sanctions against South Africa due to its apartheid policy.

– U.S. President Ronald Reagan cuts economic ties with Libya.

– Thirty-two wealthy families and nine giant conglomerates control over one-third of Canada's non-financial assets.

Entertainment & Sports

– A group of prominent Canadian recording artists record "Tears Are Not Enough" to raise money to help those affected by the famine in Ethiopia.

– Vancouver hosts the Expo '86 World's Fair from May 2nd to October 13th.

– Margaret Atwood's novel *The Handmaid's Tale* is published.

– Glass Tiger's *The Thin Red Line* is named Album of the Year at the Juno Awards.

– Dire Straits' *Brothers in Arms* picks up Bestselling Album honours (Foreign or Domestic) at the Juno Awards.

– *Platoon* walks away with Best Picture honours at the Academy Awards.

– The top-rated show on American TV is *The Cosby Show*.

– The Montreal Canadiens win the Stanley Cup.

Science & Technology

– Canadian John Polanyi shares the chemistry Nobel Prize.

– The space shuttle *Challenger* explodes, killing seven astronauts.

– *Voyageur* (an experimental U.S. plane) completes a nonstop flight around the world without refuelling.

Etc.

– Prince Andrew marries Sarah Ferguson (a.k.a. Fergie).

– The most serious nuclear reactor accident in history occurs at Chernobyl in the Ukraine.

– An explosion occurs at the Chernobyl nuclear power station in the Soviet Union.

– Actor Clint Eastwood of *Dirty Harry* fame is elected the mayor of Carmel, California.

– A train crash near Hinton, Alberta, kills 26 people.

1987

Only in Canada...

Fads & Trends

– One-dollar bills are replaced with a new coin, the loonie.

– Home renovations are very trendy.

– U.S. TV networks begin airing condom ads.

Politics & Economics

– On June 3, the final text of the Meech Lake Accord is hammered out during an all-night session in Ottawa. A three-year deadline for ratification by the provincial legislatures is announced.

– The Reform Party of Canada holds its first assembly.

– A non-party Parliamentary vote defeats a proposal to restore capital punishment by 148 to 127.

– Washington and Moscow sign a treaty eliminating intermediate-range nuclear missiles.

– On October 19th ("Black Monday"), the Dow Jones Industrial Average—a key measure of both stock market performance and the overall health of the U.S. economy–plunges 508 points, nearly twice as far as in the 1929 stock market crash that ushered in the Great Depression. The TSE 300 loses 11 percent of its value.

– Bidding wars break out as the real estate market heats up.

Entertainment & Sports

– Kim Mitchell's *Shakin' Like a Human Being* is named Album of the Year at the Juno Awards.

– Madonna's *True Blue* picks up Bestselling Album honours (Foreign or Domestic) at the Juno Awards.

– Bryan Adams is named Entertainer of the Year at the Juno Awards.

– *The Last Emperor* picks up Best Picture honours at the Academy Awards.

– *Raising Arizona*, an offbeat comedy starring Nicolas Cage and Holly Hunter, hits the movie theatres.

– The top-rated show on American TV is *The Cosby Show*.

– The Edmonton Oilers win the Stanley Cup.

Science & Technology

– The "Baby M" surrogate mother trial ends with the surrogate mother losing the case.

Etc.

– A North Korean bomb kills 115 people aboard a South Korean airliner.

– The first Canadian Starbucks shop opens in Vancouver.

– A tornado in Edmonton kills 27 people.

– The U.S. Supreme Court orders Rotary Clubs to admit women.

– U.S. presidential candidate Gary Hart withdraws from the presidential race when it is revealed that he had an extramarital affair.

– Jim and Tammy Bakker hand the PTL Club over to Reverend Jerry Falwell when it becomes public knowledge that they had defrauded the church of millions of dollars and that they had been involved in extramarital affairs.

1988

Only in Canada...

– Fifty-seven point five percent of all Canadian preschoolers are in some form of childcare arrangement.

Fads & Trends

– The West Edmonton Mall earns the distinction of being the largest shopping mall in the world.

– Canada gets its first jet-set supermodel, Linda Evangelista.

Politics & Economics

– The Supreme Court of Canada rules that existing abortion laws are unconstitutional.

– The Conservative Mulroney government is re-elected following an election in which the proposed Free Trade Agreement with the U.S. is the big issue.

– The Supreme Court of Canada strikes down Quebec's French-only sign law as unconstitutional. Quebec then employs the "notwithstanding" clause of the Charter of Rights and Freedoms to overrule the Court's decision.

– The Soviet Union begins to withdraw from Afghanistan.

– U.S. President Reagan visits the U.S.S.R. for the first time.

Entertainment & Sports

– There aren't any Juno Awards this year.

– *Rain Man* picks up Best Picture honours at the Academy Awards.

– The top-rated show on American TV is *The Cosby Show*.

– The Calgary Winter Olympics are held. Canadian figure skaters Brian Orser and Elizabeth Manley steal the crowd's heart.

– The Edmonton Oilers win the Stanley Cup.

– Runner Ben Johnson is stripped of his Olympic gold medal for using steroids.

Etc.

– Two hundred and fifty-nine people on board Pan Am Flight 103 are killed when the airplane explodes over Lockerbie, Scotland. Eleven Lockerbie villagers are also killled in the tragedy. In the end, Libyan terrorists are charged with planting explosives on the plane to retaliate for a massive U.S. air strike against Libya two years earlier.

– One million blacks in South Africa stage a three-day strike to protest new labour laws.

– Salman Rushdie is sentenced to death by Iran's Ayatollah Khomeini on the grounds that his book *The Satanic Verses* constitutes a blasphemous attack on Islam.

– Sandinistas and Contras agree to a ceasefire in Nicaragua.

1989

Only in Canada...

– Sunday shopping is still illegal in many parts of the country.

– Only one-quarter of Canadians feel confident that the government will be able to solve the country's economic problems.

– A typical Canadian carries mortgage and consumer debt equal to three-quarters of his or her after-tax income.

– Since 1987, the Canadian luxury car market has dropped by 20 percent as the yuppies' stock portfolios went up in smoke.

Politics & Economics

– The Berlin Wall comes down.
– The Free Trade Agreement with the U.S. comes into effect.
– The government passes legislation that will bring in the new federal goods and services tax (GST) on January 1, 1991.
– Audrey McLaughlin becomes the first woman to head up a major political party.
– George Bush takes over as Republican U.S. President from Ronald Reagan.
– Oliver North is tried for his role in the Iran-Contra affair. CNN devotes a tremendous amount of air time to the hearings.
– Scandal erupts when the Canadian federal budget is leaked.

Entertainment & Sports

– The SkyDome opens in Toronto.
– The *Dirty Dancing* Soundtrack picks up Bestselling Album honours (Foreign or Domestic) at the Juno Awards.
– Robbie Robertson's *Robbie Robertson* is named Album of the Year at the Juno Awards.
– Glass Tiger is named Entertainer of the Year at the Juno Awards.
– The top-rated show on American TV is *Roseanne*.
– *Driving Miss Daisy* walks away with Best Picture honours at the Academy Awards.
– The Calgary Flames win the Stanley Cup.

Science & Technology

– The Royal Commission on Reproductive Technologies is established.

Etc.

– Communist troops kill 2,000 students demonstrating for democracy in Tiananmen Square, China.
– An earthquake in San Francisco kills hundreds of people and causes the Bay Bridge to collapse.
– Two hundred and forty thousand barrels of oil spill from the oil tanker *Exxon Valdez* in William Sound, Alaska. The spill covers 1,400 square miles and costs over one billion dollars to clean up.

1990

Only in Canada...

– A *Maclean's*/Decima Research poll reveals that 69 percent of Canadians no longer see any meaningful differences between the three mainstream political parties.
– Only 23 percent of Canadians attend church regularly and just 29 percent claim to be

members of a church. In 1945, 60 percent of Canadians attended church weekly and 82 percent stated that they belonged to a church.

– The December issue of *The Financial Post Magazine* devotes a feature-length article to nannies-from-hell.

– Only 43 percent of aboriginal people over the age of 15 have jobs, compared to 61 percent of the rest of Canadians.

Fads & Trends

– Large numbers of Canadians are crossing the border to shop for bargains in the U.S.

– Bottles of Perrier water are recalled when traces of benzene are found in some bottles in the U.S.

Politics & Economics

– The land dispute at Kanesatake reserve near Oka, Quebec, leads to over two months of armed conflict between Mohawk and federal government forces.

– On June 23, Newfoundland and Manitoba do not agree to the proposed constitutional amendments, so the Meech Lake Accord cannot be ratified.

– Canadian warships go to the Persian Gulf, part of a multinational alliance that is seeking to force Iraq to withdrawal from Kuwait.

Entertainment & Sports

– The Jeff Healy Band is named Entertainer of the Year at the Juno Awards.

– Milli Vanilli's *Girl You Know It's True* picks up Bestselling Album honours (Foreign or Domestic) at the Juno Awards. The award is later withdrawn when it is discovered that the album was lip-synched. (The same thing happens to the group at the Grammys.)

– Alannah Myles' *Alannah Myles* is named Album of the Year at the Juno Awards.

– *Seinfeld* debuts on U.S. TV.

– The top-rated show on American TV is *Roseanne*.

– *Dances with Wolves* walks away with Best Picture honours at the Academy Awards.

– The Edmonton Oilers win the Stanley Cup.

Etc.

– Marc Lepine kills 14 young women at the Ecole Polytechnique in Montreal. The tragedy heightens public concern about violence against women.

– Wellesley College finds itself embroiled in a brouhaha when it invites Barbara Bush rather than a career woman to speak at its graduation ceremonies.

– Lech Walesa is elected President of Poland.

– Iraq invades Kuwait and is ordered by the U.S. to withdraw.

– Nelson Mandela is freed from a South African jail.

– Three major U.S. companies announce that they will no longer buy tuna that is caught in nets that also ensnare dolphins.

Web Sites, Books, and Other Recommended Resources

Want to explore the '60s, '70s, and '80s in greater detail? Here's a list of the web sites, books, and magazine and newspaper articles that I found particularly useful when I was researching this book.

Web Sites

1050 CHUM Toronto   *http://www.1050chum.com*
Want to know what song was at the top of the charts the week you went on your first date with that special someone? The answer is waiting to be found in the searchable database at the 1050 CHUM web site. While you're visiting the site, be sure to check out the 1050 Chum Top 300 songs of all time.

70s Preservation Society Presents 70s Saturday Night   *http://www.70s.com*
A fun web site for anyone who lived through the 70s and wants to remember them.

Advertising Age
http://www.adage.com/news_and_features/special_reports/commercials/
Find out about the hottest television commercials of the 1960s, 1970s, and 1980s by visiting the *Advertising Age* magazine web site.

Bad Fads Web Site   *http://www.adscape.com/badfads*
A celebration of anything tacky from decades gone by. It's worth visiting for the photos alone.

Canadian Resource Page   *http://www.cs.cmu.edu/Unofficial/Canadiana*
A great launching pad for anything Canadian. The music, TV, and sports links are particularly useful if you're into pop culture.

Classic Gaming   *http://www.classicgaming.com/*
Are you a die-hard video game addict? This is the site for you. You'll find reviews on all kinds of classic games. There's even an article about the first person to get a perfect score on Pac Man. (Don't be depressed. It took 20 years for it to happen.)

Classic TV: The Farrah Phenomenon - Collecting, February 1999
http://www.odysseygroup.com/coll299/ctv.htm
Can't remember what Farrah's classic swimsuit poster looked like? You can see it online at this web site. Elsewhere on the site, you'll get a chance to check out the hottest Brady Bunch collectible items. (Yes, you too can pay $100 for a Brady boys paddle ball set!)

CN Tower   *http://www.cntower,ca*
The official web site of the CN Tower will tell you everything you could ever want to know about the world's tallest freestanding structure. Did you know, for example, that two men hauled a 440 lb. piano up the stairs in just 7 1/2 hours back in 1979? Or that a Grade A egg was dropped from the 1,120 foot level of the Tower on July 27, 1979, and didn't even break? Look at all the fun you've been missing!

History Channel   *http://www.historychannel.com/exhibits/toys/crayons.html*
Do you still remember the thrill you got each time you opened a brand new pack of crayons? You know, before your baby brother got at them and broke them? If crayons have a very special place in your heart, you'll want to visit the Crayon page of The History Channel web site. Then, when you're finished revisiting your colouring book days, you can check out some of the other great pop culture information to be found elsewhere on the site.

Jam Music History   *http://www.canoe.ca/JamMusicHistory/home.html*
Wondering what happened on today's date in music history. This is the place to go to find out.

Juno Awards Online   *http://www.juno-awards.ca*
The official web site for the Canadian music industry's annual awards ceremony. Be sure to check out the site's Hall of Fame and Chronology features.

Mr. Clean History   *http://www.mrclean.com/history.html*
Yes, boys and girls, you can find anything online—including a web site that sings the praises of everybody's favourite cleaning product, Mr. Clean. You can even read an interview with the Big Guy, who will proudly tell you the story behind that earring he wears. Elsewhere on the site, you can check out some of the advertisements that have promoted Mr. Clean over the past 40 years.

Museum and Archive of Games   *http://www.ahs.uwaterloo.ca/~museum/*
Want to get a look at the world's first hand-held electronic games or just pick up some neat facts about games in general. This is the web site for you.

Network and Cable TV Guide   *http://www.geocities.com/TelevisionCity/9348/tv_guide.htm*
Find yourself humming snatches of the theme from *WKRP in Cincinnati* or *Dukes of Hazzard*? You can hear clips from these theme songs and a whole lot more at this web site which claims to be "a guide to almost all of the TV shows that have aired on television from...close to the beginning of TV itself until the near-present."

New Sixties Net   *http://www.sixties.net*
Contains links to a variety of Sixties-related topics: the Rock and Roll Hall of Fame Gallery, the John F. Kennedy Museum, the Brady Bunch Encyclopedia, and much more.

Newsworld Flashback   *http://www.newsworlf.cbc.ca/flashback/welcome.html*
An online celebration of Newsworld's 10th anniversary. Includes web links, pictures and maps, top stories, and commentary from CBC personalities on the hottest stories from 1989 onward.

Pacer Page   *http: www//lightstream.net/~jeni/pacer*
Do you have found memories of driving around in your parents' AMC Pacer? This is the web site for you. You'll find interesting facts, technical information about the vehicle that North Americans loved to laugh at, and, of course, photos galore.

Polyester Network   *http://www.hip–huggers.com/entertainment/television/primetime.html*
http://www.hip-huggers.com/entertainment/television/primetime.html
A web site devoted to everything 70s: the good, the bad, and the ugly.

Pop-Tarts Pop Trivia   *http://www.poptarts.com*
The official web site of the semi-official breakfast food of the 1970s (assuming, of course, that your parents weren't force-feeding you Life Cereal).

Rubik's Cube Java Applet   *http://www.best.com/~schubart/rc/*
A virtual Rubik's Cube for people who didn't get frustrated enough with the real thing.

Stuck in the 70s   *http://www.stuckinthe70s.com*
A celebration of the decade that everyone loves to hate by a woman whose "dimwitted" ex-husband accused her of being "stuck in the 70s."

This is the Year That Was 1980   *http://audiopros.com/1980.htm*
A fun site that highlights the best moments in pop culture for the years 1980-1989.

Toes Socks   *http://www.joyofsocks.com/joyofsocks/toesocks1.html*
Can't remember what toes socks looked like? You can actually purchase a pair online! You'll even find the dreaded mitten sock available for sale–a product that had an even shorter lifespan than the toe sock.

Toy History: Amazing Stories On How Toys Developed
http://www.drtoy.com/drtoy/toyhistory.htm
The Dr. Toy web site contains detailed stories on how toys were invented, how they got their names, and so on. So if you're eager to find out the untold story behind the Slinky or the Magic Slate, this web site is for you.

Watching TV   *http://www.civilization.ca/cmc/tv/tv00eng.html*
An online exhibit at the Canadian Museum of Civilization that includes a timeline of television history and tons of fascinating facts about The Tube.

Books

Ben is Dead Magazine editors. *Retro Hell. Life In The '70s and '80s, From Afros to Zotz.* Boston: Little, Brown and Company. 1997.

Berton, Pierre. *The Comfortable Pew.* Toronto: McClelland and Stewart, 1965.

Browne, Ray B. and David Madden. *The Popular Culture Explosion.* Wm. C. Brown Company Publishers, 1972.

Clark, Andrew. *Stand And Deliver. Inside Canadian Comedy.* Toronto: Doubleday Canada Limited, 1997.

Coontz, Stephanie. *The Way We Never Were: American Families and the Nostalgia Trap*. New York: Basic Books, 1992.

Coontz, Stephanie. *The Way We Really Are: Coming To Terms With America's Changing Families*. New York: Basic Books, 1997.

Douglas, Ann. *The Complete Idiot's Guide to Canadian History*. Scarborough, Ontario: Prentice Hall Canada Inc., 1997.

Doyle, Kevin and Ann Johnston eds. *The 1980s: Maclean's Chronicles The Decade*. Toronto: Key Porter Books, 1989.

Eaton's Spring & Summer 1976 Catalogue. Toronto: Timothy Eaton Company of Canada, 1976.

Edelstein, Andrew J. and Kevin McDonough. *The Seventies: From Hot Pants to Hot Tubs*. New York: Dutton, 1990.

Edmonds, Alan. *The Years Of Protest 1960-1970*. Toronto: Natural Science of Canada Limited, 1979.

Epstein, Edward Jay. *News From Nowhere. Television And The News*. New York: Vintage Books, 1974.

Flaherty, David H. and Frank E. Manning. *The Beaver Bites Back?* Montreal: McGill-Queen's University Press, 1993.

Gitter, Michael and Sylvie Anapol. *Do You Remember? The Book That Takes You Back*. San Francisco: Chronicle Books, 1996.

Gottlieb, Annie. *Do You Believe In Magic—The Second Coming of the 60's Generation*. New York: Times Books, 1987.

Grun, Bernard. *The Timetables of History*. 3rd rev. ed. New York: Simon and Schuster, 1991.

Hoffman, Frank W. and William G. Bailey. *Arts and Entertainment Fads*. New York: The Haworth Press Inc. 1990.

Ingham, John N. Sex 'N' Drugs 'N' Rock 'N' Roll. *American Popular Culture Since 1945*. Toronto: Canadian Scholars' Press, 1988.

Javna, John and Gordon Javna. *60s! A Catalog of Memories and Artifacts*. New York: St. Matin's Press, 1988.

Jennings, Peter, and Todd Brewster. *The Century*. New York: Doubleday, 1998.

Kleinfelder, Rita Lang. *When We Were Young—A Baby-Boomer Yearbook*. New York: Prentice Hall General Reference, 1993.

Landsberg, Michele. *Women and Children First*. Toronto: Macmillan of Canada, 1982.

Leiterman, Douglas, Robert Daudelin, Peter Morris and June Callwood. *Canadian Culture At The Crossroads*. Toronto: ECW Press Ltd., 1987.

Lewis, Laurie. *The Concerts*. New York: A & W Publishers. Inc., 1979.

Lucie-Smith, Edward. *Art In The Seventies*. Ithaca: Cornell University Press, 1980.

Melhuish, Martin. *Oh What A Feeling*. Kingston: Quarry Press, 1996.

Mills, Daniel Quinn. *Not Like Our Parents: A New Look At How The Baby Boom Generation is Changing America.* New York: William Morrow and Company Inc., 1987.

Moore Ede, Carol. *Canadian Architecture 1960/70.* Toronto: Burns and MacEachern Limited, 1971.

National Geographic editors. *National Geographic Eyewitness To The 20th Century.* Washington: National Geographic Society, 1998.

ONeil, Doris C. ed. Life. *The '60s.* Chicago: Boston, Bulfinch Press, 1989.

Owram, Doug. *Born At The Right Time: A History of the Baby Boom Generation.* Toronto: University of Toronto Press, 1996.

Panati, Charles. *Panati's Parade of Fads, Follies and Manias. The Origins of Our Most Cherished Obsessions.* New York: HarperCollins Publishers, 1991.

Pavese, Edith and Judith Henry. *TV Mania—A Timeline of Television.* New York: Harry N. Abrams, Inc., 1998.

Pevere, Geoff and Greig Dymond. *Mondo Canuck-A Canadian Pop Culture Odyssey.* Scarborough: Prentice Hall Canada Inc.,1996.

Ray, Randy and Mark Kearney. *Canadian Music Fast Facts—Profiles of Canada's Pop Music Pioneers.* London: Sparky Jefferson Productions, 1991.

Rettenmund, Matthew. *Totally Awesome 80s.* New York: St. Martin's Griffin, 1996.

Russell, John and Suzi Gablik. *Pop Art Redefined.* London: Thames and Hudson, 1969.

Stern, Jane and Michael Stern. *Sixties People.* New York: Alfred A. Knopf, 1990.

Unger, Irwin and Debi Unger. *The Times Were A Changin'—The Sixties Reader.* New York, Three Rivers Press, 1998.

Magazine and newspaper articles

Abdullah, Halimah. "Fad Fazzle: Remember Earth Shoes, Smurfs and Rubik's Cubes? And Whatever Happened To The People Who Made Us Care About Them?" *The Dallas Morning News* 11 April 1998: 1C.

Abrahamson, U. "Microwave Ovens." *Chatelaine* August 1973: 13-14.

"Age Of The Gas Guzzler Gives Way To Energy-Conscious 1980s." *The Financial Post* 19 April 1980: S1.

Aitchison, J. H. "Computers: Keys To Savings, Profits." *The Financial Post* 18 May 1963: 53.

Allen, R.T. "Tribal Customs Of Space-Age Children." il. *Maclean's* 6 July 1963: 18+.

Allentuck, Andrew. "What The 70's Might Have Been And What They Were." *The Financial Post* December 1979: 20+.

Altschul, S. "Who's Come A Long Way, Baby?" *Maclean's* 12 January 1981: 6.

"American Report." *Canadian Business* October 1967: 15+.

Anderson, D. "Change The Abortion Law Now." Editorial. *Chatelaine* September 1970: 1.

—. "How Real Are Reel-Life Women?" Editorial. *Chatelaine* July 1969: 1.

—. "Progress In The World Of Women." Editorial. *Chatelaine* May 1969: 1.

—. "Will Chatelaine Have A Male Centerfold?" Editorial. *Chatelaine* February 1973: 1.

— "Women: A Chance For A Choice?" Editorial. *Chatelaine* October 1969: 1.

—. "Women, Work And Husbands." Editorial. *Chatelaine* August 1969: 1.

—. "Women's Lib: A Short (Forgotten) History." Editorial. *Chatelaine* November 1970: 1.

—. "105 Good Reasons Why Women Should Be In Parliament." Editorial. *Chatelaine* October 1971: 1.

Anderson, I. "Both Hands On The Dials Of Canadian Culture." *Maclean's* 29 December 1980: 7+.

Anderson, P. "Business Must Adjust To Needs Of Changing Workforce." *The Financial Post* 4 April 1981: 25-26.

Appleton, F. "Games Computers Play." *The Financial Post* September 1976: 8.

Attwood, Margaret. "Atwood On Pornography." *Chatelaine* September 1983: 61+.

—. "Essays On The Millennium/2000: Survival, Then And Now: Canada's Premier Woman Of Letters Takes A Razor-Sharp Look At The State Of Canadian Literature." *Maclean's* 1 July 1999: 54.

Baldwin, Kristen, et al. "The 100 Greatest Moments In Rock Music/ The 70s." *Entertainment Weekly* 28 May 1999: 58+.

—. "The 100 Greatest Moments In Television/1970s: 1970s With Its Mixture Of Serious News And Serious Fluff, The Me Decade's TV Left Us Dazed And Amused." *Entertainment Weekly* 19 February 1999: 62+.

—. "The 100 Greatest Moments In Television/ 1980s: 1980s Just As The Medium Hit Its Stride, We Had To Learn A Whole New Vocabulary. Can You Say CNN, MTV and VCR?" *Entertainment Weekly* 19 February 1999: 82+.

Barry, Dave. "Almost 50 Is Bad, But Sixties Were Worse." *The Dallas Morning News* 14 July 1996. 10F.

Barsky, Lesley. "Overworked, Stressed Out? It's Time To Ease Off." *Chatelaine* May 1990: 106+.

Batten, J. "After Black Power, Woman Power." *Chatelaine* September 1969: 36-37.

—. "Canada's Rock Scene: Going, Going." *Maclean's* February 1968: 34+.

—. "Can Pop." *Chatelaine* September 1969: 27+.

Baxter, Clive. "Cable TV Policy May Shift Again." *The Financial Post* 25 July 1970: 1+.

—. "Success, Of A Sort, For A Mini-Summit." *The Financial Post* December 11 1971: 2.

Beattie, G. "Staying Slim: How The Beautiful People Do It." *Chatelaine* April 1969: 50+.

Belanger, J. "It's High Time Women Stopped Searching For Meaning—And Started Cooking Like Granny Used To." *Maclean's* 19 February 1966: 44.

Bentley, Rosalind. "Can't Stop The Music/Twenty Years After The Dance Craze Hit, Disco Is Still Stayin' Alive, Stayin' Alive." *Minneapolis Star Tribune* 6 August 1995: 01F.

Bergman, Brian. "The Battle Over Censorship." *Maclean's* 24 October 1994: 26.

Berton, Pierre. "It's Time We Stopped Hoaxing The Kids About Sex." *Maclean's* 18 May 1963: 66.

Best, P. "'Juggling' Consumers Want Value In 1980s. *The Financial Post* 26 April 1980: 12.

Bird, J. "Pressure Starts To Show In Trudeau's Language, Appearance." *The Financial Post* 25 March 1972: 36.

"Birth Control Pills." *The Financial Post* 1 June 1963: 26.

Blackwell, Richard. "Cutting Out Cords Cuts Appliance Constraints." *The Financial Post* 21 June 1986: C5.

Bliss, M. "How We Used To Learn About Sex." *Maclean's* March 1974: 38+.

Bliss, Michael. "What Happened In 1867? Nothing Much. So Why Bother About The Centennial?" *Maclean's* 15 May 1965: 65.

"Board Games." *Chatelaine* 25 March 1980: 25.

Booth, A. "Market Guide: Watch Hemlines." *The Financial Post* 20 August 1966: 3.

Borealis, B. "Confessions Of A TV Addict." *Maclean's* 29 December 1980: 6.

Bossin, Bob. "A Dissonant Note For Pop Music." *Maclean's* 31 August 1981.

Bower, A. "Consumers At New Low In Buying Mood." *The Financial Post* 1 August 1981: 1-2.

"Brady Bunch Here's The Story...Softheaded, Bunk-bedded, White Breaded, the Bradys Are Still Pop Icons. This Is How One TV Family Made A Generation Its Own." *Entertainment Weekly* 29 May 1992: 40.

Braithwaite, J. Lorne. "Shopping Centres Follow The Flight Back To The City." *The Financial Post* 19 April 1980.

Brown, Craig. "Lock Up Your Children, The Tamogotchis Are Here And They Want Looking After. Marriage Guidance Counsellors Were Alarmed When An American Cited A Rubik Cube In Her Divorce Petition." *The Daily Telegraph* 26 July 1997.

Bruman, C. "Games Trivial People Play." *Maclean's* 30 August 1982: 46.

Cahill, Linda. "House Of Horrors: You May Save Money, But Will Your Marriage Survive? The Real Costs Of Do-It-Yourself Renovation." *The Financial Post Moneywise Magazine* July 1987: 58-62.

Callwood, J. and others. "Do We Need Women's Lib?" *Chatelaine* November 1970: 26+.

Callwood, June. "The Unfolding Tragedy of Drug-Deformed Babies." *Maclean's* 19 May 1962: 13+.

Campbell, Laura. "Style: Joni Chic. The Look And The Voice That Haunted The Seventies Is Inspiring A New Generation Of Singers, Models And Designers, finds Laura Campbell." *The Sunday Telegraph* 8 February 1998: 06.

"Can Networks Win Sponsors For Home-Produced Shows?" *The Financial Post* 5 August 1961: 8.

Cappon, D. "Whom Should Trudeau Marry?" *Chatelaine* July 1969: 22+.

Carreck, M. "Live From Vietnam! War Could Be Bigger Than Bonanza!" *Maclean's* January 1967: 34.

Carson, S. "When New Mothers Go Back To Work." *Chatelaine* September 1981: 66+.

"CBS Is Planning A Special Next Month Celebrating All In The Family." *Entertainment Weekly* 11 January 1991: 74.

"Closing The Catalogue." *Time Canada* 26 January 1976: 9-10.

Cochran, Jason. "Encore: Remembering The King Even Twenty Years After His Death, Elvis Presley Is Honored In Ways Both Outrageous And Sublime." *Entertainment Weekly* 15 August, 1997: 93+.

Cohen, Andrew. "Specialty Channels Could Sway Broadasting Balance *The Financial Post* 18 May 1987: 8.

"Collectors: Where's Charlie? There's Room In Jack Condon's Heart—And In His Mini-Museum—For Every One Of The Angels." *People* 19 June 1995: 68.

Conklin, Ellis E. "The 70s - Those 'Happy Days' Are Here Again - But Why?" *St. Louis Post-Dispatch* 22 April 1997: 01D.

"Connected: Pac Is Back. Faqs! Facts! Fax!" *The Daily Telegraph* 3 December 1998.

Connell, Helen. "The High Price Of Culture/Back When The CRTC Was Mandating Canadian Content, There Were Dire Predictions Of The End Of Radio As We Knew It—Surprise, Surprise, Canadian Music Is Stronger Than Ever." *The Ottawa Sun* 27 March 1999: 14.

Conron, S. "How To Be Superwoman: Excerpt From Superwoman In Action." *Chatelaine* May 1980: 156+.

"Cooler Autos Coming." *The Financial Post* 19 March 1966: 54.

Corelli, Rae. "Borders Of Mirrors: Canadian Attitudes To America Are A Study In Sharp Contrasts." *Maclean's* 1 January 1990: Cover 37-38.

Cornell, B. "Microwave Update." *Chatelaine* May 1975: 24+.

Cunneff, Tom. "Take One: But Are They Mascara-Proof?" *People* 7 August 1989: 35.

Daly, M. "How Women In Power Keep Other Women Powerless." *Maclean's* March 1970: 38-41.

Delaney, M. "Pornocinema, Sexplicity, Erotic Pix." *Saturday Night* August 1969: 41-42.

Dexter, S. "Black Ghetto That Fears Integration." il. *Maclean's* 24 July 1965: 16+.

Diamant, Tisha. "Plies & Thank You, Karen Kain." *Chatelaine* 01 June 1997: 61+.

Dingman, J. "Daycare And You." *Chatelaine* July 1970: 4.

—. "Sesame Street: An Educational Show For Preschool Children." *Chatelaine* September 1970: 4.

—. "TV That's Purposely Infantile (Romper Room)." *Maclean's* 1 October 1966: 53-54.

—. "What A Nice Slum! Cue Camera One." il. *Maclean's* 17 September 1966: 58.

"Disco Takes A Dip." *The Financial Post* 26 April 1980: 6.

Donaldson, G. "From Men To Brutes To Fiends At My Lai 4: A Tardy Reconstruction." *Maclean's* July 1970: 71.

—. "State Stronger Than Dirt." *Maclean's* 3 December 1966: 2-3.

Dowling, D. "Uneasy Eaton Centre Mirrors Retail Trend." *The Financial Post* 17 September 1977: 1+.

Drainie, Bronwyn. "Meet The Post Feminist Woman." *Chatelaine* September 1986: 58+.

Dunkett, Jodi. "This Season's Toy Story: Back To The Classics/Gumby, Mr. Potato Head and Lincoln Logs Are Big With Baby Boomers' Kids." *Minneapolis Star Tribune* 15 December 1996: 09E.

Edds, J. A. "Reflections On The Demise Of A Catalogue." *Canadian Business* March 1976: 32-34.

Edelstein, Andrew. "Brady Basics. How To Explain The Enduring Appeal Of A Bunch Of White-Bread Dorks." *Newsday* 12 February 1995: 08.

Edmonds, A. "New Learning: Today It's Chaos, Tomorrow - Freedom?" *Maclean's* May 1969: 68+.

—. "There's A New Way To Have A Baby?" *Maclean's* October 1967: 40+.

—. "What Easier Divorce Will Do To Canada." *Maclean's* September 1967: 1-2.

Edmonds, Eve. "Polkaroo An Icon To Kids." *The Ottawa Sun* 28 November 1998: 31.

Egan, V.J. "You Get A Better Suit If Wife Helps You Pick It." *The Financial Post* 21 May 1960: 25.

Emberley, Peter C. "Essays On The Millennium/2000: Searching For Purpose: Spiritualism Is On the Rise As Baby Boomers Seek Meaning And Direction In Their Lives." *Maclean's* 28 December 1998: 100.

English, R. "IBM Makes A Splash In Consumer Electronics." *The Financial Post* 22 August 1981: 3.

Evans, Mark K. "Canadians Lured By U.S. Bargains." *The Financial Post* 2 April 1990: 1+.

"Everyone Wants Color TV Except Broadcast Bosses." *The Financial Post* 29 September 1962: 57.

"Farrah Fawcett. Before Or Since, Television Has Had No More Phenomenal Sex Symbol And Alluring As She Is, She Was An Angel." *People* 04 May 1989: 60.

"Fashion In The '80s: The Thermostat Look." *Maclean's* 7 January 1980: 46-47.

Fell, J. "Toy Makers Set For Big Jump In Christmas Sales." *The Financial Post* 6 November 1971: 1+.

"Finance Through The Century: A Quick Chronology." *The Globe and Mail* 29 April 1999: R8.

Fine, Jon. "Pushing 30/Young and Co. Still Crazy After All These Years." *Newsday* 17 November 1997: B02.

Flanagan, G.L. (Childbirth) "Minute By Minute On The Day Of Birth." il. *Maclean's* 22 September 1962: 28+.

Forster, W. "Problems And Pangs Of Executive's Wife." *The Financial Post* 3 June 1961: 20.

Foster, Peter. "The Edibile Man: Dave Nichol, President's Choice and the Making of Popular Taste." *Canadian Business* 01 November 1994: 112.

Fox, C. "US: Get Mikey - He Hates Everything!" *Maclean's* 19 March 1979: 33-34.

Frum, Barbara. "Insiders' Trip On How To Get Women Elected." *Chatelaine* October 1971: 38.

Frum, Linda. " '60's: A Tough Act To Follow? The Postyuppie Generation." *Chatelaine* January 1990: 48-51.

Frye, Northrop. "Why The Youth 'Revolution' Isn't." *The Financial Post* 7 December 1968: 13.

Fulford, Robert. "On Broadcasting: If The CBC Gets What It Wants, What Will It Give Us?" *Maclean's* 1 June 1963: 61.

—. "Shout Heard Around The Livingroom: Those Blasting TV Commercials. graphs *Maclean's* 6 January 1963: 46.

Gale, B. "The Quiet Heroes Of The Long, Hot Summer." *Saturday Night* September 1964: 16+.

Gale, Elaine. "A 'Jesus People' Reunion? They Never Really Left." *Los Angeles Times* 23 April 1999: A1.

Gates, Bruce. "House Market Fevers: Bidding Heats Up Fueled By More Drops In Mortgage Rates. *The Financial Post* 9 March 1987: 1-2.

Geddes, John. "Business: A Run For The Money: With A New Deal, The Magazine Debate Shifts From Culture To How To Keep Ad Dollars In Canada." *Maclean's* 7 June 1999: 54.

Gillen, M. "Back To Work - Guide To Re-employment." *Chatelaine* August 1969: 24+.

—. "Housewives: What Is Your Work Worth? Would You Believe $8600." *Chatelaine* December 1973: 20+.

—. "Lawyer: Divorce Isn't Fair To Women." *Chatelaine* July 1971: 19+.

—. "Our New Abortion Law: Already Outdated?" *Chatelaine* November 1969: 29+.

—. "Why Women Are Still Angry Over Abortion." *Chatelaine* October 1970: 34+.

—. "Why You Still Can't Get Daycare." *Chatelaine* March 1970: 28+.

Goddard, P. "Maple Leaf On Every Turntable Means Made-In-Canada Pop Stars." *Maclean's* November 1970: 89+.

Godfrey, John F. "BMW and a Brie Generation." *The Financial Post* 9 October 1989: 14.

—. "Fear, Greed And Reality." *The Financial Post* 26 October 1987: 18.

Goldenberg, S. "Now To Pay For CN Tower." *The Financial Post* 12 April 1975.

Goodykoontz, Bill. "New Craze In Recycling: Old Crazes." *The Arizona Republic* 10 June 1998: D1.

—. "Rad Fads: Who Knows If They'll Bottom Out Like Bells?" *Minneapolis Star Tribune* 4 July 1996: 11E.

Gordon, Charles. "Even Shopkeepers Need A Day Off." *Maclean's* 11 December 1989: 13.

—. "How Canadians Mistreat Heroes." *Maclean's* 5 December 1983: 17.

—. "Perils Of The Living Room." *Maclean's* 6 February 1984: 9.

Gould, A.M. "Who's Who Of Canada's Sexiest Anchormen." *Chatelaine* December 1983: 70+.

Graham, E. "Culture And The TV Soap Ads." *Maclean's* 19 March 1966: 67.

Graham, R. "Three Young Men Profit From Their Trivial Pursuits." *Saturday Night* June 1983: 80.

Gray, Charlotte. "Do Women Have A Place In the Boardrooms Of The Nation." *Chatelaine* April 1981: 56+.

—. "Should You Have More Than Two Children?" *Chatelaine* January 1985: 31.

Gray, John. "Four Fuzzy Years." *Maclean's* October 1972: 8.

Grenier, J. "There's Just No Way The PQ Can Win, Right? Never Bet On A Sure Thing." *Maclean's* 20 February 1978: 12.

Grimes, David. "Fads Of '90s No Match For Irritating '70s, '80s." *The Arizona Republic* 11 June 1998: B5.

Gzowski, Peter. "Last Chance To Head Off A Showdown With The Canadian Indian." Editorial. *Maclean's* 6 July 1963: 4.

—. "Songs To Break Up Canada By—And An Anthem That Can't Offend Anyone. Editorial. *Maclean's* 4 January 1964: 4.

—. "This Is Our Alabama." il map. *Maclean's* 6 July 1963: 20+.

—. "What's So Great About Color TV?" Maclean's 5 March 1966: 42-43.

Hall, Cheryl. "A Snap Here, A Twist There: Prolific Inventor Has Talent Forseeing What Products Can Become." *The Dallas Morning News* 8 March 1998: 6H.

Hawke. R. "Thinking Woman's Diet." Chatelaine November 1969: 46+.

Hawkins, B. "Color TV Not Far Off Despite BBG's Ruling: Digest Of Report." *The Financial Post* 2 March 1963: 11.

Hellmich, Nanci. "Benjamin Spock 1903-1998 Ground-breaking Book Made Him Pediatrician To Generations." *U.S.A. Today* 17 March 1998: 01A.

"Henry Morgantaler - Portrait." *Maclean's* 12 February 1979: 40.

Hilton, M. "Pant Suit Accepted, Maxi Next?" *The Financial Post* November 1969: 1+.

Hluchy, P. "First Corporate Olympic Games." *Maclean's* 21 May 1984: 45.

"Hockey: Russian Replay." *Time Canada* 13 January 1975: 9-10.

Hodson, B.A. "Once Again, People Are Spoiling Things—This Time It's The Computer." *The Financial Post* 18 February 1967: 25.

Hofsess, J. "How I Learned To Stop Worrying And Love Disasters." *Maclean's* February 1975: 68.

Hogers, H.P. "New Cellular Mobile Phone Gets Great Reception." *The Financial Post* 16 June 1984: 20.

"Hopes And Fears: People Are Prepared To Change; Decima Poll On The Environment." *Maclean's* 17 September 1990: 50-51.

Hopkins, T. "Disco Demolition." *Maclean's* 8 October 1979: 19.

Hutchinson, Brian. "Trouble In Big Mall Country." *Canadian Business* 01 September 1994: 68+.

Hutton, E. "Case For The Birth Control Pill And The Troubling Case Against It." *Maclean's* 22 August 1964: 12+.

"IBM Launches Personal Computer." *Marketing* 31 August 1981: 9.

"Iran: Sword Of A Relentless Revolution Ayatulah Ruhollah Khomeini: 1900-1989." *Time* 12 June 1989: 36.

Irving, M. "Now Let's See: Metre Is 3.2808 Feet And A Kilogram is 2.2046 Pounds." *The Financial Post* 24 April 1971: 41.

Istona, Mildred. "Feminine Mystique '81." Editorial. *Chatelaine* June 1981: 2.

—. "In 1990, Is Being A Wife and Mother Enough?" Editorial. *Chatelaine* August 1990: 2.

"It's Coming After All: A National Postal Code." *The Financial Post* 7 June 1969: 3.

Jackman, Philip. "Sitcom Angels." *The Globe And Mail* 11 December 1998: A28.

—. "The Ebb And Flow Of Waterbed Sales." *The Globe And Mail* 6 May 1999: A24.

Jackson, B. "Housing Trend: More Families,More Homes." il tab graph *The Financial Post* 16 February 1963: 63-64.

—. "U.S. Boom In Television Sales Will Follow Legal VHF Switch." *The Financial Post* 16 February 1963: 63-64.

Janigan, Mary et al. "Tragedy's Haunting Legacy." *Maclean's* 23 June 1986: 14-15.

Jenish, D'Arcy. "To The Brink Of Recession." *Maclean's* 16 November 1987: 34-35.

Jennings, Nicholas. "Canadian Rock Explodes! There Is A Bold New Beat Across The Country." *Maclean's* 27 March 1995: 40+.

—. "Rock Goes Gold." *Maclean's* 2 March 1987: 30-34.

Johnson, Brian D. "Sitcoms In the Fun House." *Maclean's* 13 January 1986: 42.

—. "The Canadian Patient: The Triumph Of The English Patient Raises The Question: Why Can't Canada Make Its Own Movies?" *Maclean's* 24 March 1997: 42.

"Just Sailing Along," *Marketing* 4 May 1987: 23.

Katz, Sidney. "For The Sake Of Argument Sidney Katz Says Big Families Are Bad For Parents But They're Terrible For Children." *Maclean's* 19 October 1963: 84.

—. "How All Those "Love Guides" Can Lead Us Astray About Sex." *Maclean's* November 1970: 60+.

—. "How Nuclear Fears Affect Children." *Maclean's* 15 June 1963: 23+.

—. "'Marriage Is Easy Street (For Women)." *Maclean's* 17 October 1964: 30+.

—. ""Painless" Childbirth?" *Chatelaine* February 1982: 36.

—. "Taking Healing Beyond Its Addiction to Drugs." *Maclean's* 7 January 1980: 46-47.

—. "What Television Does To Children." *Maclean's* 22 April 1961: 31+.

Kennedy, C. "Doing It Up Royally." *Maclean's* 27 June 1977: 40-41.

"Kids Source: Kelli Pryor: A Fond Good-bye To 'Degrassi High' This Month, PBS' Popular Series Begins Its Last Season. A Report From The Set-And A Salute To A Show That Deals With The Complicated Lives." *Entertainment Weekly* 12 April, 1991: 68.

Kieran, S.H. "Offers Advice To Parents: Burn All Those Books On Baby Care." il. *Maclean's* 3 July 1965: 48.

—. "Who's Downgrading Women? Women." *Maclean's* August 1968: 18+.

King, M.L. Jr. "Why The Negro Won't Wait." *The Financial Post* 27 July 1963: 6.

"King Slain In Memphis." *The Globe and Mail* 5 April 1968: 1.

Kirkby, M. "New Toys And Why Children Will Like Them." *Maclean's* 16 December 1961: 1.

Knelman, M. "Daytime TV: It's A Good And Moral Life, If You Can Stand It." *Saturday Night* January 1970: 36-37.

Krantz, Judith. "Why Paul Anka Is Everyone Else's Favourite Canadian." *Maclean's* 27 January 1962: 52.

Krivel, Peter. "Hula Hoops, Pet Rocks And Other Bad Fads." *The Toronto Star* 7 January 1999.

Lacayo, Richard. "Time 100: Suburban Legend William Levitt. His Answer To A Postwar Housing Crisis Created A New Kind Of Home Life And Culture: Suburbia." *Time* 7 December 1998: 148.

Laiscell, Ed. "Regional News In A Capsule." *Washington Informer* 11 December 1996: PG.

Landsberg, M. "Best And Worst Of Women's T.V." *Chatelaine* November 1974: 50+.

—. "TV Women: How They're Doing In Male-Chauvinist TVland." *Chatelaine* May 1974: 38+.

Laver, Ross. "Differences That Divide: Quebec's Separation Is Widely Forcast." *Maclean's* 1 January 1990: Cover 14-17.

Lenahan, Jim. "Were The 70s And 80s Goofy? You Bet, But We Still Love The Kitsch." *Gannett News Service* 9 August 1995.

Lerch, Renate. "Coleco Tries To 'Patch' Up Earnings With Cabbage Doll." *The Financial Post* 12 January 1985: 18.

Levin, Eric with Gail Cameron Westcott. "Up Front: It's Jim & Tammy Time Again! Claiming They've Been More Sinned Against Than Sinful, The Bakkers Try To Regain Control Of PTL— With No Money Down." *People* 04 July 1999: 32.

"Like Fruit Flavors? Try These Pants For Taste." *The Financial Post* 19 February 1977: 9.

Lipton, Michael A., Andrew Abrahams, John Griffiths and Craig Tomashoff. "Tube: A Cast Replays Its Happy Days." *People* 9 March 1992: 106.

Logan, Julie et al. "Dos By The Decade Did We Or Didn't We? From Beehives To Bangs, What's Come, Gone And Is Hair To Stay." *In Style* 01 October 1998: 269+.

"Long Hot Summer Helps Launch Ice Cream With A New Twist." *The Financial Post* 15 October 1966: P2.

Lorinc, John. "Next Wave: New Products And Services For Baby Boomers." *Canadian Business* August 1990: 59-60.

Lowry, Brian. "Final 'Seinfeld': How Huge Will The Ratings Be? Television: With At Least 75 Million Expected To Tune In Tonight, the Series Looks Likely To Join The List Of Most-Watched Finales." *Los Angeles Times* 14 May 1998: F48.

MacFarlane, J. "What If Anne Murray Were An American?" *Maclean's* May 1971: 78.

MacNutt, M. "Playing With Controversy: Two Social Board Games Hit The Market In Time For Christmas." *Maclean's* 7 December 1981: 56b+.

Maier, Thomas. "The Book On Dr. Spock." *Newsday* 18 March 1998: B03.

—. "The Complicated Life And Legacy Of Good Dr. Spock." *Newsday* 22 March 1998: B04.

Mair, Shirley. "Form Chart On Hobbies." *Maclean's* 27 January 1962: 19+.

"Male Sterilization: A Striking Change Since Maclean's First Report." *Maclean's* 15 December 1962: 3-4.

"Manager Lists Qualities Needed By Career Woman." *The Financial Post* 21 May 1960: 11.

Maraniss, Jim. "Lightfoot's Music A Touch Of Canada At Its Best." *Winsconsin State Journal* 11 April 1996: 6.

Marchand, P. "Love And the "Me" Generation." *Chatelaine* February 1980: 44-45.

Marcus, Ann. "Sex, Lies And Age In Hollywood." *Los Angeles Times* 29 November 1998: 22.

Marney, Jo. "Couch Potato Generation Takes Root." *Marketing* 11 July 1988: 7.

—. "Shoppers In Profile." *Marketing* 19 March 1990: 7.

Marshall, D. "But Patrick, What's Wrong With Saying #-*! On The Air?" *Maclean's* April 1970: 105+.

—. "Easy Divorce." *Maclean's* June 1969: 72+.

—. "Surprising Social Revolution We've Started With The Pill." *Maclean's* March 1967: 20+.

—. "Trudeau's Victory." *Maclean's* May 1968: 93.

—. "Viewers Of Canada, Unite!" *Maclean's* October 1968: 95.

Marshall, Robert. " The Nation's Pulse (Canadians Opinions On Political And Economic Issues). *Maclean's* 3 January 1994: 24+.

Mathias, P. "More Children, Money And Toys." *The Financial Post* 6 March 1965: 12.

Maynard, F. "New Norm: The Two Income Couple: Double The Pleasure Or Double The Stress?" *Chatelaine* June 1981: 39+.

McCandless, David. "They're Back—And About Time, Too. Fashion-The Rise, Fall And Redemption Of Digital Watches Are Charted By David McCandless." *The Daily Telegraph* 30 July 1998: 07.

McDonald, M. "Havin' My Son." *Maclean's* February 1975: 48+.

McDonald, Marci. "Community Of Dreams: A Quest For The Heart, Soul And Meaning Of Canada." *Maclean's* l July 1994: 10+.

"McDonalds Ads Most Memorable Again." *Marketing* 12 March 1990: 1.

McFadden, Cynthia. "Tennis Battle Of The Sexes." *ABC Good Morning America* 10 July 1998.

McGeachy, J.B. "About Some Things For Which Canada Will Be Remembered." *The Financial Post* 13 May 1961: 7.

—. "Are MPs Overpaid At $10,000 A Year?" *The Financial Post* 6 February 1960: 7.

—. "If We Elect A 'Socialist' PM Will The U.S. Army Invade?" *The Financial Post* 29 April 1961: 7.

—. "We're Too Self-Righteous About Racial Intolerance." *The Financial Post* 3 June 1961: 7.

McGugan, Ian. "Eh! Big Spenders!" *The Financial Post Moneywise Magazine* March 1989: 9-10.

McKay, Shona. "Eating On The Run: Fast-Food Chains Start To Lighten Up." *Maclean's* 22 October 1990: 52.

—.. "Nanny Dearest: Nagging Doubts You Had About Trusting Your Child To Someone Else." *The Financial Post Moneywise Magazine* December 1990: 22+.

McLuhan, M. "Living At The Speed Of Light." *Maclean's* 7 January 1980: 32-33.

McNaught, K. "Kennedy Steps Into Lincoln's Shoes." *Saturday Night* August 1963: 13-15.

—. "What Black Power Means." *Saturday Night* February 1967: 11-12.

McReynolds, D. "The African In America." *Saturday Night* February 1965: 14-15.

Mehr, Martin. "Television: Still Great—Or Slipping?" *Marketing* 11 May 1987.

"Microwave Oven Sales Pick Up Steam." *The Financial Post* 23 February 1974: 5.

Miller, R."Prepare To Walk Your Last 'Mile'." *Maclean's* 22 August 1977: 16-19.

Mollins, Carl. "Macleans/Decima Poll: An Uncertain Nation: Disunity May Be A Permanent Part Of A Definition Of Canada." *Maclean's* 1 January 1990: Cover, 12-13.

Mollins, Carl and Andrew Bilski. "A Sad Legacy." *Maclean's* 1 May 1995: 30.

"Montreal: What Price Glory?" *Maclean's* 6 September 1976: 22-23.

"Montreal Races Toronto For Cultural Leadership." *The Financial Post* 18 June 1960: 9.

"Moppets Galore." *The Financial Post* 2 July 1966: 6.

Morgan, Joanna. "What Some Women Really Want." *Chatelaine* December 1975: 18+.

Mungall, Constance. "Peterborough, Ontario. Could You Live In The Ultra-Average Canadian Town?" *Chatelaine* August 1975: 33+.

—. "We Lived With A Computer." *Chatelaine* April 1970: 38+.

Muwakkil, Salim. "How America Has Lost Track Of 'Roots'." *Newsday* 2 March 1997: G06.

Nash, C. Knowlton. "Maybe Canada Will Lose Ice And Mountie Image." *The Financial Post* 9 March 1963: 14.

—. "Which U.S. Aspirant Best For Canada." *The Financial Post* 20 April 1968: 7.

Negro, Linda. "Lunch Boxes Reflect The History Of Television." *Minneapolis Star Tribune* 17 August 1997: 10E.

Neil, B. "Have Phone, Will Travel: Cellular Radio Is The First Truly Mobile Phone Technology." *Canadian Business* September 1983: 102-103.

Nemeth, Mary. "The Family: Canadians See Tradition In Crisis Even As A New Poll Uncovers Enduring Strength. (Includes Related Article On Gays' Fight For Equal Rights Law In Ontario.)" *Maclean's* 20 June 1994: 30+.

Newman, C.M. "What This Country Needs Is A Good Twenty-Five Dollar Maternity Dress." *Maclean's* 2 November 1964: 50-51.

Newman, Peter C. "Behind The Polished Profile." *Maclean's* 28 March 1983: 27.

—. "Mulroney Today: A Lion In Winter." *Maclean's* 21 March 1994: 34.

—. "Shall We Dance Once More With Pierre?" *Maclean's* February 1972: 3.

"99 Things We Won't Miss About The 20th Century." *The Toronto Star* 3 January 1999.

"Nixon - Portrait." *Maclean's* August 1973: 24.

"Nixon - Portrait." *The Financial Post* 11 December 1971: 2.

O'Toole, L. "Farewell To The Gang At The Front." *Maclean's* 28 February 1983: 46-47.

Ohlendorf, P. "Mystery At Sick Kids." *Maclean's* 25 July 1983: 40-41.

Orbaum, Sam. "Ask Any Canadian." *Jerusalem Post* 12 September 1997: 23.

"Our War." *Maclean's* February 1968: 12-13.

Pappert, Ann. "Housework. How To Impose Order On Chaos." *Chatelaine* November 1979: 43+.

Porter, McKenzie. Review of "Is A Beautiful Wife Businessman's Asset?" *The Financial Post* 14 April 1962: 25.

—. "The Unmarried Wives." *Maclean's* 27 January 1962: 18+.

"Portrait (Robert Kennedy)" *The Financial Post* 20 April 1968: 7.

Posner, M. "America's High Noon Mentality." *Maclean's* 13 April 1981: 23-27.

"Quebec: Hell On Wheels." *Time Canada* 1 April 1974: 10.

Quinn, H. "Irrevocable 'nyet'." *Maclean's* 28 May 1984: 32.

Redmond, Michael. "Sunday Shopping Law Has Retailers Confused." *The Financial Post* 2 April 1990: 8.

"Rene Levesque - Portrait." *Maclean's* 1 October 1979: 21.

"Review - Lorne Greene" *Maclean's* 1 June 1963: 62.

Rhodes, A. "Chatelaine's Plain-English Guide To The Personal Computer." *Chatelaine* February 1984: 175-182.

Riddell, B. "Unwanted Credit Card On Way Out?" *The Financial Post* 25 April 1970: 1+.

Ritchie, M. and M. Gillen. "How Canada Wastes Its Woman Power." *Saturday Night* 2 April 1960: 17-19.

Robert, M. "Canadian Male Is A Lout In Love." *Maclean's* 2 July 1960: 7+.

Rockett, E. "Human Stories Behind The Irene Murdoch/Helen Rathwell Cases." *Chatelaine* September 1974: 42+.

Rodd, Catherine. "Braces Are Coming Of Age." *Maclean's* 31 August 1981: 47.

Ross, A. "Vietnam War: What Canadians Really Think." *Maclean's* October 67 1967: 1.

Ross, V. "Disco Chic Or Disco Ennui?" *Chatelaine* November 1978: 64+.

Rourke, Mary. "Hare Krishna's Mature Face The Movement And Its Members Have Changed." *St. Louis Post-Dispatch* 10 July 1996: 03E.

Ruddy, J. "...Get With The Canadian Music Scene." *Maclean's* November 1969: 61.

—. "Lights! Camera! A Little Zap Of Buttock!." *Maclean's* November 1968: 40+.

—. "Pit And The Star." *Maclean's* November 1970: 42-46.

"Sabotage Feared As 329 Die In Jet. Two Groups Claim They Planted Bomb." *The Globe and Mail* 24 June 1985: 1.

Salem, Rob. "The Laughs Of A Lifetime." *Starweek* 13 March 1999: 4+.

Salter, Michael. "Yups R Us, But Don't Say the Y-word In Front Of The Children." *Report on Business Magazine* November 1988: 19.

Schneider, Pat. "Nov 10, 1975 - 29 Died In Lake Disaster - Freighter Edmund Fitzgerald Went Down Quickly." *Capital Times* 4 November, 1998: 13A.

Schreiner, J. "Sweet, Lovely And So Plentiful—Women Rushing Into Labor Force Bringing Some Special Problems." *The Financial Post* 12 December 1964: 49.

Sclanders, Ian. "Incredible Things The Thinking Machines Are Doing For Us—-And To Us." *Maclean's* 10 March 1962: 20+.

—. "Legacy Of John Kennedy And How Congress Can Live Up To It." *Maclean's* 4 January 1964: 2-3.

—. "Look-Alikes: The Attractive Kennedys And All America. *Maclean's* 7 April, 1962.

—. "Plain Pornography." *Maclean's* 9 February 1963: 3-4.

—. "The Birth Control Explosion." *Maclean's* 21 March 1964: 16+.

—. "View From The U.S. Wasteland. The CBC Looks Fine." il. *Maclean's* 27 January 1962: 51.

"Second-Hand Computers Coming On The Market." *The Financial Post* 21 May 1966: E16.

"75 Years/1960-1973 Revolution: The Civil Rights Movement and The Vietnam War Sparked An Unprecendented Upheaval In Politics, Culture And More." *Time* 9 March, 1998: 140+.

"Sexy Ads Watered Down For English Canada." *Marketing* 14 June 1982: 2.

Sherrington, Kevin. "War On The Ice. Canada-U.S.S.R. Series That Changed Hockey Celebrates." *The Dallas Morning News* 31 August 1997: 1B.

"Shopping Malls Grow Up." *The Financial Post* 19 April 1980: 58.

Sinclair, M. "Color TV: Glorious Color Will Burst Upon (Some) Canadians..." *The Financial Post* 27 August 1966: 1+.

"Smithsonian Honors ATM Inventor." *All Things Considered* 24 September 1995.

"Social Trends—Spirituality." *Canada And The World Backgrounder* 01 May 1998.

Solomon, H. "How Nixon Mess May Affect Us." *The Financial Post* 5 May 1973: 1+.

"Some Come To Run, Others To Kill, Maim And Terrorize." *Maclean's* 9 February 1976: 17.

Steacy, Anne. "Sex And A New Hard Sell." *Maclean's* 9 June 1986: 57a-57b.

Stein, D.L. "Toy Front: The Guns Are Getting Bigger, The Dollars Are Getting Gabbier." *Maclean's* 19 October 1963: 82.

Steklasa, R. "Computers In The Home Are Almost On Us." *The Financial Post* 11 July 1981: 1-2.

Stevenson, Mark. "The Hired Hand Waves Goodbye." *Canadian Business* 1 August 1994: 12.

Stewart, W. "Proudly We Stand, The 'Butcher's Helper' In Southeast Asia." *Maclean's* March 1970: 13+.

—. "Why They Can't Burst The Trudeau Balloon." *Maclean's* January 1969: 22-26.

"Stretchy Sleeper Grows With Baby." il. *The Financial Post* 24 March 1962: 37.

"Style: Tammymania! Making Up Is Hard To Do, But A Face-Off Inspired By Mrs. Bakker's Mascara Turns Up Some Real Winners." *People* 22 June, 1987: 113.

"Sunday Law Struck Down." *The Financial Post* 2 April 1990: 8.

"Supermarkets Search For New Ways Of Selling The Same Old Things." *The Financial Post* 2 June 1979: 33.

Taylor, E.P. "Computers: Threat or Promise? Every Home Should Have One, Manufacturers Say." *The Financial Post* 9 September 1978: 5.

"Terry Fox - Portrait." *Maclean's* 28 December 1981: 46.

"Terry Fox - Portrait." *Maclean's* 30 May 1983: 34.

"The Moonies Have Landed." *The Economist* 7 November 1998.

"The Songs That Make The Whole World Sick." *The Toronto Star* 21 January 1999.

"The Way We Were, Seventies Style." *Marketing Magazine* 28 September 1998: Insert 28.

"Then & Now!: Singular Sensations Those Songs We Remember Are The Hits That Define Them." *People* 17 June 1996: 89+.

"They Won't Get Bird From Boss." *The Financial Post* 8 November 1969: 1.

Timson, Judith. "Justice For Susan Nelles." *Chatelaine* November 1983: 48.

—. "Playgirl's 'Men of Canada'." *Chatelaine* December 1983: 42.

"To Stem The Flood Of American TV." *Maclean's* February 1970: 3.

Touby, F. "CITY: The Noble Experiment That Worked - Once It Ceased To Be Noble." *Maclean's* 1 November 1976: 68d+.

"Trends: The Joking "Hello"." *The Financial Post* 8 November 1980: 9.

"TV Sales Picture Looks Very Bright." *The Financial Post* 24 February 1962: 15.

Tyrwhitt, Janice. "New Ways To Stop Youngsters From Quitting School." *Maclean's* 9 February 1963: 15-17.

Underwood, Nora. "Getting The Message: Concern About AIDS Is Slowly Changing Canadians' Sexual Habits." *Maclean's* 1 January 1990: Cover 34-36.

Unger, H.G. "New Retail Revolution." *Canadian Business* October 1967: 15-16.

"U.S. Isn't Buying Up Canada. Canadians Are Selling, And Liking It." *The Financial Post* 19 November , 1960: 3.

"U.S. Election Means Smiles And Frowns In Canada." *The Financial Post* 19 November 1960: 3.

"Valedictory Of A Decent Man." *Maclean's* 26 January 1981: 28.

Van Steen, M. "Problem Of Metric Conversion Or Why Wear A 45.46 Liter Hat." *Canadian Business* April 1972: 44+.

Viets, Elaine. "It's Baack: Old-Fashioned Streaking At Mizzou." *St. Louis Post-Dispatch* 8 November 1995: 03E.

Wadler, Joyce. "Scandal: Breaking Faith, Two TV Idols Fall. They Preached To Millions, But Their Sins Brought Jim And Tammy Bakker To Ruin." *People* 18 May 1987: 80.Wakeham, B. "Newfoundland: Those Damned Seals Again." *Maclean's* 9 January 1978: 20-21.

Walker, D. "Women Have The Capacity For Executive Posts But Traditiion Bars Their Entry To Top Ranks." *Canadian Business* August 1960: 90-92.

Walker, M.A. "All Parties Will Shift Right?" *Maclean's* 7 January 1980: 36.

Watson, E. "If It Was Good Enough For Your Mother, It's Good Enough For You." *Maclean's* 3 May 1976: 54.

Watson, Patrick. "Essays On The Millennium/2000: A Project For Canada: Now Is The Time To Create A New System Of Public Broadcasting." *Maclean's* 5 April 1999: 58.

Weiner, Caren. "Encore: The Mild 'Bunch' Here's The Story Of the Bradys' TV Debut 29 Years Ago." *Entertainment Weekly* 25 September 1998: 120.

"Will This Lower The Hems?" *The Financial Post* May 1969: 6.

Winsor, Hugh. "Pierre, Margaret Agree To Separation." *The Globe and Mail* 28 May 1977: 1.

"Wired Wizardry For Yuletide." *The Financial Post* December 1979: 9-10.

Witten, M. "New Species Of Presidential Campaign: Executives On Camera May Not Be Pretty, But They're Real." *Maclean's* 15 December 1980: 45-46.

Wolfe, M. "Television: A Propaganda Machine For Male Supremacy." *Saturday Night* April 1974: 43.

"Womanpoll: Your Views About Equal Housework." *Chatelaine* November 1985: 40.

Wong, Jan. "Tiananmen. Exposing China's Big Lie." *The Globe and Mail* 2 June 1999: A1.

Wood, T. "I Don't Believe What's In Vogue These Days." *Marketing* 20 April 1981: 28.

"Working Women Govern Retailers' Future." *Marketing* 9 March 1981: 24.

Worth, R. "Pop Shoppes Are Really Popping." *The Financial Post* 4 October 1975: C4.

Young, R.P. "Good PR Tool. Driver Education Gains Acceptance." *The Financial Post* 2 September 1961: 10.

Index

Photo Credits

About the Author

Ann Douglas is the author of nine books, including *The Complete Idiot's Guide to Canadian History* and *The Complete Idiot's Guide to Curling*. Her work regularly appears in such publications as *Canadian Living, Cottage Life, Chatelaine,* and *Homemaker's* magazines. She lives in Peterborough, Ontario, with her husband and four children. Ann can be contacted via e-mail at pageone@kawartha.com.

Other books by Ann Douglas

For adults

Family Finance 101: The Essential Guide for Canadian Parents. Scarborough: Prentice Hall Canada Inc., 1999.

Sanity Savers: The Canadian Working Woman's Guide to Almost Having It All. Toronto: McGraw-Hill Ryerson, 1999.

The Unofficial Guide to Having A Baby. New York: Macmillan Publishing USA, 1999. (With John R. Sussman, M.D.)

The Unofficial Guide to Childcare. New York: Macmillan Publishing USA, 1998.

The Complete Idiot's Guide to Curling. Scarborough: Prentice Hall Canada Inc., 1998. (With Rod Bolton.)

The Complete Idiot's Guide to Canadian History. Scarborough: Prentice Hall Canada Inc., 1997.

For children

The Family Tree Detective: Cracking the Case of Your Family's Story. Toronto: Owl Books, 1999.

Baby Science: How Babies Really Work. Toronto: Owl Books, 1998.